OF MONKEY BRIDGES AND
BÁNH MÌ SANDWICHES

from Sài Gòn to Texas

Oanh Ngo Usadi

O&O Press - New Jersey

O&O Press
www.OandOPress.com
ISBN-13 978-0-9998828-1-8

Book design by Adam Usadi
Printed in the United States of America

Dedicated to the Vietnamese boat people who lost and endured so much at sea and whose stories were left untold

In loving memory of my parents, mother and father in law

Author's Note

This book is based on my personal recollections, interviews with family and friends, and researched facts. While subject to the vagaries of memory, the events and characters recounted on these pages are what I believe to be true.

CONTENTS

PROLOGUE

"Everyone needs to shut up and calm down!" a man's voice thunders in the predawn on a wooden fishing boat filled with human cargo. "I will not turn this boat around!" Tossed wildly against the hull by heaving seas, the wet, fetid mass of us swallow our terrified cries as he shouts above us.

"I will get us to where I promised!" His words are amplified by the sudden quiet. In my eleven-year-old mind, I think the voice belongs to the captain, but as I find out later, he is more like a navigator. Our boat is leaderless. For a moment, everyone remains silent. Then someone yells, "You don't know what you're doing! You don't know how to handle a storm in the open sea!" The dispute roars back to life. One side demands that we turn around while the other insists that we keep going.

This near-mutiny takes place amid the raging waters of the South China Sea. It is the beginning of 1983, eight years after the collapse of Sài Gòn, and this boat is our means of escape from Việt Nam. Packed with 155 people and designed for near-shore fishing, our escape vessel is little more than a single open deck; the only enclosure is a small pilothouse at the aft. As the storm intensifies, my escalating panic has me agreeing with those who want to turn back.

The Night Before: January 7, 1983

The six of us—me, my parents, my brother two years older than I, and my eldest sister and her husband—arrive at dusk to board the boat for our escape down the Mekong River, into the sea, out of Việt Nam. Helping me to board are two men I have never seen before. I grab my mother's hand and edge forward into the throngs of people. Suddenly, someone wedges between us, severing our handhold. As more people pour into the gap, we are separated farther. "Chanh, find a spot anywhere and sit down for now," my mother, using my nickname, calls

1

over the crowd to me. I look for a space, but the tide of people continues to pile up behind me, pitching me forward until I fall and land on top of a woman. Certain that I have upset her, I push myself off her while mumbling apologies.

"Don't be scared," she says, helping me up. Her unexpected kindness chips away at my façade of bravery. My throat tightens, and I nod. The woman returns my nods and shifts to make room for me to squat next to her as people pack into the space around us in a seemingly endless stream.

Before the trip, my father prepared our family for what to do once aboard. We are to hide by crouching below the sides of the boat until we reach a certain point in the sea. But getting there will require an all-night trip along the tributaries of the river. At any point we can be stopped by police patrolling the river or identified by opportunistic villagers. Some of them will demand bribes not to report us and then will alert the authorities anyway to curry favor. Others, banking on a free ride, might follow us, drawing unwanted attention until we relent and take them aboard the already jam-packed boat.

After everyone has settled in, our boat begins to make its way down the river. A few passengers remain standing on the deck, posing as fishermen getting ready for a fishing trip along the coast. They go through the motions of sorting, untangling, and mending nets. From the outside, our boat must look ordinary enough—just another fishing vessel setting out to sea. But in the space just out of sight, the teeming horde jostles for room and air.

The last slivers of daylight filter through the web of fishing nets, masts, and beams hanging above me. Our escape plan would have been frightening enough on its own, but I know how terrifying a similar voyage was for my other two elder sisters and eldest brother two years before. After my siblings escaped Việt Nam in 1981, I heard my parents, in fragments of subdued conversation, talk about the horrors that had been visited upon that boat—the hunger and thirst, the storms and pirates. These stories haunt me even as I am unsure of the details. Now my mind rushes to fill the gaps in my knowledge with an awful vividness.

Since long before dawn, my family has been on the move from our remote rural village. Consumed by the singular goal of getting onto the boat, we have eaten little. On board, an all-consuming thirst displaces my hunger. In the distance, I hear the clanging of metal. Someone says canteens of water are making their way around. I strain to follow the sequence of sounds: the handle of the metal canteen hitting the body, a fleeting silence, then the glorious sound of someone gulping water. *I hope they leave some for me* I pray as the sounds make their way closer. When I think the canteen is near, I stand up, grabbing blindly into the dim light. "Hey, I'm not finished," someone yells. Others join in. "Wait your turn!" "Sit down!" But when I try to sit, I find that I have lost my spot. The mass of sweaty flesh has fused completely around my legs.

I search for familiar faces in the semidarkness and spy my family, a gauntlet of strangers between us. I know someone will come for me soon, but I can't wait. All I want is to be near my mother. I yank up one foot and plunge it forward, then do the same with the other. I am walking on a pile of people—hard shinbones, a soft stomach, even the rough side of a man's stubbled face. "Get off me!" I hear with each step.

"Nước rặc, mới biết cỏ thúi" (In putrid water, the rottenness of weeds is revealed) my mother, the dispenser of proverbs, often says. Earlier, when I fell on the woman, I automatically apologized, and she, in turn, offered me kindness. Since then, as the minutes stretch and the discomforts intensify, I sense my own social graces and those of others quickly peeling away. Around me, flailing hands reach up, grabbing at my thighs and legs to shove me off. Undeterred, I push forward toward my family. My sister excitedly calls out to me. She stands up and reaches over the crowd to pull me in. I am startled to find my mother looking almost lifeless, her face drained of color. She manages a weak smile and takes me in to hold between her knees.

For the first time since we were separated, I feel calm. My mind floats to our home deep in the countryside of Việt Nam, with its vast fruit orchard and ponds. There, I would sometimes also close my eyes and breathe deeply, but unlike this moment, when I am simply struggling for air, at home I wanted to savor the intoxicating scent of morning dew, flowering trees, and fruits. How wonderful it would feel to wade in the cool waters of the pond surrounding our house. Guavas, water apples, rambutans hanging from branches just above our heads, a tug away for the taking.

I am jolted out of my daydreaming by the sound of clanging metal. My brother-in-law quickly shoves the canteen toward me. The spit-covered container is hot from the countless hands that have already held it, and it reeks of gasoline. Obviously, it has been used to hold fuel in another life. I chug down the warm

3

water and feel instant relief. But then I start to gag, and everything that has gone down comes back up. When the stream of vomit stops, I quickly return the canteen to my lips, but before I can take another gulp, someone tears it from my hands.

The front of my shirt and pants, wet with vomit, cling to my skin. I have no idea when the water will come back. Circling my arms around my knees, still enfolded by my mother, I put my head down and again close my eyes. I think of our leaf-thatched hut, surrounded by rustling trees. I can see my brother and me running down the dirt path, straight to the two big water barrels standing sentry at the entryway. Forget about boiling the water before drinking it. Who cares about the mosquito larvae floating on the top? We scoop up the sweet liquid and douse ourselves with it, drinking and drinking until we have drained both barrels.

In a fitful sleep, drifting from one fantasy of home to the next, I manage to pass the first night of our escape. I am roused at dawn by the stirrings of thunder. Overnight, the smell of sweat, vomit, and urine has intensified. But even in that stench, another odor can be detected: the distinct scent of the sea. I have never seen the ocean and stand up to look. Immediately I fall over, thrown off balance not only by the jerking of the boat but by an overpowering dizziness. I begin retching again. As if the heavens are slowly gathering their fury, thunder booms ever closer. Streaks of lightning pierce the gray sky as bursts of wind merge into one unbroken gust. Soon thick walls of water swell up, trapping our pitiful boat inside a dome of seawater that crashes down on us with such force that it feels like a bomb detonating. Over and over the dome forms and crashes down. I burrow into my mother's chest, certain that our boat is going to break apart or flip over. Then I hear the sound of hope.

"Turn this boat around! We want to go back!"

Other voices ring out in opposition. I recognize one of them as my father's. Steely and direct, he says that our boat has to go forward because the police will be waiting for us if we turn back, and we will all be sent to prison. As one of the organizers of the escape, he is accustomed to his words being heeded, but now his is just one voice among many. "Turning around is not an option!" my father bellows. "The man was a naval officer. He knows what he's doing. Everyone needs to settle down and let the man do his job."

My father's voice, so trusted and soothing throughout my childhood, roars in my ears as the ultimate betrayal, vanquishing my fantasy of returning home. *No, not you, Ba!* I scream at my father inside my head. *Tell them you want to turn this boat around! Tell them you want to go home!*

"We are not turning around!" he continues. "We are not going back!"

The shouting dies down as it becomes clear that the side demanding that our voyage proceed has won. Now only children's whimpers and their mothers' *shush* could be heard. A certain resignation has set in: we will either make it or we will all drown.

Only the day before I thought I understood why we had to leave our home, the place of our birth and of generations of our ancestors: there would be no future for us in Việt Nam; staying would only guarantee a precarious life as outcasts. Leaving was our only route to freedom—a word invoked often in these discussions but whose meaning I only partly grasped. Now I understand nothing.

A delirious girl about my age grabs my arms, spouting a stream of gibberish while looking straight at me and addressing me as God. The consequences of turning back no longer matter. I just want to go home.

PART I: SÀI GÒN

My parents with my oldest sister in 1958

HOME

Though I was born in Sài Gòn and lived there until I was seven, the childhood home I remember most is not the capital of what was formerly South Việt Nam, a city once crowned as the Paris of Indochina; rather, it is a watery landscape covered with rice paddies and fruit orchards in Vĩnh Long Province. Eighty miles southwest of Sài Gòn, Vĩnh Long is well inside the Mekong Delta, the rice bowl of South Việt Nam. Our town, with its two-lane road and its outdoor food market that convened only in the mornings, was one of the smallest in the province. But I did not even live in the town, not even at its edge. I lived far beyond on the other side of a river. So remote, the small village of thatched huts where I lived was considered the boondocks by the townspeople.

My family's hut, like all the others, had no address. The paths leading to it, muddy tapestries of human and farm-animal footprints, had no names. There was no need for names, as our village had few visitors and no mail, electricity, or indoor plumbing. We had no soap or toothpaste. In fact, we had little other than what nature offered. Most villagers had lived on the same land, tilling the same soil, fishing in the same waters as their ancestors, for generations. Everyone except us was related or otherwise connected to each other in some way. Each family's narrative, woven of truths and rumors, was widely known.

The villagers didn't much care for outsiders from the big city. Everything about us—our accent, our clothes, our shoes, the fact that we wore shoes, and particularly our untanned skin—set us apart. The lighter sheen signaled to the villagers all they needed to know. We had never toiled under the sun and had little idea how to farm or fish, which were the only skills that mattered in a place surrounded by rivers and ponds, rice fields and orchards. The villagers were right. Our family knew little about life in the countryside. Besides my father, none of us even knew how to swim.

We arrived at our new home in 1978, when I was seven. Three years earlier, the North Vietnamese army had captured Sài Gòn, defeating the South after almost thirty years of civil war. The united country, renamed the Socialist

7

Republic of Việt Nam, set out to pursue its communist ideal of a just society in which everyone was equal economically. To save the workers from being "exploited" by profit-seeking merchants like my parents, who had owned an auto parts supply business when we lived in Sài Gòn, the new government declared private enterprise to be not only immoral but illegal. Businesses would now be owned by the state. My parents' company was shut down and our home confiscated. "Forget your sinful profit-making ways. Redeem yourselves. Leave the city and learn to till the soil," my parents were ordered. It was either jail or exile. They chose the latter.

For my father, this latest change in his fortune was not the first time his life had been shaped by the political winds of his country. When he was an eighteen-year-old student in the mid-1940s, he quit school to join the uprising against the century-long French occupation. Serving in a reconnaissance unit, he was responsible for scouting for explosive devices and traps before the rest of the troops could advance. During one of his missions, near Pleiku, in the central highlands of Việt Nam, a bomb exploded, killing many of the men in his group. The ones who survived, including him, were taken prisoner by the French army.

His parents were told only that he was presumed dead. As was customary, they continued to set a place for him at every meal. Sorrow filled the bowl of rice and rose from the cup of tea his mother placed on the family's small wooden dining table in front of a vacant chair. The ritual had roots in the belief that the souls of the recently dead lingered, not yet ready to depart the family hearth and the world of the living. So of course, he had to share in the most cherished of a Vietnamese family's daily rituals—*bửa cơm* (family meals).

After forty-nine days—the transitional period from death to rebirth, according to Vietnamese Buddhist and ancestor-worship beliefs—his parents placed his photo on the ancestral altar, next to those of his grandparents, great-grandparents, and other deceased relatives. Every morning, noon, and evening, they lit incense and stood before the altar, raising the smoldering offerings over their heads and praying for an easy transition of their son's soul to the next life. The wisps of smoke drifted past the photographs of the ancestors and then dissipated, as if being called into the past toward those long deceased. The mixed aroma of incense and food—the marker of every significant milestone in Vietnamese life—wafted through the house. Without definitive proof of their son's death, my grandparents sustained hope that he would return. "If Hòa is still alive and is lost somewhere, we beg you to watch over him and help him find his way home," they beseeched Buddha and the ancestors.

One day more than a year after her son went missing, my grandmother was in the backyard hanging laundry on a clothesline. Nearby, a sleeping infant girl, her ninth child, swayed on a hammock strung between two bamboo posts.

"Má ơi! Má ơi!" Over the noise of wet clothes whipping in the wind my grandmother heard a distant cry of someone calling out for his mother. She could make out a tiny figure several rice paddies away running toward her. She knew it was her son, though much thinner than he had been when she had last seen him. She flew down the dirt path toward the moment she had long fantasized.

Of all the stories my father told, the one about his reunion with his mother was my favorite. But I was happy to hear whatever he chose to share with me. One afternoon not long after we had moved to the countryside, while I was fishing from the deck inside our new home, a three-walled hut with one side open to a pond, my father called over to me.

"Chanh, want to see something?" He was rummaging through a briefcase on the dining table a few feet from where I was.

"Yes, yes, I do!" I answered, pulling the bamboo rod from the water and rushing to his side.

He held a rolled-up paper. Gingerly, he unfurled it. The six letters in the middle seemed to float off the page to form my father's name, Ngô Hòa. Above it in big red letters was "Tổ Quốc Ghi Công" (The Nation Inscribes Your Toil). This was the death certificate I had so often heard about.

When the Communists won in 1975, they went through decades of accumulated government records to honor those who had sacrificed for the resistance against the French and the subsequent fight for reunification. Thinking my father had died, they issued this death certificate. I stared, transfixed, at the loops and swirls declaring my father dead. "Forever and ever, the nation will remember your sacrifice in the struggle against French domination for the betterment of our countrymen's future," the document proclaimed. The signature of Prime Minister Phạm Văn Đồng—a name as well known to Vietnamese as that of Hồ Chí Minh—scrolled across the edge of the presidential seal. My father received the honor in 1978, thirty years after his capture by the French—the same year that our family was exiled from Sài Gòn for our "sinful profit-seeking ways."

I was confused. If the government owed my father a great debt, shouldn't he be rewarded rather than punished? The soldiers living in our house back in Sài Gòn and watching our every move, the strips of tape put on our possessions to indicate that they were now the property of the government, and our dislocation from the city to the countryside all felt like punishments to me. It was true that my father had not died, but hadn't he offered up his life with each footfall on the bomb-laden ground? His survival was only a quirk of fate. I had often heard him joke about his status as a living martyr and speak sarcastically of the lavish treatment the country had bestowed on him and his family. Beneath the jokes, however, his bitterness was palpable.

That afternoon I wanted to ask my father about the unfairness of it all, but I was too young to express these feelings. Instead, I asked him to tell me again about his life as a soldier. My father was in one of his rare talkative moods and began describing the constant deprivation of food, water, medicine, and sleep. He told me about night marches, his eyes refusing to stay open as his feet carried out the automatic procession. Jolted awake, he would find his arms wrapped around a tree, his unit far off somewhere. He spoke of the chills and fever of malaria. With no medicine and no blankets or extra clothes to keep him warm, the only remedy was eating spicy peppers, whose heat gave some relief from the chills.

He talked about a failed mission in which no one was captured but many of his fellow soldiers were killed. The details stayed with him: the grounds spattered red with blood, pieces of flesh hanging off trees. Somehow, he felt impelled to recover all the pieces of his fallen comrades, combing through the fields, scanning trees, and wading in ponds. However gruesome the sight, it was the stench he remembered the most. It seemed to burrow beneath his skin.

My father also spoke of the kindness he encountered. After his capture by the French, as he and his comrades made their forced march to their prison, the mothers they encountered in villages would slip into their hands some rice or a piece of corn or yucca. Perhaps they imagined their own sons filing along some other rice fields to similar fates.

Another rare time when he was talkative, my father told us that he had been beaten during interrogations. He did not go into details, and my brothers and I did not press him.

"You know, there's something worse," he said. "Sitting in your cell listening to sounds of someone else being tortured and knowing that you are next."

The interrogations were carried out to extract information about other "subversives" in the uprising, which had no shortage of idealistic young men. One of these was my father's brother, two years his senior, to whom my father was very close. Bác Hai (Older Uncle Number Two), like my father, had grown up under French colonial rule. In the early 1940s, when they were still in their teens, the brothers left their village outside Huế to attend boarding school inside the former imperial city. But in the wake of World War II, as the nationalist cry to rid Việt Nam of colonial control became more intense, the brothers, like thousands of other young men, quit school to join the uprising.

By the time my father was captured, he was still relatively new to the movement. His interrogators would discover that the scrawny, fresh-faced twenty-year-old did not have much information to offer. A little more than a year later, he was released. But my father did have something that his French captors wanted—his knowledge of the French language. Under colonial rule, Vietnamese students were taught French in school, and my father had a mind for languages. The French even asked him to consider working for them. But turning against his country and the men he had fought alongside was unthinkable to my father, though age and captivity had cooled his fire for combat.

When he was released, he looked for work in the civilian world. After recounting his story to one older Vietnamese businessman, the man gave my father some advice.

"You know you can't stay here. If you don't join the French, they'll make trouble for you. If you join the resistance and get caught again, you're not getting out a second time. Go south and seek your fortune in Sài Gòn," he advised, pressing some money in my father's palm. The wad of *đồng* felt thicker than the cost of the train ticket. Though he was in desperate need, my father instinctively extended his hand to return the charity.

"Take the money," insisted the man, whom my father would never again encounter. "It will help with rent and food your first month in Sài Gòn. And get

11

yourself a new shirt and pants. Nobody will offer you work looking like that." My father accepted the gift and headed south to Sài Gòn.

While my father might have lost the fire to fight, his older brother never did. In the coming years, Bác Hai would become deeply entrenched in the inner workings of the resistance. Led by the Việt Minh, the forerunners to the Việt Cộng, the resistance had started out as a liberation movement and had a mix of ideologies. Over time it took on a more dogged communist doctrine, but Bác Hai remained in the organization and steadily rose in rank. In 1954, after a decisive victory at Điện Biên Phủ, the uprising achieved its goal of liberation from colonialism. But the country was divided. The Geneva Accords of 1954 split Việt Nam into two at the 17th parallel, with a Communist North and an anti-Communist South.

Under Việt Minh control, North Việt Nam made clear its intention to reunite the country under Communist rule. South Việt Nam, however, was adamant about remaining separate and preserving its freedom. A fragile peace presided over the partitioned country for three years, until the tension escalated into a full-blown civil war in 1957. For the next eighteen years, as fighting inflicted a horrific toll, there would be little communication between the two Việt Nams and the two brothers. Neither my father nor Bác Hai knew much about the other's fate on the other side of the Bến Hải River, the demilitarized zone.

SÀI GÒN BEFORE

When my father arrived in Sài Gòn at the end of the 1940s, the capital of South Việt Nam was teeming with other young men also seeking to change their fortunes. Many had come from rural areas, abandoning farm life for work and educational opportunities in the big city. The money my father had been given by the kindly businessman enabled him to rent space in a tiny room shared with other fortune seekers. My father heeded his benefactor's advice and bought himself new clothes. Every night, he carefully rolled them up to use as a pillow. In the morning, he shook them out to wear in search of work.

He pursued any avenue that presented itself to make a living. He cooked and washed dishes in restaurants. He tutored students in a wide range of subjects, his knowledge at times only a lesson or two ahead of theirs. He kept the books for shop owners, a job that allowed him to peer into the inner workings of several businesses and that sparked the dream of one day having his own.

Eventually he was hired as a bookkeeper for Việt Nam Import and Export, a prominent firm that traded in wholesale fabric and auto parts. The business was partly owned by the daughter of a wealthy family. Drawn more to prayers than to business, Cô Năm (Aunty/Miss Number Five) entrusted increasingly more responsibility to the earnest, fast-learning employee. Quickly, my father expanded his role within the company. After only a few years, he rose to become its director of commerce.

As my father's professional career advanced, his personal life flourished as well. A stylish dresser with deep-set eyes, chiseled features, and two distinctive dimples, my father had his share of admirers. When he met my mother, the sister of a business associate, he was immediately smitten by the reserved bookkeeper. Distinguished by her high cheekbones and fair, freckled skin, my mother was attractive but not in the eye-turning way that my father was. It was her gentleness and kindness that attracted him. After a few months of courtship, my parents were married in 1956. My father was twenty-nine and my mother was twenty-three. In a photo taken on their wedding day, the groom looks debonair in a well-tailored suit, his lean frame evidence of a bachelor's life filled with endless cigarettes and skipped meals. The bride, in a white flowing *áo dài* (traditional Vietnamese tunic dress), beams a nervous smile. A year later, the young couple welcomed their first child, a daughter they named Thanh Loan.

Even though he was doing well working for Cô Năm, my father dreamed of owning his own business. With a growing family on his mind, he decided to open an auto parts retail shop. By now Cô Năm had come to think of my father more as a confidant than as an employee. When he sought her advice, she gave him her support, offering to provide much-needed financial backing. In return, she asked my father to remain at his job at Việt Nam Import and Export to see it through the transition.

At the time, my parents were sharing their home with two of my father's younger brothers. For some time, my father had been supporting them in their small village outside Huế. Once they were old enough, he sent for them to continue their studies in Sài Gòn. In a culture imbued with the Confucian ethic of family loyalty, it was not uncommon for an older sibling to provide for younger ones even into adulthood. My two uncles turned out to be indispensable to my parents, especially at the beginning of the business. With my father still obligated to work for Việt Nam Import and Export, the two helped my mother manage the tiny storefront. For a while, the business struggled, and its future was in doubt. But my father never wavered in his belief in the enterprise, borrowing and investing to fulfill his vision. After a few years, the business grew enough for my parents to move the store to a larger space in a more commercial section of Sài Gòn.

My parents named the store Thanh Loan Auto Parts, after their firstborn child. Located on Trần Hưng Đạo Avenue, a major artery of commerce in Sài Gòn, the auto parts retail shop could not have been in a more central spot. To its left was a busy intersection and a big outdoor market. To its right were banks, shops, movie theaters, and restaurants. The roar of motorcycles, mopeds, minibuses, and cars never stopped.

For the next decade, my parents worked to build the business as civil war ravaged the country. My father traveled a great deal, both inside and outside Việt Nam, making contacts and seeking ways to expand the business's reach. At the height of the fighting, the South Vietnamese army required all men to enlist, with only a few exceptions. My two uncles had long left my parents' house for the battlefield. In 1969, at age forty-two, my father received his conscription notice. But with four daughters and two sons to support, he met the exemption for familial obligations. Two years later, my parents added one more daughter, their seventh child—me—to complete their family. When I was born in 1971, Thanh Loan Auto Parts was thriving. By now my father was a serial entrepreneur, having started two smaller businesses—a trucking company and a tax-preparation company—and invested in several others. But Thanh Loan Auto Parts remained his flagship and his proudest creation.

With two warehouses around the city, Thanh Loan Auto Parts had become a significant supplier to retailers all over Việt Nam. My brothers and I sometimes accompanied my mother as she made the rounds to check inventory. We ran around the vast warehouse space, weaving between shelves stacked high with tires, spark plugs, and carburetors. Đà Nẵng, Quy Nhơn, Châu Đốc—the names of cities far from Sài Gòn were stamped across the boxes, ready to be shipped.

While I remember little of my parents' other businesses, Thanh Loan Auto Parts remains vivid in my memory. As was common at the time, the business storefront occupied the ground floor of our home, a narrow five-story building. Our family lived on the top four floors, which my parents had added on top of the shop's original single story. All day long, household and business employees— chauffeurs, nannies, cashiers, warehouse workers—streamed in and out of the building. I made no distinction between business and family spaces. I played hide-and-seek with friends under the shop's counters. I sat after a bath on the counter's cool surface, my legs dangling over the edge while my father combed my hair. I wanted curls, barrettes, and pigtails for my short bob, but the only hairdo my father knew was the pasted-down, hair-tucked-firmly-behind-the-ears style that only seemed to accentuate the roundness of my face. I didn't like it but felt the trade-off was entirely worthwhile. As the comb tugged and pulled at my damp hair, the world around me receded, and only I and my father remained. In those moments, I imagined he had no other care in the world and existed merely to smooth my tangled mess of hair and to soothe me.

Two years after I was born, peace was supposed to arrive. The Paris Peace Accords of 1973 called for a ceasefire between the North and the South and the withdrawal of all American troops. Việt Nam would be reunified through "peaceful means," with the South Vietnamese deciding for themselves their political future through "genuinely free and democratic general elections." But soon after America withdrew, the North Vietnamese army, sensing a weakened and demoralized opponent, renewed their offensive. Within a year, the American War, as it was called, not only resumed but surged. With Sài Gòn as its ultimate prize, the North Vietnamese Army launched full-scale attacks across the South and succeeded in capturing one province after another. By the spring of 1975, fighting had advanced to the doorstep of the capital city. After a few weeks of fierce fighting, the North Vietnamese Army surrounded Sài Gòn. Within days, their tanks crashed into the gates of Independence Palace, home to the president of South Việt Nam.

My childhood memories of Sài Gòn are quite different from those of my older siblings. They could recall the city without the backdrop of war. I have no such memory. The Sài Gòn of the days before and immediately after its fall is what stays in my mind. I remember a city with sidewalks and alleyways teeming with kids staking out spots for all kinds of games. There was *trốn kiếm* (hide and seek), a game with so many kids trying to cram themselves into so small a hiding place that someone inevitably ended up wetting himself and causing a stampede; *tạt lon* (knock-over cans), a makeshift bowling game with empty cans as pins and a flip-flop sandal for demolition; and *tắm mưa* (bathing in the rain), an impromptu street party popular with teenagers as well as toddlers.

But I also have vague memories of the sights and sounds of warfare interspersed with those of daily life: artillery fire mixing with the roar of traffic and the hawking of vendors, soldiers weaving through the crowds and at times congregating right outside our door. Near the end of the war, a small company of soldiers had moved into our neighborhood not far from our house. Among the uniformed men in green army fatigues, I have no memory of any American soldiers, only of those from the South Vietnamese Army. Even though the war was widely referred to as the American War, by 1972 the Americans had mostly left. My daily activities, from eating meals at home to going to the market with my mother to marching in the Mid-Autumn Festival with my brothers, were often interrupted by ambiguous signals. Was that lightning or parachute flares that just lit up the sky? Was that the sound of firecrackers or machine guns that I just heard? Regardless, I knew to run quickly to the nearest hiding place to huddle underneath staircases and counters.

I also remember the funeral processions. A prominent part of the Vietnamese mourning ritual is *lễ đưa tang*, a ceremony in which relatives and friends accompany the deceased on foot to the burial site. In the months before Sài Gòn fell, trails of white-clad mourners passed by our house with increasing frequency. From inside our house, my siblings and I could make out the sobs and the shuffling of footsteps. We would rush outside to join other bystanders along the street. Standing on tiptoes, we strained to catch a glimpse of the framed photo of the deceased, cradled in the arms of a male relative, leading the procession. The face staring out of the frame was almost always that of a young man.

In our house, the radio was always on. Above the static, it ticked off the names of provinces that had fallen into North Vietnamese hands: Đà Nẵng, Quy Nhơn, Nha Trang, the hometowns of my relatives. As rumors of a bloody revenge preceded the Communists' advance, thousands of people abandoned their homes and fled to any place that was still free, at least for the moment. Many, including several of my uncles and their families, ended up in Sài Gòn.

The presence of so many visitors in our house had the feel of *Tết*, the Vietnamese New Year. But the mood at this reunion was far from celebratory. I recall hearing the words *hòa bình*, meaning peace, sprinkled in conversations. My father explained that it meant the end of fighting and soldiers on both sides could go home to their families. "For you, there would be no more hiding under the counters and staircases," he said to me. I could not wait for *hòa bình*, the inspiration for the name of my father, Hòa, and one of his brothers, Bình. Its concept was the eternal dream in a land that seemed to have been forever besieged by war.

Hòa bình arrived on April 30, 1975. After three decades of bloodshed, the war was officially over. There was no longer a North and a South divided at the 17th parallel. A little more than a year later, on July 1, 1976, the country was formally reunified under Communist rule as the Socialist Republic of Việt Nam.

THIRTIETH OF APRIL

The events surrounding *Ba Mươi Tháng Tư* (Thirtieth of April) have been seared into the minds of every Vietnamese of a certain age. And though I was not yet four years old, these are some of my earliest memories. In the final days before the North Vietnamese Army closed in on Sài Gòn, a panic overtook the city. This hysteria would culminate in madness on April 29, the day before South Việt Nam's surrender. The streets were flooded with people scrambling wildly, as if fleeing an unseen monster. From our balcony, my siblings and I watched entire families running down Trần Hưng Đạo Avenue. Older siblings carried younger ones on their backs as parents lugged bags alongside South Vietnamese soldiers frantically tearing off their uniforms. Some people fled on bicycles piled high with their belongings while others pushed carts. No one bothered to pick up anything that was dropped. The streets were littered with shoes, clothes, and luggage, with broken bicycles and cars that had run out of gas, their doors still open. In this chaos, I heard an explosion. At the intersection just down the street from our house, a man was slumped in a pool of blood. Swirls of smoke and dust rose from his body.

"Ba, where is everyone running?" I asked my father.

"They're trying to get out of the country any way they can. People know that Sài Gòn will collapse soon. They're terrified of what the Communists will do when they get here."

"Shouldn't we run too?"

"No, this is our home. We're staying here," my father said.

A day later, on April 30, the North Vietnamese Army had Sài Gòn surrounded. The war was officially over. All around us, radios blasted an endless message loop: "Đầu hàng không điều kiện" (Surrender without conditions). The urgency in the announcer's voice was unmistakable, even if I did not entirely understand what the command meant. As the day went on, the hysteria of the previous days transformed into a somber quiet.

My siblings and I looked down to the streets at the long line of tanks headed toward us from Cầu Chữ Y (the Y Bridge).

"I bet they're going to police headquarters," said Cu Anh, the elder of my two brothers. Among the sites the Việt Cộng needed to capture to assert their dominance once in Sài Gòn was the police command center, not far from our house. During the war, my parents had often admonished my brothers not to play around the area, a well-known target that the Việt Cộng could bomb at any time.

Under the scorching sun, the tanks lumbered down Trần Hưng Đạo Avenue. Flying from radio antennas were billowing flags, bright red with a yellow star at the center, the symbol of the Communist Party. Trucks followed the tanks. Dangling from the sides were uniformed soldiers in bush hats and sandals cut from recycled tires. Some looked not much older than many of the teenage boys in our neighborhood. As the procession passed by, crowds lining the street waved flags while chanting, "Việt Nam, Hồ Chí Minh! Việt Nam, Hồ Chí Minh!" While some of the supporters may have been underground Việt Cộng sympathizers, many had just switched their overt loyalties to the winning side.

I was fascinated by the parade and its deliverance of *hòa bình*. But to my parents it must have felt very different.

SÀI GÒN AFTER

Peace never brought the magical transformation from the awfulness of war that I had imagined. Instead, darkness fell over Sài Gòn. Almost overnight, the boisterous city we knew, now renamed Thành Phố Hồ Chí Minh (Hồ Chí Minh City), ceased to exist. My siblings and I tiptoed around the streets and alleyways, no longer able to roam and explore as we once did.

"You can't go there. That area is now off-limits," we were told by armed police as we walked around the city during the day.

"Go home. The curfew has already started," we heard in the evening.

At home, from our balcony, we looked across the street to the night market. Not long ago it had been filled with customers in search of late-night treats. Stalls serving hot noodles and carts selling steaming buns spilled out from the sidewalks onto the streets. In bed, hearing my sisters' footsteps, I would jump up, begging to join them on their snack hunt at the nocturnal food heaven. Now the night market stood silent. The old Sài Gòn, awash in light and sound, had been lined with shops overflowing with merchandise. Hồ Chí Minh City, subdued and dark, with many shops shuttered, seemed in want of everything.

Not long after the government came to power, it implemented the *hộ khẩu* (residence status) system, a form of social control borrowed from communist China. Everyone was required to register with the local authorities to receive *hộ khẩu*. A valid *hộ khẩu* was necessary for school, work, travel, and rations, among other aspects of daily life. The new government, rooted in the communist principle that the state was responsible for the basic needs of its people, began to carry out a series of rationing programs. Only those with *hộ khẩu* could receive the rations, mainly rice and a few other necessities. But families whose members worked for the government also received such now-luxuries as fish, meat, and fabric.

I often waited in line with my mother or sisters to receive our food ration. These lines would come to represent the onset of scarcity as Western-manufactured goods along with rice, sugar, meat, flour, soap, and other daily necessities became increasingly hard to obtain. Even I could tell that our family's allotment of two small bags of rice would not last us until the next food distribution. Like everyone else, we turned to the black market. There, vendors and customers eyed each other with suspicion, since anyone could be a government spy. People conducted business hurriedly, aware that the police might swoop in at any moment, confiscating everything and sending everyone to jail.

Many other features of life from before 1975 were also banned, including music, art, and literature. Songs, even nonpolitical ballads that once filled our house, were no longer allowed. Books and films from before 1975 were deemed hedonistic and unpatriotic. My parents rushed to get rid of anything that could be considered suspicious. In our house, bookshelves stood empty and walls were barren of art. The only decorations permitted were images of the new national flag and those of Hồ Chí Minh, or as everyone referred to him, Bác Hồ (Uncle Hồ).

As the Communist Party leadership worked out their socialist reconstruction policies for the unified country, a provisional government, staffed mainly with Northern cadres, ruled South Vietnam. During this transition period, my parents were allowed to operate their businesses. However, they knew they would eventually be punished for being part of the bourgeoisie, a social class despised by the Communists for exploiting its workers in order to accumulate its own wealth. Rumors swirled that a program called *Đánh tư sản mại bản* (Smash the Bourgeoisie) would soon be implemented, aimed specifically at merchants like my parents, who did not labor with their hands. Questions loomed while my parents and other business owners awaited their fate. When would the punitive measures arrive? What personal property would be considered ill-gotten? What would they be allowed to keep and what would they have to turn over to the government? My parents held out hope that in the end they would be allowed to operate at least some scaled-down version of their businesses and that our family could remain in the city so that my siblings and I could continue our education there.

As events around them unfolded, my parents quickly lost hope that they could stay in the city or retain any ownership of their companies. Days after the Communists captured Sài Gòn, the new government began a purge of the city's residents. Soldiers and officers from the South Vietnamese Army, which included many of my uncles and cousins, along with religious leaders, teachers, writers, artists, members of non-Communist political parties, and other groups were ordered to report to specific sites to attend short reeducation programs. To their surprise, they found themselves packed into trucks and sent away to reeducation camps. Located in the far reaches of Việt Nam, the camps, called *trại học tập cải tạo*, belied their designation as "the place for the corrupt to relearn and be reborn." In fact, they were nothing more than prisons. The inmates subsisted on a near-starvation diet while being forced to perform hard labor and undergo political indoctrination. In the coming years, my father would accompany my aunts, making the days-long trek over mountains and through jungles to bring food and medicine to his brothers and nephew in these prisons where a majority of the former soldiers from the South Vietnamese Army remained for years.

It was not only those affiliated with the old regime who were sent away to these reeducation camps; anyone suspected of being anticommunist could meet the same fate. The security police, *công an*, were everywhere, watching and listening for signs of subversive activities. They patrolled the streets and wandered unannounced into homes and shops. For every *công an nổi* ("floating," or uniformed police officer) there was a *công an chìm* ("submerged," or secret police), pretending to be a neighbor. An offhand comment, a joke, anything not in praise of the new regime could be construed as anticommunist. Anyone accused of this crime could lose his job and his home and be sent away without trial. Distrust and fear infected everyone, even children. I knew to say little or nothing to anyone outside the family.

The purge of "undesirable" elements from Sài Gòn also extended to anyone without a job, villagers who had fled to the city during the war, families with fathers in reeducation camps, and entrepreneurs whose businesses and homes had been confiscated. More than just punishment, eviction was necessary to offset the population swell caused by the influx of Northerners who flooded Sài Gòn after the war ended. As victors, former Việt Cộng and members of the Communist Party came to the city in droves to occupy positions in the new state-run economy. They took over the homes, the property, and the jobs of the people they displaced.

With nowhere else to go, the evicted were forced to relocate to the New Economic Zones, uninhabited areas that had been carved out by the government for just this purpose. Far away from the city in the mountains and jungles, the exiles found themselves removed from society and from modern life. They had to start from scratch—digging canals, building roads, clearing trees—so they could eke out a living. Instead of going to school, children worked alongside their parents to turn malaria-infested jungle into farmland.

As my parents awaited their fate, my father set out to buy a piece of land in the countryside. He had decided that if we were to be exiled, our new home would not be in one of the New Economic Zones. A relative told him about a fruit orchard that was for sale amid the rice paddies of Vĩnh Long, a province deep in the heart of the Mekong Delta, Việt Nam's most productive rice-growing region. He thought growing fruit would be easier than working in the rice fields and bought the orchard.

With the orchard as a fallback plan, my parents continued to operate their businesses and did what they were told by the authorities. But there was one rule they did not comply with. This had to do with money. After the new government came to power in 1975, it imposed fines and demanded back taxes from businesses dating to the wartime years. It also closed banks, freezing accounts and sealing safe-deposit boxes. When the banks reopened, people were allowed to withdraw only a limited amount. Then, after a few months, the government issued a new currency.

These measures wiped out a large portion of our family's savings. My parents realized they had to gather a new nest egg in whatever time they had left. Risking imprisonment, they began to hide as much of their profits as possible and used it to buy gold, now the preferred, and sometimes the only accepted, currency. Their risk-taking paid off because three years later, the government would again change currency. This time around, it set a ceiling on how much of the old currency a person could exchange. Rumors circulated before the order. People flooded the market, buying up everything they could. My mother would give me and my siblings money to buy whatever we wanted. The currency exchanges might have caused much distress for the adults around me, but I remember them fondly for the frenzy and excitement that transformed the streets into a big bazaar.

Đánh tư sản mại bản finally "smashed the bourgeoisie" in the form of my parents' businesses around the same time of the second currency exchange. In

1978, without warning, a group of soldiers burst into Thanh Loan Auto Parts and ordered my parents to send all the customers away. The leader and some of his men took my father to the warehouses while the rest remained with my mother at the store.

My siblings and I watched as the men went about the process of *niêm phông*— taping up cabinets and the cash register—and securing anything else of value. "Everything now belongs to the government. Do not open or remove anything that is taped over," they warned. "If you are caught stealing, there will be consequences."

The men then proceeded upstairs to where we lived. They scanned the rooms, opening dressers and armoires and confiscating anything they deemed valuable. I remember sitting on my mother's lap watching the soldiers in their drab green uniforms. Earrings, bracelets, and rings sparkled on the table before us. As if they were playing a game, my mother would pick out an item, then wait. The men would confer among themselves and respond with a terse "được" (yes) or "không" (no). Their answer determined what jewelry my mother could keep. A pair of jade bracelets went to the pile next to us, while a gold watch ended up in the soldiers' corner. My parents were allowed to keep their wedding rings and a few other personal keepsakes. The rest belonged to the government.

It would be several months until government vehicles came to remove the things that were taped up. During this period, several soldiers remained in our house to keep guard. They took over the ground-floor store and the first two floors of our family residence. We were banished to the top two floors. The soldiers watched our comings and goings, searching our clothes and bags to make sure we weren't trying to smuggle anything out. But while the men closely watched my parents and older siblings, they paid little notice to me, and I was able to run in and out of the house freely. My mother began sewing extra pockets inside my dresses in which she would stash gold and jewelry that my parents had hidden throughout the house.

"Don't think about it. Just run outside to play like you always do," my mother told me, securing an extra safety pin over the pocket.

I flew past the guards, my dress weighed down at the waist. Down the block, my father would meet me to retrieve the goods. He buried the smuggled treasure eighty miles away in his fruit orchard.

Not all visits to our house after the war were unwelcome intrusions. A few months after the fall of Sài Gòn, my father opened the door to a man with the same deep-set eyes, coin-shaped dimples, and headful of hair as him. For one long moment, the men stood wide-eyed and speechless, then flung open their arms. As they wrapped themselves around each other, I heard: "You're alive!" "You're alive!"

My father finally turned to us and said, "Please greet Bác Hai, my older brother. He has come all the way from Hà Nội."

My siblings and I stared at the man about whom we had heard many stories and whose fate had been so much on my father's mind. On the other side of the 17th parallel, Bác Hai had had the same worries about his younger brother. When the war ended in 1975, he was a highly decorated general in the North Vietnamese Army and quickly headed south to search for my father and his other siblings.

As we gathered around, Bác Hai showed us photographs of his wife and three children. There was also one of his unit in the early days of fighting. Beneath the dense jungle foliage, the young soldier crouched beside other Việt Cộng guerillas. Not far from Bác Hai in the front row was a young Hồ Chí Minh.

The brothers were delighted to learn about each other's families and reminisce about their childhood. They recalled their fear in leaving school to join the resistance but also the solace they found in making the fateful decision together. But while the brothers may have shared similar beliefs in their youth, thirty years later their ideologies diverged dramatically. Bác Hai was a firm believer in the communist principles of economic equality and government control, while my father remained a steadfast advocate of individual freedom.

"Start a new life. Have faith in the Communist Party and in our country," Bác Hai advised my parents when he left. At the dawn of the new Việt Nam, my parents did want to have faith. They hoped to be able use their skills to help rebuild the war-torn country. But as they were to learn, the new government did not want their kind of help.

25

In the summer of 1978, after months of living among soldiers, my parents lost their *hộ khẩu*, and without this legal residence status they lost their legal status to stay in the city. But while my parents might accept a life in the countryside for themselves, they refused to accept it for their children. "You won't be farmers," my father repeatedly told us.

Their plan was for my two brothers and me to follow my parents to the countryside. Then, when we were old enough, my father would find a way for us to return to Sài Gòn to continue our education. My four older sisters would remain in the city, since students who were already in high school or college there were allowed to finish their schooling. But they needed a place to stay. My father turned to the only person he knew in Sài Gòn who had a house that was big enough and who would be willing to take in four boarders, his former boss Cô Năm.

In communist Việt Nam, the currency with the most value was not money but power or connections to power in the new government. My father suspected that Cô Năm had such a connection through an uncle who was a high-ranking government official. One clue was that my father and Cô Năm were both merchants in the same business, but though the government confiscated her business, she was allowed to keep her house—an enormous villa in the middle of Sài Gòn. My father should also have had this currency because of his older brother. But Bác Hai did not offer, and my father did not ask. He knew that his brother, the principled idealist, would not betray his beliefs, even for family.

Cô Năm agreed to take in my sisters. In postwar Việt Nam, she had turned fully to a life of prayers and meditation. These prayers would turn out to have a profound impact on my life.

I first heard them when I came along to help my sisters move into their new home in Sài Gòn. Inside the villa, the strong scent of incense in the air led me to a curved flight of stairs where I heard faint chanting and the periodic clanging of a bell. I followed the sounds up the stairs, then down the hallway to a slightly open door.

Inside, an older woman, sitting erect on a reed mat on the floor, her legs crossed over each other, was chanting. I realized that she must be Cô Năm. Wearing a long, billowy gray robe, she resembled a Buddhist nun except her hair wasn't shaved close to her head but tied up in a bun. In one hand, she was holding a bell; in the other, a short metal rod. It looked as if she was sleeping, only her lips were moving. Suddenly, she opened her eyes, then tapped the stick against the bell. As I turned to run, I heard, "Chanh, stay!" She knew me and my nickname. "Come inside," Cô Năm said as she stood up and walked toward me. Uncertain of how to greet a nun, I opted for the standard salutation.

"Con thưa Cô Năm" (Good afternoon, Aunty Năm), I said while bowing my head and folding my arms in front of my chest. She smiled and extended her hand to me. Inside the room, redolent of incense aroma, an enormous statue of Buddha, bigger than any I had seen in anyone else's home, looked down from the altar. Moments ago, I had wanted to flee; now I wanted to stay.

"Cô Năm, I don't know the prayers," I said.

"You can watch and listen, then repeat what you hear. Or you can just watch and listen," she answered.

For the rest of the afternoon, I sat beside Cô Năm on the reed mat, my legs crossed, palms pressing together in front of my chest. Following her lead, I sounded out words from a small book whose sounds had no meaning to me. When the rhythm became familiar, I pitched my voice to match her chanting. No matter my efforts, our voices remained separate, my staccato stops and starts peppering her flowing notes. Through the windows, children's laughter spilled in from the streets outside. Normally, I would have dropped whatever I was doing to join in the fun. That day, the games held no sway.

Every afternoon from then on, I would beg my parents to take me to the villa. Immediately I would run upstairs to chant with Cô Năm, then listen to her sermons about Buddha and his teachings. She taught me about karma and reincarnation and the ways to live a life of compassion for others with less concern for my own interests. She showed me how to clean the incense bowl and arrange the fruits on the altar. She demonstrated the proper way to greet a nun or monk: pressing her palms together at the chest to resemble a lotus bud then bowing her head slightly while reciting the mantra, "Nam Mô A Di Đà Phật" (Homage to the Infinite Light). I was drawn to everything inside the incense-filled room—the prayers, the teachings, the aroma, even the dull ache from sitting erect for so long.

"I'm thinking of a Buddhist name for you. It's a very big honor," Cô Năm said one afternoon. But before the event could take place, my family was ordered to leave the city.

In the summer of 1978, my parents, brothers and I left Sài Gòn to begin a new life in the countryside of Vĩnh Long. For all of us, but especially for my parents starting over at ages fifty-one and forty-five, the acclimation would prove more trying than we had ever imagined. The orchard, only eighty miles away but decades back in time, would test the limits of our survival instincts, taking my father to the edge of death more than once.

from Sài Gòn to Texas

PART II: VĨNH LONG

A recent photo of the area near our village in Vĩnh Long, Việt Nam.

A WATERY LANDSCAPE

T he move was the first trip to our new home for everyone in our family except my father. During the prior year, as it became increasingly evident that we would be forced out of Sài Gòn, my father spent as much time as he could in Vĩnh Long. He oversaw the construction of our thatched hut and familiarized himself with life and the people in what would be our village.

It was late morning when we boarded the bus to our new home. People who got on first squeezed into seats; those who came later squatted on the floor beside vegetable-and-fruit-filled baskets and wire cages holding ducks and chickens.

Throughout the trip, we were often asked, "Do you have authorization to travel?" Under the new regime, movements of any distance were tightly controlled and required various forms of permits. At different checkpoints, my father presented our papers and gave the same answer, "We're traveling to Vĩnh Long. We're not carrying goods to sell." Our bags were opened and searched for the commonly traded contraband: rice, MSG, sugar, meat. Since my father had already moved bigger household items by boat, we carried with us only some clothes, detergent, toothpaste, medicine—basic necessities that would be hard to obtain in the countryside. Since the buying and reselling of merchandise was forbidden, anything in excess of what was considered enough for personal use would be confiscated and the accused detained for questioning. The quantities we had were deemed small enough that we were allowed to keep everything in our bags.

As our bus rolled down pothole-filled roads, I sat on my mother's lap, transfixed by the continuous rice paddies passing by our window. Across flooded fields, rows of cone-shaped hats (*nón lá*) atop stooped bodies appeared to move in formation. My father said it was the start of rice planting season and the farmers were transplanting rice seedlings. Beneath the blazing sun, the men and women were completely covered except for their eyes, hunched over, shin deep in mud. With one hand holding a bundle of rice saplings, their other hand worked fast, taking the stalks, one at time, and depositing them into the soil.

In one unplanted paddy, a water buffalo dragged a plow across the soil to prepare it for rice seedlings to be transplanted. Each step involved an arduous extraction of its leg from the mud. A farmer waded a few steps behind. At the crack of his whip, the giant beast immediately picked up its pace only to slow down after a step or two, its eyes cast downward and its hide caked with mud. I finally understood the expression referring to the iconic animal of the countryside, "Life as hard as that of a water buffalo."

The rice paddies I saw through the bus windows were interspersed with rivers and canals. Canoes of different sizes crisscrossed the waterways. Some boats were laden with fruits and vegetables, others with fishing nets and gear. A few resembled floating homes with children sleeping and mothers cooking beneath a shelter. My father said that we were well inside the Mekong Delta and getting close to Vĩnh Long. It occurred to me that our new home was not land, but more water broken up by land.

By late afternoon, our bus arrived at an outdoor depot. After retrieving our bags and taking them to the side of the road, my father asked us to wait as he disappeared into the crowd. When he returned, he was accompanied by two bicycle rickshaws, peddled by two men. Their muscles contrasted with the age etched into their sun-beaten faces.

The rickshaws took us and our belongings along a two-lane road, past carts selling orange and sugar-cane juice. Huts made of thatch, or coconut palm leaves, lined the sides of the road. Some were so small that they resembled toy houses. I wondered how a family of any size could fit inside. A water buffalo with a teenage boy riding on its back lumbered alongside the traffic of pedestrians, bicycles, and bicycle rickshaws. An occasional a bus roared past us, each overflowing with goods on the roof and packed inside with passengers, their arms and legs hanging from windows and doors.

When we reached a brick manufacturing plant, my father asked the drivers to let us off. We entered what seemed like a village. Children ran and played on dirt paths, grandmothers lay on hammocks fanning themselves, and mothers prepared food over wood stoves. In the distance, columns of smoke meandered upward toward the clouds. My father said that the smoke came from the back of the brick factory.

As with any major enterprise, the factory was owned and managed by the government, which also provided housing for all its workers. The path to our new home cut through the clusters of brick huts where the workers lived. All around the village, red banners hung on walls extolling Hồ Chí Minh's greatness and Việt Nam's victory against foreign domination: "Nothing is more precious than independence and liberty"; "Bác Hồ will live forever in our hearts and in our future." Loud speakers perched on tall poles blasted news from the government interspersed with the proclamations on the banners.

Our path ended at the edge of a Mekong River tributary. A row of huts lining the river's shore teemed with activities. By the water's edge, some women washed dishes and cleaned fish and vegetables. Further out in the water, a few rinsed clothes as children swam and splashed.

"Our house is over there," my father said, pointing to a bank of trees far out in the distance on the other side of the river. A man leaped off a canoe tethered in the river and rushed over to us. My father told us that the man lived in our village and would ferry us across the river. The guide took our belongings and loaded them onto the canoe. Then it was our turn to get on.

On the canoe, we moved tentatively, as if we were toddlers learning to walk. Whenever any of us shifted, the canoe dipped precariously to one side. Instinctively we all leaned to the other side, only to cause the boat to again dip too low. After several near flips, our guide ended up jumping into the river to hold the canoe in place.

"Ba, so we have to cross this river every day to go to school?" I asked.

"Yes," he answered.

After we had settled in, the guide leaped out of the water and back onto the canoe. Standing at the rear, his hands clutched the top of two crisscrossed oars. Slowly he steered us away from shore, aiming the bow of the canoe toward trees in the distance. Every time his arms pushed forward, our boat jumped, listing over the small brown ripples. In the open river, the air, infused with the scent of mud and water, felt noticeably cooler. The mass of greenery ahead of us gradually emerged as distinct leaves and branches. On other side of the river, we pulled up beside a small dock that jutted out.

"This is your new home," my father announced.

The guide tied up the boat and began helping us off. Taking turns holding his hand, we scooted along the canoe then climbed up a set of stairs leading to the top of the dock. We walked off the wooden slats into a forest of trees. Nestled among leaves were brightly colored fruits—pink water apples, golden guavas, red hairy rambutans. Surrounding each tree, even those without obvious fruit, distinct fragrances filled the air. It felt as if I had entered an entirely different world of sights, sounds, and scents unlike anything I had experienced in Sài Gòn. I had never paid so much attention to my breathing or the air around me. As I looked around, a long brown twig, close to my feet, suddenly transformed into a snake, slithering to chase after a salamander. My father said that in our new home, we would need to pay attention to our surroundings at all times. Besides snakes, there were also scorpions, giant centipedes, bats, toads, and countless other creatures camouflaged among leaves and twigs. They could cause serious harm if we accidentally came in contact with them.

The dirt path we were on ended at a very shallow pond. A bridge made of scrap metal spanned a muddy bottom covered with a thin layer of water. The corrugated platform, rusted in parts, looked precarious. I hesitated, but my brothers didn't seem bothered and weaved around me to race each other across. Copying them, I took off running but immediately lost my balance at the first bounce of the swaying bridge. Only by grabbing fast onto the handrail was I able to catch myself from falling off into the mud.

On the other side of the bridge was our house. It was similar to the other huts I had seen, only bigger. The front was covered with palm leaves; the back, roofed with corrugated plastic. Even though the plastic roof provided better protection from rain, it made this part of the house hotter and much noisier. Even a light rain sounded like artillery fire. In time, however, I would find the amplified sound of rain oddly comforting, especially during the nighttime.

Our hut was divided into two separate living areas, one slightly raised above the other. The structure was supported by columns that were a mix of wood and metal fence posts. Like the metal bridge, these materials were also leftovers from the war. Other artifacts such as empty flare canisters and bomb casings were repurposed as washing basins, rice storage containers, and feeding troughs for livestock. They were prized for their seeming indestructibility.

The higher level of our hut had a floor tiled with red bricks. It was split into two rooms: a large space with three beds where we would all sleep, and a small open area filled with light where we would keep our family altar. From the big mansions in Sài Gòn to the simple huts in Vĩnh Long, every household I had been in had a similar room for worship. Ours contained a tall cabinet lined with photos of my deceased grandparents and great grandparents and a statue of Buddha. There was also a small pot for holding incense sticks.

On a wall in the altar room was my favorite painting, the only one that had followed us from Sài Gòn: two horses stood side by side; one, mounted by a general, rested its head on the other. It always appeared to me as a two-headed horse. Next to the painting was a small clock, an object that would draw the most stares from our neighbors. Upon entering our house, many would look surprised at the wall and proclaim, "Is that a clock? Wow, such wealth!" The sentiment was entirely understandable in a place where a pair of store-bought shoes or a shirt without patches was considered a luxury.

Our living area was adjacent to and one step down from the altar room. Partially perched on stilts and missing a wall, it was open to the orchard. Its floor was a mixture of clay and mud that extended to a metal ledge or deck that hung over a pond. I hadn't realized, until my father pointed it out, that this pond circled around our house and was the same one I had almost fallen into when I crossed the metal bridge upon first entering the orchard.

I use the word *pond*, but in English, it might be more accurately referred to as a moat. A previous owner had long ago dug out four of these moat-ponds inside the orchard. Three surrounded small islands of fruit trees and were intended for raising fish. The one circling our house provided water for daily use and a safe and convenient place to store our canoe when it was not in use. Connected to the river by a canal, the pond drained and refilled itself with the tides. At high tide, the water rose close to the deck. At low tide, it receded to just a few inches above its muddy bottom.

By the entrance to our hut stood two big barrels which we used to store water from the pond to supplement rainwater. The job of fetching water belonged to my brothers. After filling the barrels, Bảy or Cu Anh would drop a white rock called *phèn* into the silt-infused water and swirl it around. Known as potassium aluminum sulfate, or alum in the West, the water-purifier compound worked like magic: overnight, the brown river water would turn crystal clear, the sediments clumping together and settling to the bottom. The treated water might look pristine, but drinking it without boiling first would most likely result in severe stomach cramps or worse. Consumed by thirst, I often didn't wait for the boiled water to cool down enough and would rush to drink. Having a slightly scalded palette and numb tongue was a near-constant sensation in my new home.

Inside our orchard, there were seven or eight bridges, only two of them made of scrap metal. The rest, like most others in our village, were *cầu khỉ*, or monkey bridges. Monkey bridges were usually made of a single log spanning a stream. Most were only a few feet above the water, though some could be at dizzying heights. Many had a handrail, others no support at all. Fancier monkey bridges resembled a makeshift scaffold—a series of logs tied together with vines, propped up by supporting poles driven into the mud below. To anyone encountering a monkey bridge for the first time, it might seem that only a monkey could meet such an acrobatic challenge. But the inspiration for the name came from another source: the distinctive posture, stooped and monkey-like, that one must maintain when crossing.

In the beginning, none of us was eager to attempt these scary crossways. But quickly we realized that there was no other way to get around. Our mother would make us practice on a coconut log that was wider and less bouncy than the typical bamboo stalk. A helpful villager advised us that the key to keeping one's balance was to look ahead and never at our feet or at the water.

We would learn to cross the different bridges by doing whatever it took to do so without falling. Initially I would hold the handrail with both hands and scoot slowly sideways, if only I could ignore the inevitable laughter from onlookers. Over time, Cu Anh managed to become almost as skillful as the villagers, even able to run across a monkey bridge while carrying a heavy load. I never developed my brother's skills. On rainy days or when running away from village dogs, I would, on occasion, fall into the mud, but somehow I always managed to emerge intact.

In the countryside, we all noticed the quiet that enveloped us. The whirl of traffic and other noises of the city had vanished. Our daily life revolved around the pond surrounding our house. At low tide, I waded in the mud to catch *ba khía* (small, dark-colored crabs indigenous to the Mekong Delta) and to chase after the few remaining fish. What I caught was usually not enough for a meal. To carry out actual fishing, I had to wait for high tide, a period when most of our daily activities took place. Surrounded by abundant water, we bathed, washed clothes, and prepared food. Like fishing, these activities were done right from the deck inside our house.

During the day, my brothers and I raced each other to climb trees in search of the best fruits. We filled our stomachs with guavas, tangerines, longan, rambutans, stopping only when our teeth balked at biting into yet another sour fruit. In the pond, we transformed land games into water sports. In the beginning, when we hadn't learned to swim, we cut down old banana trees, ones that were no longer productive, and clung to them to stay afloat in the water. As our water skills advanced, our games became more elaborate. While my mother rinsed dishes, I often swam nearby. "Chanh, go swim somewhere else," she said, pointing to the ripples of grease. I paid no attention to her chiding, as I knew a fun game awaited. Invariably, a spoon or ladle would slip out of her fingers and I would get to be the hero, diving to retrieve the lost utensil.

Nighttime in the countryside was different. On moonless nights, kerosene lanterns were our only source of illumination. Oil, even scarcer than other supplies and bought on the black market, was measured by the drop. We lit only two lamps: the smaller one was portable; the bigger one stayed put on the kitchen table in the middle of the house, lit only for a short time to conserve oil. Under the flickering light, Cu Anh hurried to finish his homework while my father stayed glued to the battery-powered shortwave radio, listening to *Voice of America*. Back then I knew the broadcast only by its acronym, VOA, which I assumed was a Vietnamese word. I thought it was the only program on the radio, delivering forbidden news of a world beyond Vietnam. America, Australia, the United Nations—the names streamed into our darkened home. What I heard about these faraway places seemed so alien that I could not relate in any way. I knew almost nothing of the world outside Việt Nam. At the slightest noise from outdoors, my father immediately turned off the barely audible broadcast and rushed to put the radio away.

Many things I welcomed during the day terrorized me at night. The quiet, so peaceful earlier, became oppressive. The animal noises, rowdy and boisterous, resembled screams in the absence of light. During the day, I loved that our house had only three walls. The missing wall turned the deck into one long diving pad and a most convenient place for fishing. In the dark, I only saw the open expanse as an invitation to robbers, rats, snakes, anything and anyone that wanted to drop in. I yearned for a house filled with light and a fourth wall. But what I longed for most of all was a bathroom down the hallway, like we had in Sài Gòn, instead of an outhouse several monkey bridges away, rising above the water like a poor man's mausoleum.

Even the trees that I loved to climb turned ominous in the dark—perhaps none more than the *vú sữa* (breast milk) tree outside my window. During the day, I searched among its branches for the round green fruits the size of a baseball. Inside was a juice so sweet and purely white as to be indistinguishable from milk. At night, my mind could not quiet the ghost stories that I had heard about mothers who had died in childbirth and their preferred place to congregate. On the limbs of the *vú sữa* tree, these brokenhearted mothers, surrounded by an endless supply of milk, would nurse the babies whom they never got to care for in life.

These nighttime torments metastasized through my mind, leaving me wide-eyed in my bed. To calm myself, I would trace the shadows that the moonlight occasionally cast on the mosquito net draped around me. The softest sound, the slightest movement would send me diving beneath the thin blanket, even on the hottest nights. Often, I ended up gathering my bedding and running to my brothers. Mindful of my parents' rule not to share the boys' bed now that I was older, instead of squishing my pillow next to my brothers' heads, I put it by their feet, then squeezed myself into any tiny space on the bed. As long as I could feel a toe touching my hair, the rustling of leaves no longer came to my ears as footsteps of an intruder or of a ghost but only as what they were, lulling me to sleep.

OF CANOES, BEES, AND OTHER STORIES

A s in the city, the only sure way to keep anything from being stolen was for someone to stand guard. And thus the chore I dreaded in Sài Gòn followed me to our new home in the countryside. In both places, my job meant long stretches of boredom.

In Sài Gòn, my watch was over a bicycle. "Chanh, come with me," my mother would call out. I must have been around five when I first heard the cue that always seemed to come in the middle of some fun game. I grudgingly hopped on the back of her bicycle, which she then pedaled to a black market a few blocks from our house. While my mother shopped, I stayed next to the bicycle. Around me, vendors and customers haggled over prices. One time a man came over and offered me some candy. Another time, a woman gave me some coins. They said that they needed to talk to my mother and asked me to go find her. Even though I wasn't entirely sure, I sensed dishonesty behind their friendliness. "My mom said I can't leave," I answered each time. They did not press more and quickly left. These interactions were my first lessons in assessing people's motives and trusting my intuition. The ride home from the market was much more fun. Holding the bike handle with one hand, my mother would reach into the front basket with the other. Rummaging around, she would pick up something, then extend her hand behind to me. In her palm, I would find some sticky rice or boiled peanuts. Whatever annoyance I still had would instantly disappear.

In the countryside, the object under my watch changed to the canoe. As there was no secure place to store it on the other side of the river, and I wasn't old enough to take it back home by myself, my job was to keep watch while my mother went around the brick factory selling fruits that she couldn't sell at the market. If I was lucky, there would be some children's games nearby for me to join. If not, the minutes felt endless while I waited for my mother to return to row back home.

Rowing back and forth across the river was something we did daily to get to school, the market, or anywhere in town. The process involved two parts: getting the canoe from the pond into the river and then paddling it to the other side.

The first part was simple when the tide was high. We could hop on the canoe from the deck inside our house, paddle around the pond, then paddle through the canal leading into the river. Things were more complicated at low tide, when only a small amount of water remained in the pond and none in the more elevated canal. We could still get around the pond by pushing the oar against the mud. By the entrance to the canal, however, we had no choice but to roll up our pants, get off the canoe, and push it across the mud. The act always left our clothes and bodies smeared with muck.

In the river, any combination of wind and rain would force a confrontation between our efforts and nature's might. Despite our furious paddling, the tiny houses on the other side at times did not grow any bigger and even seemed to shrink. But no matter how much my arms ached, I knew I could not rest until we got to the other side.

Once we reached shore, Bảy and I still had a trek to complete our daily commute to school. We had to walk through the brick factory, then along the busy thoroughfare. The barren school structure was nothing like the tall building of my elementary school in Sài Gòn. It comprised six or seven adjoining classrooms with open doorways but no doors. With no electricity, we relied on light and wind coming through open windows. Younger students, including Bảy and me, attended classes in the morning, while older students, Cu Anh's age, attended in the afternoon.

In the fall of 1978, I started first grade in the countryside. Every morning before school started, we stood in formation around the flagpole in the center of the courtyard. Amid a sea of white shirts, dark blue pants, and red kerchiefs, we sang songs in praise of Bác Hồ and the Communist Party, such as "Last Night I Dreamed I Met Uncle Hồ." I came to know the lyrics by heart: "He had a long beard and white hair. With adoration, I kissed his cheeks. So happy, I sang. So happy, I danced. He smiled, praising me as a good child. He nodded, praising me as a good child." We also recited slogans about freedom, liberty, and independence— weighty concepts that I did not fully understand. But around me, people did not appear to embrace these ideals. Instead, everyone, even children, seemed afraid of saying or doing anything that could cause trouble with the government. Mindful of my parents' advice, I knew not to refer to our family's background lest it draw attention to our status as outsiders and unpatriotic holdovers from the old regime.

Around my neck, the red kerchief felt tight and uncomfortable. The symbol signified that we, good and obedient students, were part of the Youth Pioneer—future leaders of the Communist Party. The irony of our elevated status was not lost on my father, who would jokingly ask us to remember to look kindly on our parents in the future. Turning serious, he added that we would never be free of our past. Our family's association with the old bourgeoisie would always follow my brothers and me as it had my sisters in Sài Gòn, limiting their school and employment prospects. In the communist society, our family would never be fully accepted. As soon as school let out each day, I quickly reached for the end of the scarf. In one swoop, my neck was free.

"You have to keep up with the kids in Sài Gòn," my father often said. I had a feeling that they were much more prepared than we. At the very least, I suspected that they had more books than we did. Our class of thirty first-graders had only a few, which the teacher took home with her every day to prevent theft.

Paper to write on was also in short supply. On the molasses-colored pages, I knew to press the pen only lightly so that ink would not bleed onto the back. But as the low-quality paper was so thin, ink often bled through anyway, rendering the backside useless. Perhaps using a pencil might have helped, but students never used pencils to write. In the countryside, as had been the case in Sài Gòn, students wrote using an ink-dipped pen. Before we learned to trace the letters of the alphabet, we had to learn how to use an ink pen: how to dip the tip into the ink, how long to wait so as not to flood the ink chamber, and how to extract the pen without splattering ink all over.

With limited materials, students in the countryside turned to a writing surface that never ran out: a handheld chalkboard. We used it to work on math and practice spelling. During a test, our teacher would call out a question, then wait for us to write down our answers. When finished, we held up the boards as she went around the room checking our work. At her signal, we swiped the boards clean, ready for the next question.

"King, Teacher, Father": the hierarchy of reverence was ingrained in me and other children at an early age. Ranked even above one's father, the teacher was the representative of knowledge and our moral guide. Students were not to challenge or contradict opinions of the authority considered beyond reproach. In Sài Gòn, my kindergarten teacher always wore a white *áo dài*, the traditional knee-length tunic worn over long pants. She spoke sternly when praising us and when doling out our punishment. Being disrespectful, talking in class, doing subpar work, all could result in lashes with a ruler on one's open palm. The number of lashes depended on the infraction; the severity of the strikes, often on my teacher's mood.

The teachers in the countryside were less formal in their dress. Most opted for the uniform of women in the countryside, a blouse over loose black pants. Despite their appearance, they still seemed to possess that air of infallibility. Except for my first-grade teacher.

"SHUT UP! Shut up, all of you uneducated, ill-mannered bastards!" She yelled from her desk in front of the blackboard. My hands gripped the wooden bench as my eyes fixated on the dirt floor, like those of every other kid around me. Our silence hung in the hot air between her pauses. I wondered what could have ignited such wrath. Anything, it seemed, as I would discover. For the rest of the school year, the name-calling continued amid bursts of rage. During the tirade, she would wave her hands and shake her head, loosening her hair held in a bun with two chopsticks. For most of my first-grade year, Scary Teacher—the name my classmates and I took to calling her—terrorized me during the day as the ghosts and monsters of my imagination did during the night.

Most of the people in our village were rice farmers with a small parcel of land around their homes to grow fruits and vegetables. Our family was one of the few that had a slightly larger fruit orchard but no rice field. Soon after we arrived, my father was given the nickname Ông Ba Vườn (Old Man Number Three with the Fruit Orchard). Around the village, every head of the household had a nickname that was also used to refer to his family. My mother was called Bà Ba Vườn, or Old Woman Number Three with a Fruit Orchard. My brothers and I were known as Con Ông Ba Vườn, or children of Old Man Number Three with the Fruit Orchard. A person's actual name was rarely used; often it was not even known. In fact, using an adult's name without a title is considered very disrespectful. The biggest insult a kid could hurl at another was to call out his or her father's real name.

"Ngô Hòa," a boy once yelled out as my brothers and I walked by. The call to battle—most likely discovered after some snooping around for information about the new family from the big city—immediately halted my brothers' steps. They passed whatever they were holding to me, ready to fight.

Despite their moniker, my parents lacked a green thumb. The trees inside our orchard didn't appear as lush or productive as those around us. We had a few of each kind of fruit—longan, water apple, orange, guava, mango, rambutan, soursop, pineapple, papaya, and others, including several varieties of banana. While we had plenty of fruits to eat—at least in the beginning when things had not become so desperate and theft was not so rampant—we never produced enough to earn much of an income. Even though the temperature didn't vary much throughout the year, the harvest seasons tended to vary for different fruits. Some grew better during monsoon season; others thrived in the dry season. So the income, however meager, was distributed throughout the year.

Every few days, we would collect enough from the orchard to fill least one or two small baskets to sell at the market—the only one in our town and a half-hour walk from the brick factory on the other side of the river. On those mornings, we would leave our house when it was still dark, since markets in the countryside convened long before dawn and were mostly over by the time the sun came out and the heat intensified. After ferrying us across the river, my father or brother would return home with the canoe while my mother and I continued to the outdoor marketplace.

Once there, we staked out a spot on the ground next to vendors selling vegetables, meats, live chickens, and ducks. I would organize fruits with long stems, like rambutans or longans, into bundles, putting the most attractive ones on the outside along with a few decorative leaves on top. After laying out our produce on the straw mat, we sat on wooden blocks and waited for customers.

The people who came by taught me much about human nature. I remember a woman wearing a much-patched-over blouse surrounded by many young children. She usually bought eleven, or multiples of eleven, of whatever fruits we had. "Equal amount for each kid," she told me. Often, she couldn't come up with enough money and had to put some fruits back. But sometimes, when counting her change, she would press a few coins into my hands and tell me to go buy myself some sweets.

I also remember another woman with a beautiful jade bracelet and meticulous hair held in place by a porcelain chopstick. Her bulging eyes nevertheless reminded me only of a salamander. The woman often showed up soon after we arrived at the market. Walking back and forth, she would sidle up to any customer seeming interested in a certain item, saying that my mother had already agreed to sell it to her. When my mother insisted that this was not the case, the woman would pretend to be confused and repeat her insincere offer at a price so high that the customer almost always left. At the end of the market, she would tell my mother that she didn't have enough money and could pay only what she had in her pocket. As a child it took me some time to understand this woman's sly deceit.

At the market, I noticed some vendors buying banana leaves to use as wrappers for their merchandise, as there were no plastic or paper bags. Until then I had not thought that anyone would pay for something so abundant. Banana leaves drooped down from trees everywhere. My mother explained that gathering and cleaning the leaves provided value. Deciding that this was work I could do, I proceeded to find customers willing to buy from me. A fishmonger agreed and said that she preferred "wilted brown banana leaves, not green ones."

Prized for the tissue-soft texture, such wilted leaves were used mainly as toilet paper. Each morning afforded only a small window of time for their harvest—the period after the sun had evaporated the dew, but before the heat had become intense, turning the leaves brittle. A few times with Bảy's help, I gathered some bundles and brought them to the market. The fishmonger's pay was not much, but the satisfaction of making money stayed with me.

It seems that trees with the tastiest fruits often bear the fewest. Animals, insects, and humans vie for these sweet fruits. I would often see weaver ants—big red ants whose jaws could cut through bigger insects, not to mention human skin—scurrying up and down in long lines on their branches. In contrast, trees with bad fruits were free of pests. I first observed this phenomenon in two types of mango trees. The sand mango had an exquisitely smooth texture and a balance of tartness and sweetness. Each tree had only a few fruits. On the other hand, the stinky mango, with a vile odor and a taste equally terrible, hung in bunches, mostly untouched by bats and birds. When we first moved to the countryside, my brothers and I pinched our noses and bit into one, only to spit it out immediately. It was only later, when food became scarce, that we came to appreciate their abundance.

If the stinky mango was God's mistake, the durian was his glory. From the moment my mother let me taste its sweet creamy flesh off her fingers, I was sure this fruit with its intense fragrance had to be the food of the heavens. Round and covered with big, sharp spikes, the durian even looked like it came from another world. Around the Mekong Delta, the home of the durian, everyone seemed to share my love for what was nicknamed the king of fruits. In Sài Gòn, this was not the case. Some likened the smell to that of rotten food and raw sewage and blamed it as the cause of their persistent headaches. So strong was their opposition that durian was banned in many public spaces.

When we first arrived in our orchard, my brothers and I were excited to discover a tree with the tell-tale oblong-shaped leaves, green and smooth on one side, brown and fuzzy on the other. Every day, we scanned the canopy, hoping to find a durian. It took a few years for us to spot a small bud covered with tiny thorns. The bud grew to the size of a coconut, then stopped growing. Its thick green husk gradually turned golden. Soon a crack appeared in the center of the fruit as the air all around took on the distinctive scent. I wanted to hold the fruit in my hand and feel its spikes against my skin, but I knew that I needed to wait. Unlike other fruits, the durian could not be picked and was only ready to eat after it had fallen on its own to the ground. While waiting, I was afraid that a thief would come for it, ripe or not.

It was around this time that my uncle, Dượng Mười, (Uncle Number Ten, the husband of my father's youngest sister) sometimes stopped by our house to plan the escape from Việt Nam with my father. When I mentioned to him my fear of our durian's being stolen, he told us a story about his grandfather.

Dượng Mười's grandfather also loved his durian tree and kept careful accounting of the number of fruits he had. One morning he noticed one was missing; the following morning, another. With no trace of their having fallen on the ground, he concluded that a thief must have climbed up the tree during the night to steal the fruits. He decided that under his watch the thief would have no more.

When dusk came, the grandfather climbed up the tree to a safe distance away from the potentially lethal missiles. The thorn-covered fruits, each weighing several pounds, tended to fall at nighttime. He found a sturdy branch, then settled down for his lookout. The night went on without incident, but as the chirpings of crickets gave way to the crowing of the rooster, he heard loud crushes of leaves beneath the tree. In the dim light, he made out a shadow of a man.

"Thief, stop where you are!" his grandfather shouted down. The trampling immediately stopped.

"You'd better leave and don't come back!" he continued. He had expected to hear footsteps dashing off, instead he heard, "I'm not scared of you, old man!" followed by what sounded like rummaging around the ground. A fusillade of rocks suddenly shot up from below, grazing his grandfather's arms and legs.

"I'm coming back tomorrow. If I see you up there, I'm going to cut down the tree!" the thief called out as he ran off.

The rocks rattled my uncle's grandfather but ended up only refueling his resolve. The next night he was back in the tree, armed with his own pouch of rocks. But as it turned out, he never had to use them, that night or any of the nights that it took until the last durian fell down. Perhaps the thief did come back only to turn around when he spotted his foe up in the tree. For all his bluster, maybe he feared a determined old man after all.

"No, you cannot climb up the tree to guard the durian. If it's stolen then it's stolen," my father said before we even asked. We did not have long to worry. A few mornings later, I found our durian on the ground, pinned to a layer of wet leaves.

Like other firsts—first child, first customer, first visitor during the *Tết* new year holiday—the first fruit of a tree embodied a special honor. There was no question that we first had to present it to the ancestors. And afterward, my father would be the one to open the fruit and have the first taste.

After my mother cleaned the durian of dirt and leaves, she placed it on a plate in the middle of the altar. Throughout the day, while my parents were at work, I ran in and out of the altar room, stopping each time to look up. What was inside the thick rind to produce such an overpowering scent extending far outside our house? The thought drove me to climb on top of a chair to take down the plate holding the durian. On the floor, oblivious to the gaze of my grandparents from the altar, I pressed my nose against the split in the husk. My fingers grabbed at edges of the slit and in one quick motion pulled them apart. The durian split open. The long-awaited first fruit was no longer whole but two halves. But inside, the two pockets were hollow, with not a trace of the ambrosia that I had expected to find.

Until now, my misdeeds had comprised mostly fighting with Bảy, being rude to my parents, or interrupting adult conversations. The punishment—a harsh reprimand from my mother or a slap across the cheek from my father—had always been doled out on the spot, catching me unaware. This time felt different. I had no idea what punishment awaited me.

As panic lurked, I cut out some thread from a spool and tied together the two halves. I then climbed on the chair and placed the fruit back on the altar. While waiting for my parents to come home, I sat on the floor, staring up at the bandaged offering and the photos of my grandparents. Their faces, once approving, now appeared to scowl in judgment. Even the clock, with its louder-than-normal ticking, seemed to signal its disapproval. I finally heard my parents' footsteps and rushed over to pour out my story. When I finished, I heard a chuckle.

"So Chanh, you like durians that much?" my father said, smiling.

I nodded.

"Go find your brothers and you can open the other sections. Maybe you'll have more luck," he continued.

Later, with everyone gathering around me, I pried open the rest of the durian. In all the remaining pockets, there was only one small pod. My father took a small nibble, then passed it to my mother, then my brothers, then me. But, instead of a sweet creaminess that I had expected, the long-awaited fruit tasted bland and

47

chewy. My father was quick to point out that such off flavor was not uncommon for the first fruit of any tree, an explanation that did little to ease my disappointment.

My parents' lack of knowledge about farming also extended to raising livestock. While most of our neighbors had only a few varieties of animal, we kept a whole menagerie: ducks, chickens, turkeys, pigeons, rabbits, pigs, and several types of fish. Feeding them was an all-consuming, never-ending task.

Among the livestock, the turkey, or *gà Tây* (Western chicken), was the meanest. Even though no one around us raised turkeys, my father wanted to experiment. He thought of the turkey as an oversized chicken with similar temperament and habits. If we were going to raise chickens, he said, why not raise a bigger chicken? It could replace the hen to hatch a bigger clutch of eggs, producing more baby chicks at one time, besides yielding more meat in the end.

But the turkey did almost nothing my father had planned. It never quite developed the desire to brood, the urge to sit on a pile of eggs day and night with little thought for eating or drinking. Quite the opposite, eating seemed to be the only thing on its mind. It stripped leaves off every tree within its reach and poked at any chicken or duck that came close to it at feeding time. The Western bird eventually wore out its usefulness. Though, in the end, my father was right about one thing: It did yield a lot more meat than a chicken.

After the turkey's departure, the hens and ducks resumed hatching their own eggs. Of the batches of ducklings, one stands out in my mind. Among the golden-fur ducklings was one brown baby chick. Immediately we realized that a chicken egg must somehow have gotten mixed in with the pile of duck eggs. As fowl were known to be quite protective of their young, we had no idea how the mother duck would react. In the following days, we kept close watch over the group, but as it turned out, the chick didn't need our rescue. The mother duck didn't treat it any differently from the rest of her brood.

Each day, she took her babies a little farther from the nest to look for food. After a few weeks, when their soft fuzz had grown into a thick coat, she led them to the pond next to our house. In one swoop, she slid down the bank, then waddled over the mud into the water. One by one, the ducklings followed, pressing their webbed feet against the wet mud to slide down as she had done. In the water, they spread out their tiny wings, then reached high in the air while dipping their heads in and out of the water.

As his siblings frolicked, the baby chick remained on the shore, cheeping loudly. From the pond, his mother quacked back, as if to tell him to get in the water already. After a while, the chick stopped pacing and began the tentative descent. But without webbed feet, he couldn't slide down the mud. Instead, he had to dig in his claws to hop down, barely catching himself from toppling over. As he approached the water, he resumed cheeping loudly.

A few feet away, the mother duck swam back and forth, quacking the same message as before. This time, the chick refused to budge. On land, the differences between the chick and his duck siblings had not mattered and had in fact given him an advantage. His claws, distinct little pick axes, could stir up dirt to get to the worms that their fused-together feet could not. His pointed beak, unlike their round bill, could break apart even the sturdiest soil. In the water, these features would prove useless if not deadly. He needed webbed feet to propel through water, a round bill to burrow into the mud, and a waterproof coat to stay afloat. Hard-wired evolutionary instincts must have stirred something in the chick, preventing him from jumping in the water to certain suicide.

After a while, the mother duck proceeded to lead the ducklings farther out into the pond. The chick hopped alongside on the mud. When the brood had drifted far from shore, he turned around and ran up to higher ground, where other chickens had gathered to dig for worms.

For a long time, the saga of the chick continued to captivate my attention. With few books and no TV or neighborhood games, life in our village lacked entertainment options. The suspense of what would happen to the chick provided novel excitement. I would follow it around to see how it fared on its own. After the initial separation, the chick never returned to its duck family. Within a few months, bright red combs developed above its head and long arching feathers grew out from its tail. Most impressive were the sharp spurs

49

above its back claws, weapons it used to attack dogs, cats, and other predators. The once tiny ball of fuzz had blossomed into a rooster, quite capable of fending for itself. But eventually, like the rest of the livestock, it too became our dinner.

In school, I quickly realized the power that came with having an older brother. "I'm telling my brother" was a threat I directed freely at any perceived bully. Usually, it was enough to stop the harassment, although I did sometimes have to run over to Bảy. As my brother broke from his friends and games of marbles or hacky sack during recess, I recognized the look of annoyance. Still, he always extended his hand to let me drag him along.

"You guys had better stop bothering my sister," he said when I deposited him in front of the enemy. That was all it took for the bullies, boys my age and a couple of years younger than Bảy, to back away and for me and my friends to return to jumping rope. The exercise invariably led to thirst, which often happened in the tropical heat.

At school, thirst was our constant companion. We knew to just bear it until we got home, but occasionally my friends and I would sneak into one of the neighboring yards seeking relief. The owners, aware of the parched mouths hovering just outside, bolted covers over their water barrels. All had dogs. At the edge of the yard, we paused to check. Only if the guards were sleeping did we tiptoe to the water barrel. As quietly as we could, we worked together to remove the lid. Using our cupped palms, we scooped up the unboiled water, drinking and drinking with little thought of likely stomach cramps. Our drinking invariably woke the dogs. At the first hint of their stirring, we trampled over each other to run off. Luckily, they never chased us far, trained to get the intruders just out of the yard.

While there was no drinking water, bathroom, or nurse's office at the school, we did on occasion receive vaccination shots. In the courtyard, we stood in line with our shirt sleeves pushed up, inching toward a pot of water boiling over a wood fire. I watched the nurse retract the needle from my arm, then put the used syringe into boiling water to clean. When finished, she repeated the process with the students in line behind me.

We had school six days a week, Monday to Saturday. Most days, school let out before noon at the clanging of the bell in the middle of the courtyard. The stream of students spilled out onto the street alongside traffic. Girls walked in pairs holding hands or linking arms while boys sauntered in groups, draping arms around one another's shoulders. Most lived in town and had a shorter commute home than the few of us who had to cross a river. By the water's edge inside the brick factory, Bảy and I readied our lungs to summon across the river for our mother to come pick us up, just as she had dropped us off in the morning.

"Má ơi!" We bellowed into our hands curved around our mouths.

On calm days, our screams for pickup arrived at our mother's ears as intended. In bad weather, the winds hurled our voices far downstream. Since our mother expected us at the same time every day, she almost always showed up. But sometimes, distracted by the daily rhythms of farm life, she would lose track of time and forget about us if she did not hear our call. In that case, we would scream even more loudly, then settle down to wait. Around us, kids squatted along the riverbank, eating lunch. These waits felt interminable as my stomach growled. I remember watching a boy bite into a long red pepper. His other hand was holding a small bowl of freshly-cooked rice with a dollop of *mắm ruốc* (fermented shrimp paste) perching on top. It was a simple lunch even for back then. But when hungry, I sometimes find myself thinking back to the steaming rice with *mắm ruốc* and spicy pepper as a meal I would want.

Another time while awaiting our pickup, I watched one of Bảy's friends climb up a coconut tree. Keeping his feet gripped to the sides of the trunk, he propelled himself upward with his hands, much like a frog hopping. Once on top, he secured himself on a large palm leaf. Screaming loudly, "Coconut falling! Coconut falling!" he reached over to twist a coconut until it broke from the stem to fall on the ground. After a few fruits, he began the descent. When he was almost at the bottom, suddenly he lost his balance and fell backward. After a heavy thud, the boy was spread out on the ground, his arm twisted at an odd angle from his body. Several neighbors immediately rushed over and carried him inside the nearest hut.

A few days later, the boy was back playing with Bảy and the other kids. His arm was wrapped in a homemade cast held straight with bamboo and dressed bright yellow with turmeric. The potent ginger-like root was known for preventing infection and speeding up healing. When the wrapping came off, his arm remained crooked, the forearm perpendicular to the upper arm, dangling near his chest. After the accident, his nickname became Chín Quẹo (Crooked Ninth).

While the ghosts and monsters I feared during the night existed, as far as I knew, only in my mind, my fears during the day—of drowning, snakebite, stepping on sharp objects, falling off bridges and out of trees, getting fish bones stuck in my throat, discovering a leech on my body—were actual dangers. Some had simple remedies such as pouring ash on a leech and waiting for it to let go instead of rushing to pull it off, or swallowing uncomfortably big clumps of rice to dislodge a small fish bone. Others were not so clear-cut. Of all my fears, stepping on a rusted nail and contracting lockjaw reigned supreme. I did not know much about the condition except that it was a horrible way to die, and I believed I could get it if rust got into my blood.

Surrounded by water and mud, we had long ago discarded our footwear for the firm grip of bare feet. Getting punctured and scraped was all too common. If the cause was a rusted nail or piece of metal, panic would take over. Dropping to the ground, I squeezed hard around the cut, then bit on it to extract more of the tainted blood. After rushing home, I would wash the wound, then dab it with *thuốc đỏ* (red medicine).

Known as Mercurochrome in the West, the red liquid antiseptic was the closest thing to Western medicine in our village. People used it for every break in the skin, from superficial cuts to severe burns. We also used it to treat our livestock—the pig that scraped its snout while reaching for scraps beyond the pen, the roosters fighting almost to the death during mating season, the chicken that accidentally stepped on a smoldering wood fire. That last incident I remember well.

As *thuốc đỏ* was particulary effective in treating burns, the chicken's injuries healed without complications but left it without most of its claws. Still, the resilient hen could defend itself and dig for food. What it could no longer do was grab onto tree branches for a prolonged period. One morning, Bảy discovered its body floating in the pond, a victim of what we assumed was a failed attempt to sleep in a tree, a chicken's preferred nighttime resting place.

For illnesses *thuốc đỏ* could not cure, the villagers turned to herbs and other folk medicine. The most popular remedy was *cạo gió*, which literally means "scratching off wind." An excess of bad wind in the body was believed to be the cause of many sicknesses. The process of *cạo gió* involved scraping lubricated skin with a spoon to release the bad wind from the body and restore internal balance. So deeply embedded in the Vietnamese culture, *cạo gió* is as emblematic as *nước mắm* (fish sauce) to the national identity, even though the former was imported from China long ago.

Despite its popularity, I did not much like receiving *cạo gió*. "Má, I don't feel so well," I said, gently tapping on my mother's *nón lá* (cone-shaped hat) as she sat beside the banana trunk slicing food for the pigs. I knew my complaint would result in the dreaded treatment, but being near my mother and having her undivided attention was worth the tradeoff. With livestock to care for, fruits to harvest and sell, vegetables to plant, meals to cook, my mother was always busy. Her chores often continued into the night, illuminated by a small kerosene lamp flickering by her side. In my bed, I was sometimes stirred awake by the sounds of sloshing water. Without looking, I knew they came from my mother washing clothes. Guilt tugged at me to get up to help or at least just to keep her company. A few times I was able to overcome the pull of slumber, but often I just fell back to sleep.

The transition to the countryside was hardest on my mother. Overnight, her world shifted from running a business with my father and living in a home with help and modern conveniences to merely surviving in a backwater of preindustrial farm life. When we first moved to the countryside, I would sometimes hear my mother lapse into a tirade of complaints. But the longer we stayed, the more she seemed to accept the reality of our lives. While my mother worked, I often stayed by her side, copying whatever she did and peppering her with questions. "Chanh, I'm too tired to talk," was her response to many of my inquiries. Her grievance would show no stronger expression. She mostly exuded quiet endurance, a trait highly valued in Vietnamese society.

Upon my complaint of not feeling well, my mother always broke from her work to put her palm against my forehead to feel if I had a fever. Regardless, she would tell me to go get the stuff. The stuff was a spoon and a small diamond-shaped glass bottle filled with *dầu xanh* (green oil). Rubbed onto the skin or sniffed, the medicated oil released a menthol-scented heat believed to bring relief to various kinds of aches and pains. Many Vietnamese keep a small bottle in their shirt pockets, ready for a quick sniff or rub. In postwar Việt Nam, the beloved oil, like other daily necessities, disappeared from the markets. When my parents managed to buy a bottle of *dầu xanh*, they would sometimes find only green water inside.

After retrieving the two essentials of *cạo gió*, I headed for the wooden divan in the back of the house, then lay face down. After lifting up my shirt, my mother put a few drops of oil on my back and spread it around. Almost immediately, I could feel the heat seeping into my skin, then radiating outward. This part I did not mind. What came next I never learned to appreciate. Using the sharper edges of the spoon, my mother scraped at my oiled skin. As the metal edge went up and down, I imagined bad winds being pulled out from my muscles to congregate in the deep red lines now appearing on my back. The redder the scrape marks, the more sickness was extracted. Even though my back felt like it was on fire, I kept silent, but somehow my mother always seemed to know my limit. Just as I was about to scream for her to stop, she moved the spoon to a fresh patch of skin to resume scraping. A light pat on my shoulder was my cue that *cạo gió* was over.

"Má, how red were the lines?" I always wanted to know. Although I had not wanted the *cạo gió* remedy, I often felt better afterward.

Worse than receiving *cạo gió*, however, was performing it, as my mother sometimes asked me to do for her. In bright daylight, my harried, always-on-the-move mother lay motionless before me. I could not help but imagine that she was dead, even though I could feel her body rise and fall with her breath while I spread the oil. With the creatures that flooded my imagination at night, I could conjure fighting back. The idea of a life without my mother or father had my mind in a chokehold. All I could summon was a vast expanse of nothingness where everything and everyone, including me, ceased to be. I knew my mother was not dead, yet I could not tame my fears. Often, I would ask questions merely to elicit a response. My mother either remained silent or told me to be quiet. The reprimand I did not mind, but I dreaded the silence.

Besides the turmoil in my head, there was the worsening ache in my arm as it took much effort to keep up the sweeping motion of the spoon. I would rush from one spot to another, scraping furiously to prove that I was hard at work. Abruptly pulling down her shirt, I announced that it was all done. I would tell my mother that I was able to extract many deep red lines. She never seemed to doubt me. Turning chatty, she would thank me and proceed to extol the virtues of the most wondrous remedy.

Around our village, each day began with a wake-up call from nature's perennial timekeeper. Long before the first ray of daylight, the rooster unleashed its crowing, louder and harsher in the beginning, then softer as dawn approached. All the animals woke up starving and demanding food. The pigs banged their heads against the gate, trying to break out of their pen. The chickens and ducks formed a barricade in front of our house, jumping over each other to press up against the door, clucking and quacking loudly. The longer the animals had to wait, the more destructive they became.

The animals with the most insatiable appetite were pigs. In a pen situated a pond away from our house, we raised two. Several times a day, we fed them a mixture of sliced-up banana trunk and rice bran, a diet that perhaps was not substantive enough, because they always seemed to be hungry. While we poured their food into the trough, they rammed up against each other to get closer. Barely missing our fingers, they often knocked the bucket from our hands, then continued to devour the food strewn on the floor of their pen and now mixed with their excrement. Our days were filled with their incessant cries for food. As my mother raced around during the day, she often hummed the ditty, "Heo kêu, con khóc, cơm sôi" (Pigs are crying, children are wailing, rice is boiling). The short simple song perfectly captured the frenzy of life for a mother in the countryside.

After we fed the animals, it was our turn for our breakfast. On rare occasions, we might have some leftover rice from the previous evening's dinner. Over a small wood fire outside, my mother transformed it into my favorite dish—fried rice. A sprinkle of fish sauce and black pepper, when the condiment was still available at the market, signaled the end of her cooking. My mother scooped out the hot rice, infused with the scent of lard, into five small bowls. After setting aside a portion for my father, she let me, the youngest, choose first among the remaining four. While everyone waited, I weighed my options. The less-filled bowl might be the best choice. Compacted, it might hold more than the bowl topped high. But then, the fuller bowl might just have more.

"Come on, pick one already!" one of my brothers would say, forcing me to a decision.

After I chose mine, my brothers then took theirs. No matter how sure I was just a moment ago, my brothers' bowls, now in their hands, always seemed to have more. The smell of cooking had the animals gathering around us. But often we couldn't wait to go inside and ended up eating with the chickens, ducks, cat, and dog circling at our feet. Between bites, we held the bowls high above our heads, keeping the just-fed-but-already-hungry mouths from stealing our breakfast.

Most mornings there were no leftovers from the night before, and my brothers and I had to go search for food. We could fish or dig for yucca or yam, but neither guaranteed success. Even if we succeeded, we still had to clean and cook what we found. So, although we yearned for proteins and starches, we often resorted to the quickest and surest food—fruits. Our games often revolved around the search for fruits. Our favorite was to race each other up a tree to see who could get to the top first.

One afternoon while Cu Anh was at school, Bảy and I decided to race up a guava tree, a favorite in our repertoire that we had forgotten about for a while.

Within seconds of our ascent, Bảy was already much higher than I was. Every time he moved, the branches jostled.

"Bảy, don't eat everything! Save some for me," I called up.

Suddenly I heard a frantic scream.

"Get down! Drop down now!"

"What? Why?" I looked up to see what had happened. As if an eclipse had emerged out of nowhere, above me loomed a huge shadow, obscuring everything. It was Bảy, falling and frantically grabbing at the tree to break his fall.

I no longer cared to know the reason. I knew whatever came for Bảy would also come for me. I let go my handholds and dropped down. Through the jumble of leaves and twigs that whipped at my face, arms, and legs, I grabbed onto anything I could to slow the fall.

I landed on my back on the wet ground, stunned, and Bảy followed an instant later, landing on top of me. I screamed, "Get off me!" but he didn't need any encouragement—he leaped to his feet and sprinted away, shouting: "Run! Bees!"

I scrambled after Bảy, terrified because I knew that if he had disturbed their nest, the whole swarm would be furious, intent on stinging the closest living thing that might have done the damage. I could hear their angry droning behind me as I raced after Bảy.

The buzzing grew fainter as I ran, but after twenty or thirty yards, my legs began to slow. I reached behind my thighs and felt what I thought was mud. I looked at my hands. They were covered with blood. I slowed almost to a stop. "Bảy, help me! I can't run anymore," I called out.

Bảy turned back toward me. His eyes widened—I thought at first it was because he saw my bloody hands, but he was looking behind me. The bee swarm was clearly catching up. Bảy then seemed to be struck by a sudden inspiration and started to run away from me. I thought I was being abandoned, but then I saw where he was headed—toward a pond directly ahead of us.

He yelled, "Chanh, jump in!" as he hurled himself into the water.

I ran as well as I could, recalling the words of caution that I had heard from my father for years: "Do not jump in any water if you don't know for sure what's underneath. You don't want to be impaled by a broken branch."

I had no idea what lay beneath the water lilies and algae. Bảy and I had never swum in this pond before. Unlike the one surrounding our house, it was intended for fish farming and connected to the river only by a small drain. Its water was usually still and green, but now it was heaving from Bảy's cannonball.

I didn't hesitate—there was an outside chance that I might be badly injured, maybe even fatally skewered, by whatever lurked below the pond surface, but I was almost certain that I'd be stung horribly if I stopped. I flung myself into the water.

Every cut and scrape stung with the same startling intensity. But nothing had jabbed into me. As I sank to the bottom, the initial burn dulled to a prickling sensation. I held my breath and hovered above the mud, forcing myself to remain still. I was sure that if the bees sensed our movements, they would remain on top to wait us out. Around me, the water had taken on a slightly pinkish hue. My thoughts turned to water snakes and eels. I imagined them zipping toward the source of the blood, searching for my wounds so they could feast on them.

The fear forced me up to the surface. I swam over to a denser patch of water lilies and hid underneath. Nearby, I saw that Bảy had his own water-lily protection. The long dark roots of the water lilies surrounded his face like a flowing mane; the big green petal perched on top of his head like a hat. The disguise had turned my brother into a quite pretty girl, a sister close to my age that I had always wanted. The swarm of bees was nowhere in sight. We took no chances and remained in the water for a long while before we decided it was safe to get out.

Once we finally climbed out of the pond, I noticed for the first time that Bảy was missing something.

"Hey Bảy, where are your shorts?" I called out.

"What? What are you talking about?" He said, looking down.

Like most boys outside school, he was normally naked from the waist up, wearing only a pair of shorts. Now he was completely naked. The shorts were gone. We both burst out laughing.

The following week, Bảy and I were walking past the same guava tree. I felt a finger poking at my back.

"What?" I asked, turning around. Putting his finger to his lips, Bảy signaled with his other hand for me to look up. Above us was a lush canopy dotted with plump guavas. Peeking out on the side was an enormous hive, swarming with bees. A few feet below the hive, the stump of a broken branch stuck out. Hanging from it was a pair of ripped shorts.

The lunar New Year, Tết, is the most important holiday in Việt Nam. The weeklong national celebration is like Christmas, New Year's, and Thanksgiving all rolled into one. Marking the arrival of spring, Tết usually falls between late January and early February. The first three days are the most significant and reserved for visiting relatives, friends and teachers. Shops and markets are closed. Adult children are expected to travel home. The older the parents, the more imperative the obligation is on the child. The longing of a soldier away from home on the battlefield during Tết is the theme of countless Vietnamese songs and poems.

This most festive holiday also serves as a communal birthday. Since birthdates were rarely mentioned, I didn't know mine or that of anyone in my family. What mattered was a person's Chinese zodiac animal in a twelve-year cycle. I knew by heart the zodiac for almost everyone around me. My sign is the pig, the same as that of my second sister, Chị Ba. The first day of Tết marks the transition of one zodiac animal to the next, when we all turn a year older, including a baby born only the previous day. Because Vietnamese consider a newborn as one year old, the baby, only two days old, would be two after Tết.

In the countryside, Tết festivities were much more subdued than what I remembered from Sài Gòn. Our house, like all those around us, was still filled with yellow *hoa mai* (apricot blossom) and red decorations. Red and yellow are colors believed to bring good luck. Absent around our village was the continuous popping of firecrackers and lion dancing which, for me, was the most entertaining feature of the celebrations. During the New Year, dance troupes visit homes and businesses to bring good luck for the coming year. Dressed up in costumes with lion heads and long dragon tails, the performers synchronize their movements to the loud beatings of drums and gongs to mimic the actions of lions. The climax of the performance comes at the end when the dancers reach up high, at times by stacking on top of each other or climbing over chairs or tables, to get to their reward: a small red envelop filled with new money called *lì xì*.

On the first morning of Tết, my siblings and I would wear our new clothes, traditional gifts from parents, while lining up to wish them good health for the coming year. They then would give us our *lì xì* or lucky money. Sometime after our arrival in the countryside, Bảy and I stopped receiving new clothes and red envelops. My parents still gave us money, though the bills were not pristinely new as *lì xì* was supposed to be, lacking that crisp new smell which, for me, was the defining scent of the Tết.

59

While my parents might have skipped some traditions, they, like the villagers, strictly followed the key ritual of the holiday that celebrates the concept of letting go and renewal: cleaning. Days before Tết, our family did little but clean. We always started in the altar room, polishing to a shine the altar table, including every worship ornament. We then moved on to the kitchen, the second most sacred part of a Vietnamese home, scrubbing everything clean of soot. After that, there was still the rest of the house and the surrounding yard to sweep and tidy up.

The other major preparation for Tết was cooking. What we made had to last through the first three days of the new year, when work was considered bad luck and thus taboo. The food synonymous with Tết is *bánh chưng*, a sticky rice cake filled with mung bean paste and pork belly and wrapped in banana leaves. Days before Tết, extended families would gather to prepare these cakes and *bánh tét*, a log-shaped variation popular in the South. Preparing and wrapping the cakes would take all day. Boiling and draining them would extend long into the night. In the countryside, my mother and I joined a neighbor's family in this Tết tradition. While working, the women sang and talked. From them, I learned the story of *bánh chưng*'s origin.

Four thousand years ago, King Hùng Vương wanted to bequeath the kingdom to the most deserving of his sons. "Bring me the most delicious dish you can find. One that is worthy to be on the altar and shows your love for our land and devotion to the ancestors," the king commanded. Prince Lang Liêu, the poorest of his sons, decided to use the ingredients of everyday life. Using sweet rice, mung bean, and pork, he made two cakes which he named *bánh chưng*, molding one in a square shape to symbolize the earth and the other in a round shape to represent the heavens. The King chose Prince Lang Liêu's simple creation over his brothers' sumptuous offerings. Simplicity, piety, the significance of rice—*bánh chưng* encompasses what Vietnamese society values.

Apart from all the festivities surrounding Tết, what I loved most about the holiday in the countryside were the visits from my sisters. In the days leading to their arrival, my mother would save all the chicken and duck eggs and set aside the best fruits for the beloved guests. During their stay, mealtimes were more boisterous, resembling the ones I remembered from Sài Gòn. "Chanh Cưng" (Adored Chanh), my second sister Chị Ba would call me. At night with my sisters next to me in bed, the monsters and intruders of my imagination never showed up. As Chị Ba caressed my hair while telling me stories of her life in Sài Gòn, I easily drifted off to sleep.

In Vietnamese culture, rice is a life-sustaining force surpassed only by air and water. Consumed at every meal in some form—whole grains, broken-up grains, thick noodles, thin noodles, wrappers, sheets, rolls—rice is the key ingredient in main dishes, side dishes, sweet desserts, savory snacks. Commonly referred to as white gold, rice also plays a symbolic role in all of life's major milestones: birth, marriage, and death.

There are countless words to describe rice in its different stages. *Lúa* refers to rice still in its husk; *gạo*, after the husk has been removed; *cơm*, after it has been cooked. *Cơm* also means a meal. Only the time of day differentiates meals: *cơm sáng* (breakfast), *cơm trưa* (lunch), and *cơm chiều* (dinner).

Apart from the grain, every part of the rice plant is also used. The stalks, after having been dried, are woven into baskets and used to line roofs and walls of homes. The husks, the outer shells of the rice grains, are used as cooking fuel and fertilizer. The bran, the dust between the rice grain and the husk, feeds livestock on land and fish in water.

The *S* shape of Việt Nam resembles two rice baskets on a pole. The Red River Delta of North Việt Nam and the Mekong Delta of South Việt Nam—two agricultural powerhouses—form the baskets on the opposite ends of the less fertile soil in the middle. Legend has it that rice was a gift from the heavens to nourish the Vietnamese people. The plant was supposed to grow easily to feed the entire populace. But the messenger from above made a mistake by switching the pouches of grass and rice. As a result, grass grows effortlessly, while rice demands intense backbreaking labor.

A bowl of white rice, the embodiment of this toil, commands respect. The concept that rice is never to be wasted, not even one grain, was instilled in all of us at an early age, and this reverence took on even greater significance in the countryside. Somewhere in the heavens, I had been told, someone was keeping track of all the rice I left uneaten. In the afterworld, I would have to consume a maggot for each grain wasted. The thought terrified me as far back in my childhood as I can remember. At the end of each meal, with chopsticks still unfamiliar between tiny fingers, I stayed glued to my seat, prying off every bit of the precious grain still stuck to my bowl.

The Vietnamese phrase *ăn cơm*, which means "eating rice," refers to eating a meal, regardless of what is consumed. Mealtimes are daily occasions of great anticipation. Fathers come back from fields as mothers break from chores and children rush home from school to gather around the table or on the floor. As a child I looked forward to every meal. Lotus-flower salad, fried salted dried fish, catfish melon soup—the supporting dishes might vary at each meal, but rice remained a constant. With my stomach growling and chopsticks ready to be deployed, we waited for our father to start. Only after he had taken the first bite, followed by my mother, could my brothers and I begin.

Myriad rules, summed up in countless proverbs dispensed by my mother, governed our behavior at mealtimes. "Ăn coi nồi, ngồi coi hướng" (While eating, be mindful of how much food is left in the pot; while sitting, be mindful of your place at the table). Do not take too much. Do not eat only the best foods. Do not play with your chopsticks. As the youngest, my place was next to the pot of rice so that I could refill everyone's empty rice bowls, and thus my meals were often a series of interruptions. Though my mother might overlook certain rules, she always insisted on our waiting for my father to commence the meal.

The consumption of rice is considered a sacred communion, never to be disturbed. Unless invited, guests knew not to show up around mealtimes, when arguments also took a reprieve. However angry my mother might be, she would stop yelling at us while we ate. Whatever punishment my father was about to dole out, he would wait until we finished eating. Heaven also paid heed. It is believed that lightning would never strike anyone while he or she ate. I often sought comfort in this mercy. As lightning flashed and thunder boomed, I held on to my rice bowl. The chewing never stopped.

THE EDGE OF FAMINE

Việt Nam should be awash in rice. The fertile soil of the deltas was formed over millennia from an accumulation of silt deposited by the Mekong River and its many tributaries. Irrigated by an intricate maze of canals, the fields could be cultivated to produce two or even three rice crops a year, enough to feed everyone in the country and many more beyond its borders, as in current-day Việt Nam. But throughout Vietnamese history, war often disrupted farming, causing rice production to stall or plummet. Hunger and sometimes even famine would ensue.

This was the case during World War II, when Việt Nam was under the double occupation of France and Japan. Before the war, the occupiers had forced Vietnamese farmers to set aside rice farmland to grow cotton and jute, cash crops deemed more profitable than staple crops such as rice or corn. In 1944, drastically decreased rice production in northern Việt Nam was further reduced by droughts, pest infestations, and massive flooding. Amid the severe food shortage, Northern Vietnamese had few means of receiving outside help. The frequent airstrikes by the United States and its allies against occupying Japanese forces had destroyed many roads and transportation facilities, cutting off the transport of food and materials from the South. Of the dwindling remaining rice supply, the Japanese and French militaries seized much for their own troops. Hundreds of thousands, perhaps as many as two million North Vietnamese, are estimated to have died from starvation during this period. The famine helped spark the uprising against foreign domination that later turned into the civil war, lasting three decades.

When peace finally arrived in 1975, it was expected that the rice harvest would rebound in abundance. But the opposite happened. Within a few years of peace, rice production in the Mekong Delta had decreased to a level lower than when the war ended. Unlike previous instances, the food shortage this time resulted not from bombs or other wartime destruction but from misguided policies of the communist regime.

When Việt Nam was formally reunified in 1976, the communist government set out to collectivize rice fields in the South as they had done earlier in the North, even though the efforts had not yielded much success. Fruit orchards, like the one my parents owned, were excluded in this first wave of collectivization. In the communist experiment, farmers had to turn over to the state not only their rice paddies but also all their farming equipment, including the water buffaloes that plowed the soil. In the communal, government-owned fields, every able adult, including people like my parents who had contributed no land, was required to work to cultivate rice. The state provided seeds and fertilizer and took care of other farming needs. At harvest, the rice crop was distributed based on the amount of labor contributed by each household and the number of people living in it. The communist goal was to transform the Mekong Delta's "rice bowl" into an "iron rice bowl" with no cracks for anyone to fall through.

"From each according to his ability, to each according to his need," was a much-cited slogan under the communist paradigm. Reality, however, did not conform to this ideal. Angered at being forced to hand over their lands and properties, many farmers would rather destroy their equipment and slaughter their water buffaloes than turn them over to the collective. With no distinction between good or bad-quality work and no individual reward or penalty system, few saw any incentive to work harder than their neighbor. Growing rice is notoriously labor intensive. After a heavy rain, paddies must be drained, sometimes one bucket at a time. Before collectivization, the arduous task was carried out routinely in our village; but after, the act was rarely seen. Instead of devoting the extra effort, many chose to tend to the small vegetable gardens or orchards they still owned around their homes.

Some farmers even took to sabotaging communal assets. I remember walking around the village after a harvest. Alongside the dirt paths, golden carpets of the yellow-husked *lúa* lay drying in the sun. A group of farmers were ahead of me, complaining and cursing loudly about every aspect of collectivized farming. Suddenly, one of the men stopped talking. He reached down to grab a handful of pebbles, then flung them into the rice.

On top of self-destructive acts were self-serving ones. Long before every harvest, when the rice grains were still green and too underdeveloped to be eaten, thieves would come at night to cut down swaths of the stalks. Theft was so rampant that a few farmers were assigned guns to keep guard. After the harvest, people would surreptitiously set loose their chickens near where the rice was drying. In the past, no one would have thought of feeding livestock precious rice grains instead of just the husks or bran.

It came as no surprise that under the communist regime, rice production drastically decreased at each harvest. By the time we arrived in Vĩnh Long in 1978, the food shortage was already widespread but still manageable. Within a short time of our arrival, however, the economic disaster would get much worse. Although the collectivization of farmlands bore the most blame, a series of events coincided around this time to push people in our village and across the Mekong Delta from hunger to the edge of famine.

First was the floods. In the countryside, water was not only our salvation but also our doom and always in our thoughts. As water fell from the sky, all life rejoiced. Animals frolicked; humans collected the crystal-clear droplets in barrels. Rice paddies grew lush while vegetable gardens and orchards blossomed. We prayed for rain, but almost as often, we prayed for it to stop.

In 1978, the prayers for rain to stop went unheeded. The Mekong Delta experienced some of the worst flooding in its history. Across the region crisscrossed by rivers and swamps, floods were an annual occurrence. The only factor that varied was the magnitude. The period between June, when the river began to rise, until November, when it receded, was known as rising-water season. In our village, rumors of a bigger-than-normal flood often preceded its arrival. People could tell in advance, because it took weeks for the snowmelt from the river source in the Tibetan Plateau or the typhoons along the way to reach us.

Sometime after our family arrived at Vĩnh Long, we began hearing warnings of an impending flood. Villagers had rushed to drain their ponds of fish. As we weren't aware of the practice, we did nothing with ours. When the rain arrived, we noticed people in canoes waiting in the river in front of our house. Armed with buckets and nets, they scooped up the fish overflowing from our ponds into the river. Their bet on our ignorance paid off with a windfall of fish.

As the rain continued, the water around us kept rising. The swelled river and ponds flooded rice paddies already inundated with water. In the waterlogged fields, the young rice stalks had no chance of taking hold. The flood washed away boats, homes, and even people. Stories of hardship and tragedy abounded.

The misery I felt most keenly was around our house. The rising water overwhelmed me in every way. At the height of the flood, the lower part of our house was submerged in water, becoming part of the pond. To get around, we had to wade or paddle in the canoe. Tending to ourselves was already drudgery enough; still we had to care for the animals. Each day was an unrelenting struggle to move them to dry ground and to find enough food to feed the hungry horde.

When the rain finally stopped, the ponds and river gradually returned to their normal level. Around our house, the torment continued. The air retained the musky damp while the floor remained a wet, slick mud. We slipped and fell as we walked around. After some drying out, the floor turned into a sticky clay. Each step was a noisy struggle to lift our feet.

For all the misery it caused, the flood brought an unexpected present for me in its aftermath. Not long afterward, a girl about my age came to live with her grandparents in the house behind the orchard. I was happy to have a playmate close by. I called my new friend by her nickname, Lượm, which means found, with a sense of having been picked up from the ground. As long as I knew Lượm, I never thought to ask what her real name was.

In the countryside as in Sài Gòn, a child's actual name was often used only in school. Outside school, my friends and I usually referred to each other by our nicknames. The most common were numerals indicating birth order. The practice provides a ready supply of names to big families. The firstborn is called Hai (Two), the second-born, Ba (Three, though *Ba* also means Dad), the third-born, Tư (Four), and so forth. The practice of skipping number one had roots in the belief that the evil spirits liked to steal firstborns. By starting at number two, parents hope to sidetrack the spirits.

Following this tradition, I called my four sisters Chị Hai, Chị Ba, Chị Tư, and Chị Năm. *Chị* means older sister. I called my brothers Cu Anh (Older Boy) and Bảy (Seven). I really should have included the title *anh* (older brother) with their names. For some reason, I never adopted the formality, a lapse that my parents let pass.

When departing from the norm of birth order, nicknames usually alluded to some characteristic of the person, as in the case of my older brother. Instead of Sáu (Six), he is called Cu Anh, older boy. At times the nicknames could confound even the most imaginative of minds. Such is my nickname, Chanh, meaning lime. Actually, Chanh was only half of it. The other part specified exactly what kind of lime I was: the salted kind. *Chanh muối* is a lime pickled in salted water, used to make a distinctively Vietnamese lemonade.

Unlike the nickname Bảy (Seven) or Cu Anh (Older Boy), which had a counterpart in almost every household, Chanh Muối was a one-off. It never failed to elicit laughter from anyone hearing it for the first time. I never cared for it.

"Why Chanh Muối? Do you think I'm salty or sour or both? Who came up with it?" I had asked my parents over the years. Behind their bemused smiles, the answers never quite satisfied, and the details varied with each telling. It seemed that my grandmother had some trouble pronouncing Oanh, and Chanh was close enough. As for Muối (Salted), the description was tacked on by someone and the name stuck.

"Don't call me Chanh Muối! Just Chanh!" I lashed out when the teasing would not let up. Around our neighborhood in Sài Gòn, my insistence had made no difference. In the countryside, I offered only the shortened version. In a place populated by many strange nicknames, mine would seem downright bland.

"Overbite," "Stunted," "Ugly," a few kids answered when my brothers and I asked them their names. Why such unpleasant names? we wondered. The reason became clear once we grasped the outsize role that superstition had over the villagers.

Among the farmers, few people had much education beyond basic schooling. With little scientific understanding of the world, many sought explanations in supernatural beliefs. The evil spirits were blamed for all kinds of misfortune in a place where deaths and illnesses struck often and with seeming randomness. The first month and year of a baby's life were joyous occasions, since many newborns did not pass these milestones. The fear of evil spirits stealing babies took on even more layers than in the city. It was widely believed that the spirits preferred not only firstborns but also the more attractive children. To trick the spirits, many parents would only refer to their child by a most unappealing name despite having conferred on him or her an official designation of beauty. The more trying the circumstances, the more hideous the nickname.

Even among the more unpleasant nicknames I had heard, the name Lượm struck me as particularly sad. When she was born, her parents must have had some hope of a good life for their daughter. Yet by the time she came to live with her grandparents, she had been reduced to someone discarded then picked up off the ground.

From my parents, I knew that Lượm's father had died fighting for the South Vietnamese army when she was just an infant. In the Vietnamese patriarchal culture, bloodline matters a great deal. It was not customary for a man to raise a child who was not his or related to him by blood. Perhaps in abundance, a man could afford such generosity, but not in a place like our village, where rice was counted by the grain. Here, long-held traditions, much like superstitions, bound everyone's actions. A woman would be ostracized if she chose to ignore them. Customs prescribed that if a widow wanted to remarry, she had to give up her child to a relative on the father's side. If that was not possible, then the child would go to a relative on the mother's side. Following this tradition, when Lượm's mother remarried, she gave Lượm to her paternal uncle.

Lượm's uncle took her into his already large family. They shared what little they had until the flood came, destroying much of the rice harvest. In the past, when farmers still owned their land and could choose what to grow, they could switch to yam or other crops when weather or insects made rice-growing conditions unfavorable. Under communist rule, the collectivized farmlands could only be used to grow rice. Facing starvation, many farmers, including Lượm's uncle and aunt, fled to drier land to look for work. Unable to take their younger children along on such a journey, many left them in the care of relatives. Before leaving, Lượm's uncle delivered her to her paternal grandparents—our neighbors behind the orchard.

Lượm did not go to the school across the river that Bảy and I attended. Had we gone to school together, I would have known her official name. Instead, she went to a one-room hut inside our village where kids of different ages learned mostly to read and write.

When not in school, I often ran over to Lượm's house. We would play games that I could never get my brothers interested in playing. Lượm and I braided each other's hair and made jewelry out of banana leaves. We searched for touch-me-not plants, competing to see who could make the tiny leaves fold inward the fastest. At low tide, we looked for the perfect clay to mold into bowls and pots for playing house. We even tried smoking cigarettes and chewing betel leaves, pilfering the ingredients from her grandparents. The excessive coughing and gagging quickly convinced us to give them up.

Of all our games, our favorite was jumping rope. With one end of the rope tied to a tree, one of us would hold the line taut for the other to jump back and forth. The game favored agility and endurance, two traits I had in abundance but Lượm seemed to have even more. Until I met Lượm I had not thought to cheat, as all the kids would pounce at the first hint of anything untoward. By chance I found out how easy it was to do so with my new friend. I remember the first time I felt the spurs of the rope brushing against my leg and not stopping to give up my turn. Determined to win, I kept jumping until I reached past Lượm's score. I had expected Lượm to say something, but she never did.

"Lượm, I never touched the rope," I volunteered after collapsing in a heap.

"I believe you," she said.

Did she not see that I had cheated? I searched her expression for any sign of suspicion, but detected none. From then on, I began to cheat in increasingly obvious ways. Beyond winning I wanted to see how far I could push Lượm before she noticed.

"I picked up the chopsticks just in time," I said even though the ball had bounced twice, not once, as the rules dictated.

Time after time came the invariable response, "I believe you."

In time, I concluded that Lượm had to know that I cheated. I was also certain that she would never confront me. I never asked her why, just as I never asked her another question that also loomed in my mind when we were together. What was it like growing up without a father and mother? In the beginning, I assumed that my cheating somehow did not bother Lượm. As I came to know my friend better, it occurred to me the answers to these two questions might be related. Perhaps Lượm never said anything to me because growing up without parental love and getting passed from one relative to another, she had learned to adapt by not making too much fuss over anything. Her silence didn't necessarily mean that she was not upset. I had two parents, more food than she did, and a roof that did not leak torrents when it rained. Filled with riches, I still wanted more. The thrill of winning dulled to shame, and I stopped cheating.

After the successive typhoons and floods came even more devastation to the economy. In 1978, only three years into peace, Việt Nam was again at war. After years of isolated clashes along the border with its neighbor Cambodia, Việt Nam launched a full-scale attack against the Khmer Rouge (Cambodian Communists) when it began crossing over to massacre Vietnamese peasants as it had millions of its own people. The Vietnamese invasion into Cambodia succeeded in removing the genocidal Khmer Rouge and its leader Pol Pot from power but garnered little support in the international community. Việt Nam was denounced for its aggression and subsequent occupation of Cambodia. Many Western countries joined the trade embargo against Việt Nam started earlier by the United States at the end of the Việt Nam War.

After its victory in Cambodia, Việt Nam was still not done with wars. In 1979, it became embroiled in another when China, which had backed Cambodia, retaliated. Fighting lasted only a few weeks, but subsequently China too ceased all trade with Việt Nam.

These wars battered an already weakened economy while severe economic sanctions imposed by the West and mostly indifference from Việt Nam's allies meant there was little outside aid. Việt Nam would enter one of its darkest periods. At the market in our town, vendors had little to sell, and people had little money to buy. Many items not locally sourced, such as garlic, onions, MSG, and white sugar, vanished. The merchandise that was left was often counterfeit or doctored. Vendors diluted gasoline and filled the bottoms of rice bags with less desirable grains or even dirt to make them appear fuller. Amid the scarcity, mistrust spread. Customers came to the market with their own scales, sniffing, tasting, and inspecting every aspect of the merchandise before buying.

When we first arrived at Vĩnh Long, my mother was usually able to sell all the fruits that we had brought to the market. She would use the money to shop for food, sometimes splurging to purchase 100 grams of beef or pork. A few years later my mother and I would leave the market without having sold all the fruit, even at very low prices. In the afternoon, she would walk from hut to hut in the brick factory village, offering the leftovers for whatever people would pay.

Hunger began to dominate my thoughts. As soon as I finished eating one meal, I was already looking forward to the next. We still had three meals a day, but with very small portions. Around the village, many made do with only two meals a day, one at mid-morning and another in the late afternoon. Even with just one or two small bowls of rice per person, my mother still could not make our rice ration last until the next harvest. We always had to buy more at the market.

For a long time, I didn't understand the connection between our ability to afford the extra rice and the outings into the orchard my father sometimes made at dusk. Carrying a shovel, he seemed jittery as he left our house. My brothers and I knew not to inquire too deeply when he told us it was adult business. But we suspected it had something to do with the bank of fruitless shrubs behind the house. Our parents often warned us not to go there. But without fruits on top or edible roots beneath, the tangled branches held little interest to us or to any robber—which was precisely what my parents had hoped. By the dim light, my father would dig up some of the gold that he had buried.

Most people in our village had no savings to spend on supplemental goods. They had little more than a subsistence lifestyle. Apart from switching to two meals a day, people devised other ways to stretch out the meager food supply. To fill out the pot of rice, they would mix in other grains or roots. Instead of regular cooked rice, people took to eating rice porridge. The watery gruel, made by adding extra water when cooking rice, was not very filling but yielded more volume. Sometimes people added even more water to make soup. The broth, skimmed off the top of the pot while the rice was boiling, was quite bland but at least had some flavor.

In the scarcity, many resorted to eating *bo bo*, or sorghum, when it was available. The dark cereal, donated by the Soviet Union, one of Việt Nam's few remaining allies, had to be soaked overnight and took much longer to cook than rice. The tasteless cereal used to serve as animal feed, but it had become a staple for many Vietnamese. In time, *bo bo* would become a synonym for the severe shortages of this period.

We were all hungry. But from the sunken eyes of those around me, I sensed a hunger that was different from mine, a deprivation that compelled neighboring children to steal and drink a whole jar of liquid pork fat, as I happened to witness one day. Their hunger seemed more desperate, exuding an urgency and menace in its quest for relief. People cared only about filling their stomachs and those of their children. Finding enough food just for the day and maybe the next was the driving force for every action. People combed the ground for snakes, mice, rats, anything that moved. They cleared the air of birds and bats. They drained the streams and ponds of even the littlest fish. They cut down bananas still green and barely bigger than fingers. The gritty and hard young fruits could not be eaten raw and had to be boiled. The starch substituted for rice. Had people waited just a while longer, the bigger fruits would have been more filling.

But had they waited, the bananas might not have ended up in their stomachs, since anything that could be stolen often was. While many villagers commiserated with my parents during the day, some took liberty with our property at night. With uncanny skill, the thieves could bypass us and our dog to snatch chickens, ducks, and somehow even a pig known for its loud squealing. They plucked fruits off our trees, leaving a few on those near our house but stripping bare the ones furthest away. They dug up yucca roots, stripped corn from stalks, and cut off bamboo shoots. I woke up one morning to find even a fish I had caught and stored in a bucket inside the house stolen.

Within a few years of our arrival, birds, bats, and snakes all disappeared. Even the once abundant *tra* fish became scarce. The huge, energetic fish lived in ponds beneath outhouses, consuming waste. When abundant, they turned upward, piling on top of each other with their mouths open every time the outhouse was used. They lunged at anything that came down, even rocks. In the beginning, I was terrified to go to the bathroom with them lurching in the waters below. In time, I got used to them and even found them entertaining.

Not long ago, none of us would think to eat them. But when nets and hooks stopped catching other kinds of fish, we turned to the still-plentiful source of protein. My father was the first in our family to taste it. At first, I could not suppress the image of their churning open mouths. Soon I stopped making the association altogether. As food became scarce, we wasted nothing, not even the chickens suddenly falling ill and dropping dead on top of each other. Sautéed, fried, or boiled, the mound of meat transformed into meals we craved. I dug into the rare abundance, pushing away the persistent thought that we too might succumb to whatever illness caused the chickens to die.

As hunger tightened its grip, people committed increasingly desperate acts. When my brothers and I first heard the loud boom, we had no idea that someone had thrown a grenade into the river. Immediately we ran in the direction of the sound and arrived at the dock to watch in amazement a frenzy of canoes on the water. Through the slats on the dock, I saw a few small fish floating by in the water below. As we watched, more canoes shot out from the riverbank, bumping into each other and racing to the various clusters gathering throughout the river.

"There're a lot of fish over here!" someone called out. In one swoop, the canoes turned and lunged toward the voice, converging at a spot in the middle of the river. People frantically scooped up whatever floated by, depositing them in buckets lining their boats.

My brothers and I ran back to our house. Loading all the nets and buckets we had onto our canoe, we paddled furiously toward the frenzy in the river, where fish as big as my hand and as small as my fingers floated all around on the surface. We raced other canoes vying to get at the bounty. Dead or almost dead, the fish barely resisted when we scooped them up with our nets.

Laughter and excitement filled the air. The hordes of canoes zipping through the river resembled a parade. My brothers and I called out to each other and our neighbors, bragging of our hauls. The fish overflowing from the buckets would be our dinner, breakfast, and lunch for days and weeks to come. Anything not eaten right away would be cleaned, coated in salt and left to dry under the sun. When dry, the salted fish could be preserved almost indefinitely. A quick soak in water to rehydrate and lessen the saltiness was all the preparation needed before cooking the dried fish.

When my parents came back from working in the rice fields, my brothers and I rushed to show them the buckets of fish waiting to be cleaned. We talked excitedly about the explosion and race to gather the unexpected bounty. My father shared none of our enthusiasm.

"Did you think about everything that was killed that didn't float to the top? he cut in before we could finish, as angry as I had ever seen him. "Is this the last time you want to fish from the river?"

My father was not the only one in our village to express outrage. Days later, officials came by our house to ask if we knew or saw the person who threw the grenade in the river. They spoke of the same disastrous consequences my father had mentioned and made it clear that the practice was illegal. The investigation went on for a while, but we never found out who was responsible.

In the next few years, there would be two more explosions. My brothers and I knew immediately to jump in the canoe and paddle in the direction of the telltale boom. Each time, the number and size of our catch decreased dramatically, as did the frenzy and excitement. The lackluster mood of the canoes idling on the river surface must have mirrored the sparse aquatic life remaining underneath.

In the countryside, every household had pets: dogs to chase away robbers and cats to chase away mice. My father adopted a puppy, my first pet, shortly after we arrived in our new home in Vĩnh Long. We called her Lem. The name, meaning smeared with dirt or soot, befit a mutt with off-white fur scattered with patches of gray resembling grime. When Lem came to live with us, she was still pining for her mother and missing baby teeth, and I was still wearing dresses and speaking with a distinctly Saigonese accent. We grew up together. She shed her baby fur and teeth; I shed my footwear, billowy frocks, and the shade of pink on my skin. We swam together, fished together—my feet, her paws, bare and always caked with mud.

When she was about two years old, Lem, normally ravenous, suddenly stopped eating. No food, not even the rare chicken bone, could entice her to change her mind. When coaxing did not work, we tried force. Bảy pried open her mouth while Cu Anh fed her a spoonful of sugar water mixed with precious medicine that my parents had saved from Sài Gòn. At first, she resisted, spitting out what was put in. Then she became too weak and just let the medicine spill out. Lem lingered for about a week, then died.

My father told us that he thought Lem had been poisoned. In a land of venomous snakes and scorpions along with farmers known for feeding poison to roaming dogs suspected of snatching chickens and ducks, the source of the toxin could be many things. Still, I wanted to think it was nature and not man that was responsible for Lem's death.

Shortly after Lem died, a fully grown, gaunt-looking dog wandered into our house looking for scraps. Her name was Luốc, and she belonged to a neighbor. Over time, the sporadic visits became more frequent, spilling over to mealtimes.

"This will be enough for the dog. Don't feed it any more," my mother would say, setting aside a small scoop of rice before we sat down for our meals. Unable to resist the sad eyes staring up at us from beneath the table, my brothers and I would drop some of our food on the floor for the uninvited guest. In time, the skin around Luốc's ribcage thickened and her stomach filled out. She ended up living with us full time, which her owners did not seem to mind.

One evening, Luốc was nowhere in sight when my mother set out her food. We suspected something must have happened, as no human or animal had ever not come when called for food. Putting away her dinner, we went around the orchard to search for her. At the far edge of our property by the fence separating our land from the neighbors', Bảy and I saw something writhing in the mesh of barbed wires. We rushed over to find Luốc drenched in blood and contorted in a pile of twisted wires. She looked up with relief when she saw us. In the past, Luốc had gotten entangled in wire fences while chasing prey. The entanglement this time, however, was much more serious. There were gashes all over her body. Some were so deep that I could make out the layer of yellow fat beneath the fast-congealing blood.

Immediately, Bảy and I set out to unravel the crisscrossed wires, teasing out the barbs strand by strand from the matted skin and fur. While we worked, I thought about lockjaw and wondered if a dog could contract it. The possibility almost seemed hopeful as Luốc would have to survive long enough for the condition to set in. As we pried off the last barbs, two men from our village passed by and offered to help. We thanked them but declined their offer. Bảy and I both noticed that Luốc had stopped struggling so much and her breathing had grown more labored.

"Bảy, do you think she she'll make it?" I asked.

"I don't know. It doesn't look good," my brother said.

With the last wire removed, Bảy lifted Luốc up, cradling her in his arms as we ran home.

When my mother saw us in the yard, without even asking what had happened, she ran to get a mat and spread it on the ground. We crouched around Luốc while my mother wiped away the mud and blood from the wounds. Except for the rising and falling of her stomach, Luốc stayed inert. The eyes that used to stare at us with such eagerness appeared vacant while the pauses stretched longer between her breaths. I had never witnessed a dog dying, but it was clear that she was close to it. Suddenly Luốc exhaled loudly. Her stomach deflated and then the legs went limp. We waited for Luốc to take another breath, but it never came.

It was getting dark, and I knew the task that awaited us had to be completed soon. I could sense none of us wanted to get started. We lingered around the mat, trading stories about Luốc and how she had come to live with us. My mother recalled the time Luốc, while rummaging around the kitchen for food, discovered the prized stash of black pepper. After tearing into the small pouch, Luốc started sneezing. The sneezing fit continued while she raced to the deck to gulp down water from the pond. Bảy shared that he learned to hide from bees by copying Luốc. He once saw her charging into a bush only to back out running, trailed by a swarm of bees. When she passed a pond, Luốc suddenly stopped running and flung herself into the water.

After a few more stories, my father said we needed to get going with the chore. We scattered to gather shovels and pick axes when I heard footsteps and the familiar hooting call. When we first moved to the countryside, I often mistook the low guttural sounds for the noises of animals, but quickly I learned that hooting was how visitors announced their presence. I looked up to see two figures crossing the bridge to our house. As they came closer, I recognized them as the same men from before who had offered to help us untangle Luốc.

"Chào Anh Chị Ba," the men greeted my parents.

"We saw the kids with the dog. It looked like it was in pretty bad shape. We didn't think it was going to make it," one of the men said.

"Yes, it just died a little while ago," my father said.

The men looked at each other, then at us, but remained quiet.

Finally, one of them said to my father, "Anh Ba, could we save you the trouble of burying it? We could take it away for you," his voice was barely audible.

I glanced at the men and then at my father. I knew burying Luốc was not what they had in mind.

In our new home, I had learned to separate the animals that I cared for from the meat that I ate. In the beginning when I picked at a piece of chicken, I thought of the baby chick that ate out of my hands, then grew into the chicken that loved to be petted. Over time, I stopped making such associations. But this was different. Luốc was not a chicken, duck, or pig. She was my fishing companion and playmate.

Yet I also knew well the hunger that loomed over all of us. In hunger's clutches, there was still a stigma attached to eating dogs. Bats, rats, snakes—the men in our village freely exchanged recipes for the meat found more often at drinking gatherings than at family meals. Few, however, would volunteer that they ate dogs. It was believed that a dog could tell if someone was a dog eater. Found in such company, it would bark frantically, then run away to hide.

My father's silence hung in the air. The longer it went on, the more certain I became of what his only answer could be. Luốc was already dead; she could either rot in the ground or feed someone. I forced the rationale into my head.

"Yes, you can take it," I finally heard my father say.

Vietnamese believe that losses come in threes. After the loss of our two dogs, news of my third loss arrived without any warning. One morning, I was surprised to see my parents coming back early from working in the fields.

"Cu Anh, Bảy, Chanh, come here," my mother called out before they reached the yard. I could tell something was wrong. We ran and gathered around them. My father spoke softly.

"Your friend, Lượm, died last night."

My mother said Lượm had started to have diarrhea and vomiting a few days ago, but her grandparents didn't realize how sick she was, as she kept telling them she was fine. On the morning of the day she died, Lượm was still working alongside her grandparents in the fields, insisting that her ailment would soon pass. By the evening, she suddenly became much worse. No longer able to get up to go to the bathroom, she soiled through all her clothes while begging for more water. But whatever she took in, she instantly discharged. The layers of blankets and mats her grandparents wrapped her in couldn't keep her from shaking. Throughout the night, as her condition rapidly deteriorated, it was clear that she needed urgent help, but there was no choice for her grandparents but to wait for daylight. Only Lượm couldn't wait.

While my mother spoke, I heard her words clearly, but my mind could not absorb their ultimate meaning. Lượm could not have died; the thought was incomprehensible.

My father had a long list of dangers for us to avoid in the countryside. Near the top was a whirlpool. The spiraling vortex, he warned, could appear anywhere in the river, sucking in everything nearby, drowning even the strongest swimmer. As my parents' words swirled around me, I felt as if I had been pulled into a most powerful vortex.

I did not go to Lượm's funeral. I can't remember the reason, but most likely it was because my parents did not want us to catch what she had. In the days after her death, everyone was terrified of what might be lurking around us. We boiled water for every need, not just for drinking, as we had been doing. Everyone in the village contributed to her burial. Some gave money to buy wood and nails for a coffin. Others brought food for the communal meal. My mother gave some of my clothes for Lượm to be buried in.

Even if her grandparents could afford a more extravagant farewell, it couldn't have happened. In a culture that places great emphasis on age and status, a younger person must always show respect to his or her elders. An elder would not bow down to a child, either in life or in death. As a child, Lượm had committed the biggest breach to this natural order by dying before her grandparents. As customs prescribed and circumstance dictated, she had to be buried quickly, without any elaborate funeral rites. There was no time or means for anyone far away to travel to the funeral in our village. Sometime after, Bảy and his friends saw a woman running from a hastily tethered canoe toward Lượm's grandparents' hut. In hysterics, she called out for Lượm. Without a doubt, they all knew she had to be Lượm's mother.

Misfortune seemed to hover all around us. Not long before Lượm's death, a girl in Bảy's class also succumbed to a similar stomach illness. Perhaps it was dysentery. A young expectant mother died while giving birth. Drowning, even in this place where children learned to swim almost as they learned to walk, was not uncommon, especially after a big storm. When someone disappeared and was thought to have drowned, boats bedecked with white masts would troll the river. The searchers blew on horns, blasting out the dreaded summons for everyone to be on the lookout for a washed-up body.

I remember the first time I heard the terrible sound. Running home, I headed straight for my bed to bury myself in whatever blankets I could find. With my hands pressed tight over my ears, I still could not escape the awful sounds of the dirge. I never again felt free to swim in the river. A banana trunk or any long log floating among the flotsam would have me screaming and bolting for dry land.

A few weeks after Lượm's funeral, I finally worked up the nerve to go to her house. Despite everything I had heard, part of me still believed that I would find her waiting for me. At the edge of the yard, I looked for my friend at our usual playing spots. No one was around except for a few chickens pecking at the wet ground. Stepping over the clumps of dirt that the chickens had stirred up, I made my way to the house. Inside, the tiny room smelled of her grandmother's betel leaves and slaked lime and her grandfather's cigarettes.

Certain that no one was home, I went to the small area behind the house where I sometimes saw Lượm and her grandmother preparing food. That day there was no soup bubbling or rice boiling. The wood stove stood beside the soot-blackened pots and pans stacked empty on each other. Spying her grandparents inside their vegetable garden, I ran to them.

"Con thưa hai bác," I said (Good afternoon Uncle and Aunty).

"Chanh ơi!" her grandmother called out, turning to look at me. The words then spilled out in one anguished jumble. I could see her teeth stained black-red from years of chewing betel.

"We didn't want Lượm to go, but the spirits had different plans for her. They wanted her to be with her father. We heard them come for Lượm that night. They made noises to show us they were there. Bác Hai fought them off with the knife that he had put under the bed. He warned the spirits to go away and leave Lượm with us. But they refused and took her." She stopped talking to wipe her eyes with the back of her hand.

"We all have our fates, and Lượm's fate is to be with her father," she added.

Fate, the concept of predestination, permeates the Vietnamese culture, offering acceptance and perhaps comfort. But that afternoon, it gave me neither.

The five years that I spent in the countryside are distinctly sectioned in my mind into three periods: before Lượm, during, and after. Her death ended our friendship and exacerbated my fears. Three years later, I would come close to what my friend must have felt when she was sick. Delirious from a similar stomach illness while in Sungei Besi, the second of our three refugee camps, I would think of Lượm.

The scholar precedes the peasant, but when the rice runs out, it's the peasant who precedes the scholar. The well-known Vietnamese proverb befits an agrarian society that holds a deep reverence for education. Its ending, however, makes clear the shift in priorities in times of shortage. Amid the hunger during the time when rice came very close to running out in our village and across the rest of the Mekong Delta, my parents did not want to flaunt their status as educated city folks and were quick to discard vestiges of their old life: pants that required a belt, jewelry—including their wedding rings—and soon even shoes. Beyond deflecting envy, the change in attire was pragmatic. Jewelry easily slid off in the water and often interfered with movement; form-fitting pants made jumping in and out of the canoe difficult; and footwear of any kind guaranteed disaster when crossing bridges.

Despite these and other efforts to assimilate, my parents didn't make much progress inside the tiny village of intertwining bloodlines and wariness for outsiders. The government didn't help matters when they singled out my father to be among the handful of people in charge of running the rice cooperative.

Sometime after we arrived in Vĩnh Long, the regime that had condemned my father's capitalist know-how asked him to tap into this knowledge. In setting up the cooperative communes, Communist Party members needed people with business skills to manage the bureaucracy. Among farmers, the former entrepreneur was an obvious choice. My father was assigned a role as vice head of the cooperative.

Each day my father worked alongside the villagers in the rice fields. A fast learner, he was capable in his role, but he sensed the farmers only saw him as an entitled bourgeois who had contributed no land to the cooperative and had no business telling them what to do. As the rice crop continued to shrink at each harvest, people became more disillusioned, casting their ire particularly against those in charge. In my father they found an easy scapegoat. Fueled by alcohol, their anger would turn into violence.

With few options for entertainment, the men in our village often turned to alcohol for relief. On dirt floors in homes throughout the village, they would gather to drink, eat, and talk after a long day of labor under the sun. So inseparable are the acts of drinking, eating, and talking, there is a Vietnamese word to describe it: *nhậu*. Over a few pieces of fish or meat, or if none was available, some crunchy sour fruit, the men ate and drank into the night. Wine distilled from fermented rice was the only alcohol available. My father was sometimes invited to these *nhậu* gatherings, which he understood as the only way to gain trust and acceptance.

"Ba, don't go," I said whenever I saw him heading out in the afternoon.

"I won't come back late," he said, prying my arms off his waist. But I knew it was not true. I would not see him until long after we had already finished dinner. He would walk into the house only to head straight to sleep. Not a heavy drinker, my father would come to dread these gatherings, mentioning how there was never a good time for getting up and leaving while still sober.

Walking around the village, I could always tell whenever there was a *nhậu* gathering ahead. The loud voices immediately prompted me to alter my path even if it meant going much farther out of the way. But at times there was no alternate route to bypass the rowdiness, and all I could do was quicken my pace.

Nhậu might have been the source of happiness for men, but it was the cause of misery for many families. In tiny huts already crowded with people and livestock, the loud carousing took over the little living space. As the afternoon merged into the evening, the wine continued to fill the men's glasses around wailing children and animals demanding to be fed. For some families, the money spent to buy alcohol was the last *đồng* they had.

At times, the misery did not end there. In their drunkenness, some men turned on their wives and children. I remember one family that lived not far from us and raised pigs for a living. The shortest route to our house was through their front yard. A few times I witnessed the father in a drunken rage swinging his hands and feet at his wife and their four children. Their cries would summon neighbors to intervene. The man's father, who lived nearby, was often the first one to run over when he himself was not drunk. For that day, the beating might have halted, but another *nhậu* gathering always loomed.

"He didn't know what he was doing. He was drunk," was the excuse I heard often. The odious behavior spurred by alcohol would one day spill onto my father.

It was a typical afternoon. Bảy and I were home while Cu Anh was at school and my father was working in the rice field. My mother was in the front yard slicing up a banana trunk for the pigs, with me as her helper. As the sword-like machete slid back and forth over the banana log, big round rings fell onto the ground. When the pile mounted to a certain height, my mother put down the knife. It was my cue to scoop up the wet strands and deposit them into a bucket. Around us, chickens and ducks wandered about, now and then poking their heads into our stash. As hungry as they all were, none wanted the tasteless staple that only the pigs would eat.

Suddenly I heard someone calling out for my mother, unmistakable panic in her voice. I looked around to see a woman running toward us on the other side of the bridge. I recognized her as Cô Sáu (Miss/Aunty Number Six), the secretary of the cooperative. Before reaching us, Cô Sáu had already started talking loudly and fast. I could not follow all the details about a farmer with a gun and my father, but it was clear he was in danger. My mother asked Cô Sáu to take her to my father.

"Chanh, help your brothers feed the animals and make dinner," my mother called back before taking off. As the women's cone-shaped *nón lá* retreated from view, my fears alternated between that for my father and that of being left alone. The receding sunlight had replaced the heat with a mellower warmth, which meant we only had a few more hours of daylight left. I had to find Bảy quickly and tell him what had happened. I didn't know where he was until I remembered where he could be found most afternoons these days.

He was glued to a book called *Tam Quốc Chí* that my father had brought home from a trip to Sài Gòn a few weeks earlier. Translated from the fourteenth-century Chinese novel *Romance of the Three Kingdoms*, it is the epic story of three warring kingdoms at the end of the Han dynasty. Our dog-eared copy, dense with tiny words, had cast a deep spell on my brothers. If both happened to be at home, they would fight for its possession to read until the last drop of daylight, then spend the rest of the night dissecting plotlines involving feudal lords, dragons, and astrology magic.

While Cu Anh was at school in the afternoon, it was Bảy's time for reading. As soon as he was done with his chores, he would rush to a short wooden extension parallel to the scrap-metal deck and hanging over the pond. With a bowl filled with guava or some other fruit by his side, he hunched over the enormous book, remaining like a statue until dark. Despite my initial interest, the historical novel never captured my attention as it did my brothers'.

Relieved to find Bảy at his usual perch, I quickly told him all that I knew. Only two years older, he always seemed to know what to do whenever we were in trouble. But not that day. After I finished talking, Bảy said nothing and looked as scared as I felt. In the distance, I could hear the pigs banging against the pen, rooting loudly.

"Bảy, say something!" I pleaded, having never seen my self-assured, bossy brother at a loss for plans.

"Chanh, don't be scared. I'm sure Ba is all right," he said, springing back to life as if tapped by a magic wand. "So we'll feed the animals. Cu Anh will be back soon to help us." My brother's sureness calmed me even as I was aware that he did not know any more than I did.

Before feeding the pigs, we first had to prepare their food. That meant slicing the unfinished banana trunk. My mother had never let us use the machete despite our vigorous lobbying. That afternoon we finally got our wish to wield the fearsome knife. Around us, chickens milled about looking for food. Every now and then, some would stop strutting, freezing in mid-motion. Just as suddenly, they would unfreeze, turning their heads from side to side while flickering their eyes wildly, seeming as if they had just recovered some lost memory. The chickens gradually tightened their circle around us, pecking not only at the ground but also at our legs and arms. Their constant badgering for food normally annoyed me to no end. That day, I welcomed the distraction.

By the time we finished feeding the animals and preparing our dinner of rice and *rau mồng tơi* (wild spinach) soup, daylight had all but disappeared. Cu Anh lit the kerosene lamp and set it in the middle of the table as we waited for our parents. I must have fallen asleep at dinner, because the next thing I remember was Cu Anh carrying me to my bed. Wiping the mud off my feet, he told me to go to sleep.

I woke up to sounds of morning activities. In the back yard, my father hunched over the kerosene lamp, taking it apart to fix something. Nearby, my mother squatted on the ground beside a water basin, washing clothes. The morning looked like any other, as if nothing had happened the day before. I ran to my father.

"Ba, what happened to you yesterday? Did someone try to shoot you?" I asked, wavering between wanting to know and being afraid of his answer. That morning, my father did not tell me much other than that he was fine and for me not to worry about him. But over the years, I found out from him and others what had happened.

The previous afternoon when my father was heading back to the rice fields after the midday break, he saw a man staggering toward him in the distance. As the man got closer, my father recognized him as one who had given up more land to the collective than most in our village. Waving his hands and gesticulating wildly, the man repeatedly called out to my father. Detecting trouble, my father thought of walking away, but he suspected the man might be carrying his gun. It was the middle of the rice harvest season, and the man was one of the few farmers temporarily assigned guns to guard the crop—a coveted privilege in the tightly controlled police state where gun ownership was a rarity, available only to those in trusted positions with the government.

"Ông Ba Vườn, I want to talk to you," the man called out, slurring his words. Sensing no better alternative, my father moved closer. While still an arm's length away, the man reached out and grabbed my father by his shoulders.

"Ông Ba, you had no farmland and contributed nothing. How is it that now you have as much as me?" he said, his breath reeking of alcohol. Before my father could answer, the man pulled out a gun wedged between his trousers and stomach and pointed it at my father. "Let's go," he said, "I'm taking you to the police station and demanding my land back." Weighing the option that perhaps the gun wasn't loaded, my father hesitated. The gunman reached up and shot into the air. "Let's go," he repeated, returning the gun to the back of my father's head. The heat from the just-discharged nozzle replaced the coolness of the metal, garnering immediate compliance.

The forced march went unnoticed past one rice field after another. As they walked, the gunman continued his rant, haphazardly waving the loaded gun. It was about noon, so many farmers had gone home for lunch and a nap to escape the day's most intense heat. Suddenly, before my father could make out what was happening, he found himself tackled to the ground along with the gunman.

As he had hoped, some farmers, upon coming back to the field, had heard the gunman's rant and understood the situation. Deciding to take matters into their own hands, they sneaked up behind the gunman and wrestled them both to the ground. After some time, the local authorities arrived. My mother showed up just as everyone was led away to the police station, where the interrogation extended into the night.

The gun incident had a profound impact on our family. In the days after, we all seemed to be on edge. The change was most distinct with my father, who seemed much more nervous and jittery than I had ever seen him. At night, he stopped sleeping inside our house. "The gunman was sent away, but his relatives are still here. Your father's afraid they might come for us. He wants to be on the lookout," my mother explained the first time I saw my father heading out into the dark orchard. He held a kerosene lamp in one hand and a blanket folded inside a reed mat in the other. Bảy thought these nightly excursions were great adventures and often begged to come along. Despite my brother's insistence, my father always made the trips alone. In my bed, I would think of my father lying on the thin mat, surrounded by insects, snakes, and other creatures of the night. I no longer thought of him as invulnerable.

The father protects, the mother nurtures, and the child obeys. This theme recurs in proverbs and songs that my mother sprinkled amid endless lectures about life lessons. At every opportunity, she had an adage ready. "Công cha như núi Thái Sơn. Nghĩa mẹ như nước trong nguồn chảy ra" (A father's toil towers like the ranges of the Thái Sơn Mountain. A mother's love flows ceaselessly like a stream at its source). "Con không cha như nhà không nóc. Mồ côi mẹ, lót lá mà nằm" (A child without a father lives in a house without a roof. A child without a mother scavenges leaves to lie on). "Cá không ăn muối, cá ươn. Con cãi cha mẹ, trăm đường con hư" (Fish rot without salt. Children rot if they contradict their parents).

Growing up, I copied my mother and sang the ditties, at times without much thought. Over squares of hopscotch and between bounces of balls, my friends and I sometimes included such jingles of parental sacrifice and devotion among the playful tunes that we hummed, synching their rhythm to our games. The proverbs go on to prescribe, "Một lòng thờ mẹ, kính cha. Cho tròn chữ hiếu, mới là đạo con" (Worship one's mother; respect one's father. Fulfilling the calling is the religion of the child). Somewhere in my childhood, the seeds of filial piety took root, sprouting entwining vines of loyalty, love, and duty.

In my young mind, my father was like the Thái Sơn Mountain itself, a timeless and indomitable protector of my life. He seemed capable of defying death. How else to reconcile the calligraphy extolling his wartime sacrifice with the fact that he was still with me? The gun incident would catapult me into a different mindset. My father no longer seemed invincible—rather, quite the opposite. In his constant brushes with death, I came to suspect that he must have either used up or come close to using up all his luck. Even his age, more advanced than that of most of my friends' fathers, came to represent something else. Before, I had equated his advanced age with wisdom. Now, I could only think of it as a liability. Going forward, I concluded, my father would need my protection as much as I needed his. The notion of my father's being both my protector and my charge would crystallize into an unwavering conviction as I grew older.

ESCAPE FROM VIỆT NAM

I t was in the months following the gun incident that I first heard my parents mention *vượt biên*. The phrase, brimming with secrecy and danger, means crossing the border. As one side of Việt Nam faces the sea and the other edges up against Laos and Cambodia, the border could be with either land or water. But from my parents' conversations, I only took *vượt biên* to mean crossing the border by boat. I also understood it to be the most forbidden of all illegal acts. Just the thought of *vượt biên*, if revealed to the wrong people, could land all the involved adults in jail.

In planning our escape, my parents never explicitly informed us of their plans, but neither did they conceal them. They discussed and strategized as we hovered in the background. Gold bars, bribes, rendezvous points—words and concepts that I did not entirely understand—dominated the whispered conversations. These discussions were the ultimate adult business. I knew not to pry into any details and to never repeat what I had heard to anyone outside the family.

Around this time in 1981, almost five years after the first reunion with his older, communist brother, Bác Hai, my father made the trek to Hà Nội, on a detour from his trip to bring supplies to his nephew and younger brothers in reeducation camps. My father confided in Bác Hai that his faith in the new government had run out. He could no longer foresee a future for our family anywhere in the place of our birth. He told his brother of his plans to escape and said goodbye, certain that it was the last time they would see each other. As it turned out, they did meet again, twenty years later in Texas.

In our village, there was one person outside our family who knew of my parents' plans: Chú Tư Huệ. With more education and interest in the world than most in the village, Chú Tư was one of the leaders of the cooperative. As the vice head, my father worked closely with Chú Tư. Before the communist takeover, he had grown a flower called *huệ* (lily) for a living, hence his nickname Chú Tư Huệ (Uncle/Mr. Number Four Lily). He and his family of five young children lived on a small plot of land next to Lượm's grandparents.

Most nights after dinner, I heard footsteps outside our house.

"Anh Ba ơi! Anh Ba có ở nhà không?" (Older brother number three! Are you home?) rang out the familiar voice.

Over countless hand-rolled cigarettes and cups of *chè*, a dessert soup of mung bean and homemade sugar, my father and Chú Tư talked into the night. They spoke mostly of their disillusionment with the new government—no small risk to take, as anyone could be an informer. But from the beginning, the men sensed they could trust each other. In my father, Chú Tư saw an entrepreneur whom he admired. In Chú Tư, my father saw someone who, in different circumstances, could have been a savvy businessman. When my father confided in him about our plans to escape, Chú Tư offered his support. He often told my father that he too would consider leaving Việt Nam with his own family if he had money.

My father proposed a plan to Chú Tư that he thought would benefit both families. He suggested that Chú Tư move his family to the back half of our orchard, an area much bigger than the small plot of land on which he and his family were living. Living behind us, Chú Tư could keep an eye on the orchard and deflect questions from the local police regarding our whereabouts during our escape attempts. This was especially important if our escape failed. Any escape attempt, even the most well planned, could unravel at any stage from the beginning until the end. At sea, the unravelling could result in death. Closer to home, it often meant imprisonment, resulting in the loss of home and work, the punishment the government doled out for anyone suspected of *vượt biên*.

By living right next to us, Chú Tư could shield us from prying eyes. In the rice fields, he could make up excuses for my father's absence. In exchange for his help, Chú Tư would receive half of the orchard immediately. The other half would be taken over by the government after we left, whether we succeeded or not.

Chú Tư accepted my father's proposal. Three years after we had arrived in the countryside, his family moved onto our orchard.

With the police always lurking and watching, there were few means to verify information, and deals were made on faith and trust. Those deceived had no recourse, as they could not go to the police. The lack of transparency or accountability enabled con men to prey on the desperate. Scams to steal and extort gold were rampant. Finding trustworthy collaborators was a monumental task.

By luck, my father did not have to search long to discover that a distant relative was organizing an escape for his extended family. My parents had decided that our family would not leave together. Besides reducing the financial loss if the escape failed, splitting up also increased the chance that at least a part of the family would make it out of the country. Cu Anh would be in the first group to leave, as he was near the age of conscription and would likely have ended up part of Việt Nam's occupation of Cambodia. In school, he had been learning jungle survival skills and bomb evading and defusing techniques. The two youngest of my older sisters, Chị Năm and Chị Tư, would join him. The organizers' price for the passage was four taels (37.5 grams) of gold for each of my sisters and two taels for my brother, a children's discount.

When my father informed his siblings of the escape plans, two of my uncles, former South Vietnamese soldiers who had recently come back from reeducation camps, decided to escape with their young families.

One of my uncles, Dượng Mười (Uncle Number Ten, the husband of my father's youngest sister) paid some of the cost of his family's passage in labor by helping to scope out the escape routes and by registering the boat in his name. For months before the escape, Dượng Mười and the organizers took the boat along potential routes down the Mekong River to the sea. Through bribes and connections, they had secured permission to ferry bricks to Rạch Giá, a coastal town on the Gulf of Thailand ninety miles west of Vĩnh Long. Besides providing scouting intelligence, these trips served to familiarize the local police with the boat, so that on the actual day it could pass by without suspicion.

For one of the trips, Dượng Mười stopped at our house, which was on his way, to discuss plans with my father. At night, he would regale my brothers and me with stories, such as the one about his grandfather and the durian tree. By serendipity, his visit coincided with an incident in which my father again found himself with a gun pointed at his head, but this time it was a robbery.

In hindsight, it was inevitable that someone would come for the most valuable commodity right inside our house: the bags of urea fertilizer lining our storage room. The fertilizer came to us not long after we had arrived at Vĩnh Long. Urea, a source of nitrogen, came in the form of white granules and required a relatively dry storage environment. With limited storage space, the government needed people to volunteer room in their homes to stockpile farming materials that it supplied to the cooperative. A typical dwelling in our village had only one room, walled off into separate living spaces by thatched dividers. Our house, with an extra room in the back protected by a plastic roof, did not go unnoticed. Given little choice by the cooperative, my father agreed to provide the room as storage space.

On the day of the fertilizer delivery, canoes weighed down with heavy bags weaved around the pond and up to our deck. After carrying the fertilizer a few feet to the storage room, the men unloaded the bags on top of wooden platforms raised above the floor to keep away moisture. When they finished, the room, except for a small pathway, was filled. The distinct smell of urea—the faint odor of urine and sweat— seeped out into the rest of the house and remained with us thereafter.

From then on, farmers showed up at our house at all hours. They would present my mother a slip of paper authorizing the amount of fertilizer to take back to the fields. In a notebook, my mother carefully recorded the details of the transactions. The deliveries and distribution of fertilizer contributed to the ever-lengthening lines of canoes waiting in the pond.

Shortly after one such delivery, my uncle Dượng Mười stopped by our house on one of his scouting missions for escape routes. Dượng Mười did not want to draw any attention to himself or to the visit that could potentially unravel the plans for escape. He stayed close to our house and quickly hid when he thought someone was coming. After lunch, when we thought our neighbors would most likely be inside for the midday nap, we showed him around our orchard. When we approached the barbed-wire fence separating us from our nearest neighbors—an older, wiry man with a very appropriate nickname (Strong Old Man Number Four) and his wife—we showed Dượng Mười a hole beneath the fence, one that we believed thieves had been using to slip in and out of our property.

When I went to bed that night, my father and Dượng Mười were still in deep conversation planning the escape. I fell asleep to muffled discussions of patrol boats, rendezvous points, big fish (main boat), and small fish (canoes).

"Chanh, wake up!" I heard my mother's voice at a whisper. Leaning close to my face, she murmured, "Keep quiet and stay in the bed."

"Why? What's ...?" I began, when her hand clamped over my mouth. In the faint light, I could make out my mother shaking her head, her forefinger pressed against her lips. She looked scared, which frightened me.

From the other side of the wall near the back of the house, I heard unfamiliar voices and immediately realized that my nightly torment had become a reality. Our house was being invaded.

"Don't look at my face. Sit close together and don't move," a voice said from my brother's side of the room.

Through the mosquito net draped over my bed, I saw a young man, not much older than Cu Anh, standing next to my brothers' bed. In his hand was a knife. I quickly turned toward my mother, burying myself in her chest. In the darkness, I listened for the noises coming from the back of the house. The mix of voices combined with a steady march of footsteps, periodically interrupted by a thud of something heavy landing on the ground. This went on for a while until I heard a faint cry coming from far beyond the orchard. The footsteps immediately halted.

"Don't move!" the intruder said as he ran off toward the back of the house. The cries from the orchard grew louder and clearer. Soon after, I heard a loud splash crashing into the water, then in quick succession, two more splashes.

"Stay here!" My mother called out to my brothers and me as she jumped down from the bed. We ignored my mother's command and took off running after her toward the storage room. The scene we encountered left no doubt of a robbery abandoned in mid-progress. Bags of fertilizer lay scattered from the edge of the pond to the storage room. Inside, we found my father in the corner, blindfolded, his hands tied behind his back. We all rushed to him.

"Are you all right?" we asked.

"Yes, yes, I'm fine," he answered with the familiar response.

As we all helped untie him, my father told us what had happened. Earlier in the night, he was awakened by a hand on his shoulder and opened his eyes to a gun pointing in his face.

"Keep quiet. Let's go to the back of the house," the gunman ordered. Immediately my father realized we were being robbed. He intentionally avoided looking directly at the perpetrators' faces, but not before he had noticed that there were three men. Two later followed him to the fertilizer shed. One stayed behind.

Inside the storage room, the leader told his subordinate to tie my father up. As the rope went around his wrists, my father sensed a certain nervousness in the movements of his captor, who fumbled with the cord. It occurred to him that the robber might have thought my father knew him. It wasn't true, but my father feared his fate was sealed. Blindfolded, he tried to make sense of his surroundings. For a long while, like us in the other room, he also listened to the march of footsteps. Then came the cries beyond the orchard that took everyone by surprise.

"Ăn cướp! Ăn cướp!" (Robber! Robber!) the voice called out.

When the robbers heard this, they quickly fled in panic. It was then that we all heard the loud splashes as each of them jumped into the pond and escaped. It had happened so quickly that it took a while to figure out the sequence of events or that my uncle, Dượng Mười, was not in our house. Later, when he returned, he told us his version of what had happened.

After talking to my father earlier in the night, Dượng Mười had retreated to the altar room to sleep. He was still awake when he heard voices that he did not recognize. He quickly moved to a darker corner, leaning against the wall to listen. The words faded in and out but were clear enough for him to know that my parents were being robbed.

Were the robbers armed? Scattered both inside and outside the house? How many of them were there? He didn't know. As a former soldier in the South Vietnamese army, Dượng Mười had experienced ambushes in the night. What he did know was that he needed to get help.

Dượng Mười crawled down from the altar room to the lower floor. As the noises all seemed to come from the back of the house, he tiptoed past the kitchen in the front and then outside into the dimly moonlit orchard. Surrounded by the thicket of leaves, he wasn't sure which way to proceed, but he vaguely remembered our tour of the orchard and started running. Just when he thought he was lost, he found himself staring up at the barbed-wire fence. He crawled through the hole that we had pointed out to him earlier in the day. On the other side, he continued running while bellowing out loudly.

"Ăn cướp! Ăn cướp! Nhà Ông Ba Vườn bị ăn cướp! (Robbers! Robbers! Ông Ba Vườn's house is being robbed!). The screaming woke our neighbors Strong Old Man Number Four and his wife. They rushed out of their hut, a kerosene lantern dangling from their hands. Dượng Mười ran to the light and told them what was happening. When he finished, all three ran around the village, combining their voices to sound the alarm.

By morning, news of the robbery had spread before my father reported to the local security station. Many villagers came to our house to hear for themselves what had happened. Later, I would gather from my parents' conversation that among those who came, some were most likely involved and wanted to find out what we knew. But we did not know much, not then or ever. The police never caught the robbers, nor were they able to trace the canoes to anyone.

For a while after the robbery, my father resumed sleeping outside in the orchard at night. This time, I did not have to ask my mother the reason. Fear for my father and our family exploded in my mind as I viewed every man who came to our house with suspicion and dread. An uneasy sense of being watched hovered over me as soon as darkness fell. I abandoned my nightly routine of bathing by the deck, where the robbers had tied their canoes. I stayed glued to my parents and brothers and begged one of them to come with me whenever I needed to go outside. Before the incident, I could ignore my fear by running fast, then closing my eyes for the few moments that I needed to use the bathroom. After, I found doing anything by myself in the dark increasingly difficult.

Some weeks after the robbery, my siblings' *vượt biên* took place as planned. The afternoon before the escape, my sisters, uncles, and their families gathered at our house. My mother had prepared a special meal to present to the ancestors. After the food had been carefully arranged on the altar, we, starting with my parents, took turns lighting incense and paying our respects. My father and uncles, normally models of stoicism, looked visibly shaken as they whispered their prayers. The wisps of incense smoke rose above their murmured voices, taking to heaven their pleas for guidance and protection during the sea voyage.

After the ceremony, I followed my mother to our sleeping area while everyone else remained in the altar room to help take down the food and set up for our final meal together. "Má, what's that?" I asked when I saw my mother roll up some pieces of paper. "Đô la. American money," she said, her voice dropping to a whisper even though only the two of us were present. I had often heard đô la mentioned along with talk of gold bars. Until that moment, I had assumed that it was some sort of rare metal even more precious than gold. My mother stuffed the rolled-up money along with a few pieces of jewelry into the waistband seams of my sisters' pants. She explained that the đô la and gold would help my siblings in the safe harbor where my parents hoped they would find themselves. For the power they seemed to possess, the green pieces of paper before me looked so ordinary.

Everyone continued talking long after dinner. "Are you scared?" "Will you be all right?" "Where will you be?" I wanted to ask my sisters these and other questions. Sensing that they didn't know the answers themselves and my probing would only make matters tenser, I mostly listened while they talked. Soon my father said everyone needed to go to sleep, as the escapees had to leave very early in the morning.

When I woke up, it was already bright daylight. The chatter from last night was gone, and I knew I was too late. I had planned to get up with everyone to say goodbye. On my bed, I found a red bracelet and two đồng on top of a note. "For you to buy some candies." I recognized the handwriting as that of my third sister, Chị Tư.

For the rest of the day, my parents said little to Bảy and me while they went about their chores. At mealtimes, my mother prepared food for us, but she and my father ate little. At night, when my brother and I went to bed, they stayed up. A heavy tension hung over my parents, turning more oppressive each day.

On the third morning, my father left for Sài Gòn. In his absence, I sensed a rising panic in my mother. Three days later, he came home. Immediately I could tell he had good news. He told us the organizers had received a telegram from Thailand indicating that my siblings' boat had made it to land and that they were all right. In that instant, the heaviness in our home lifted; our parents came back to life and to us. In the days that followed, I would learn that for many on the boat, things had been far from all right. I heard "pirates," "rape," and "kidnap,"—words whose meanings I only vaguely understood. But the little I did understand was enough to terrify me.

My father began making frequent trips to Sài Gòn to send and receive mail. As Việt Nam became increasingly isolated under the trade embargoes, there was little communication with the outside world, particularly with the West. International telephone service was unheard of, while international mail service was severely limited and had to go to one of Việt Nam's major cities. My uncle Cậu Hai (my mother's oldest brother) and his wife, who had a legal residence status in Sài Gòn, had several children living abroad. This fact, although never openly discussed, was known by the local government. Viewed with suspicion, families with relatives in the West nevertheless could still receive outside communication. It was understood that the letters and packages, often taking weeks or months to arrive, if they arrived at all, would be subject to searches and theft. Anything deemed antigovernment was confiscated, the intended recipient harassed and detained. By using my uncle's address, my father was able to conceal that he had children who had left Việt Nam, knowledge that if revealed would cast suspicion on our family and jeopardize our future escape attempts. Cậu Hai and his wife had no such qualms, as they had no desire to leave Việt Nam.

Sometime after my siblings' escape, my father came home from Sài Gòn with one such letter sent to my uncle's address. Songkhla Refugee Camp, Thailand: the unfamiliar words appeared beneath Chị Tư's name on the envelope. Inside, I would learn of the horrors that visited their boat in its five days at sea—the thirst, hunger, storms, and six brutal attacks by Thai pirates.

Cu Anh described the pirates' repeatedly ramming their much bigger ship into the refugees' rickety boat while shining bright lights onto the screaming mass of refugees. Wielding machetes and other weapons, the thugs stormed aboard, threatening to kill anyone who fought back. After separating the men from the women, they forced the men to jump over to their ship. The transfer not only made it easier for the pirates to search for gold but also to carry out their savage assaults on the women. My sisters described how they copied other women in dumping oil and urine on themselves to appear unappealing. They couldn't be sure if it was their actions or the mere luck of where they happened to be standing on the boat, but in the end, they were spared. Many other women, including young girls, were not.

In one of the attacks, when the waters were particularly choppy, my brother said he misjudged the height of the pirate ship and fell into the ocean while jumping across. A few others who made the jump after him also fell in the water. In the chaos, no one heard their screams for help as the waves continued to push them farther into the ocean. Cu Anh was sure they were all going to drown. By chance someone finally heard their cries and summoned for help to pull them aboard.

The pirates who came later were even more vicious. Unable to find valuables in a boat that had already been ransacked multiple times, they resorted to extreme measures: pulling out gold fillings from inside people's mouths, torturing people who they suspected might still be hiding gold somewhere, throwing overboard anyone showing the slightest hint of resistance. Given to wanton destruction and indifferent to the consequences, they pried open panels and floorboards looking for valuables that might be hidden among the crevices, then smashed engines out of anger when they could find none.

However horrific, the tortures and rapes were not the worst of the brutality. The grimmest fate befell the six young girls whom the pirates took with them. In the immediate aftermath, their mothers could not stop screaming, a few fell silent, turning mute.

By the time my siblings' boat reached shore, it was sinking, listing on its side, broken and damaged, much like the people it carried. The shell-shocked refugees staggered onto land, many men wearing only their shorts. The pirates, familiar with the hiding places for jewelry and dollars, had even stripped people of their clothes.

Everything I knew about my siblings' escape horrified me, but the kidnapping of the young girls, only a few years older than I, haunted me the most. At night in my bed, I often thought of them calling out for their mothers and of their mothers' anguish, unable to fathom how anyone could endure such suffering.

After a year of staying in various refugee camps in Thailand, my siblings arrived in America. Their letters described a new life in a small town in Texas. My father explained that Texas, only one of fifty states in America, could fit much of Việt Nam, Cambodia, and Thailand combined inside its borders. Until then, I had not realized that the faraway mystical country called America was so vast. I read and reread the rare letters in which my siblings talked about school and work and their impressions of a town called Port Arthur. There was a mention in Cu Anh's letter concerning his job cutting grass after school that defied my vision of the distant land.

In English, the words *grass* and *weeds* have different meanings and connotations. Both, however, translate as *cỏ* in Vietnamese. With no concept of a lawn, I only thought of *cỏ* as weeds, despised for invading rice fields and vegetable patches, to be plucked at the first sprout. Except for inaccessible places along riverbanks, I rarely encountered tall *cỏ* in fields and vegetable gardens. They would have long been grazed by hungry animals. In his letter, Cu Anh wrote that every two weeks he got paid for cutting *cỏ* around someone's house. I imagined my brother going around the person's home to cut down weeds so out of control that they could not be plucked by hand and had to be slashed with knives and big scissors. As America was a land of riches and plenty, I couldn't understand why its people would live in homes overgrown with weeds that could grow so fast.

One afternoon after my father had returned from a trip to Sài Gòn, he called excitedly for Bảy and me to come over. "This is for you from your siblings in America," he said.

He handed us a brown, waxy paper package that sounded as if filled with marbles. In the middle of the bag, two big letters "m" were joined together, surrounded by button-shaped candies in bright colors. Even though the present was sealed, I detected a familiar scent of chocolate, a candy I had once tasted in Sài Gòn. For so long, I had not thought about a food that I had equated with sublime deliciousness almost on par with durian. Back in the city, we each could have only a small square of chocolate to try. I couldn't believe all those candies in the bag belonged to just me and my brother.

I tore open the bag, took out one piece of candy and gave another to my brother. Holding the candy between thumb and forefinger, my brother and I inspected it from different angles, then looked at each other, and in unison, popped the chocolate pieces into our mouths. As the hard shell dissolved into a sweet creaminess, my taste buds burst to life. My brother looked at me with an expression that must have mirrored my own excitement and immediately offered up a plan: "We should eat only two more pieces and save the rest. Every day we should eat just three, all right?" Normally I would challenge Bảy even when we agreed, as I generally disliked being bossed around. That day I had no objections.

Until the M&Ms ran out, eating them was the highlight of each day. Sitting by the deck inside our hut with our feet dangling over a pond, we competed to see who could finish eating them slower. It wasn't long before we gave up figuring out what the small "m" imprinted on each candy meant, but we continued our debate regarding the colors. My brother thought each had a different flavor, but I was sure they all tasted the same. Long after we had finished all the M&Ms, I thought about them at night as I drifted off to sleep, my hunger tamed by the fantasies. Before my siblings' gift from America, I had thought that durian was the only food from the heavens. After, I knew there was another.

Under any circumstances, M&Ms are delightful treats, but back then, their hold over my brother and me was complete. Their power had much to do with the fact that it had been so long since we had last tasted pure, clean sugar. When we first arrived in the countryside, white sugar was still available at the market. Soon, we could only find brown sugar sold in blocks. In time, it also vanished along with much of the other merchandise.

My father, born with a sweet tooth, began to experiment with raising honeybees. The honey I remember only vaguely, but the stings I remember well, the saving grace being that honeybee stings hurt much less than those from wasps or yellow jackets. After the bees, my father turned to making sugar from the sugar cane that we grew. The process was laborious, involving much cooking and straining. After rounds of testing, he proudly showed off what he had produced.

"Chanh, taste this," he said, handing me an oversized chopstick that he had just swirled around a big vat. The thick brown syrup tasted sweet but had a strong earthy smell that made my stomach churn. But life in the countryside had conditioned us to make do. With no soap, we used the detergent brought from Sài Gòn for washing ourselves, and when I suspected that the harsh chemicals made my hair fall out, I just used less and rinsed more thoroughly. In place of toothpaste, we used salt. After losing my toothbrush in the pond—a common occurrence—I used my fingers to clean my teeth while waiting for a replacement. But as much as I craved sweets, I never acquired a taste for my father's homemade sugar.

There was someone in our family who loved it, though: our dog Lu Lu. She came to us as a puppy sometime after Luốc had died from the barbed-wire fence entanglement. By chance, Bảy and I discovered that we could soothe the tiny pup that cried endlessly for her mother by letting her suck on our fingers dabbed with the sugar-cane syrup. Lu Lu could not get enough of the treat and continued to eat off our fingers long after her teeth had grown in.

As she grew older, Lu Lu became quite attached to Bảy and me and followed us everywhere. Fishing, swimming, climbing trees, even going to the bathroom, we were often not alone. For a while every morning before heading out to school, my brother and I would run far into the orchard with Lu Lu by our side. Waiting until she was distracted while tearing into a coconut shell or chasing after a lizard, Bảy and I would run back home to hop onto the canoe for school.

It didn't take Lu Lu long to figure out our ruse. From then on, at the slightest sound of our footsteps in the morning, she would run straight to the canoe, perching herself firmly in the middle. With an energetic puppy accompanying us, the ride across the river was anything but calm. Each time she leaned over to drink from the river, the canoe tipped precariously. The frustration continued once we reached shore, since she insisted on following us to school. My parents had to hold on to her while we ran off. Back at home, Bảy and I kept trying out new tricks to keep Lu Lu from following us in the morning. But eventually, she would find a way to outsmart all our efforts.

By the time Lu Lu came to live with us, we all had become proficient rowers. Crossing the river no longer caused much angst except in severe weather. One morning while paddling to school, I noticed a small piece of black driftwood

99

bobbing a distance behind us. Its trajectory seemed deliberate, unlike those of other river debris tossed randomly by the currents. As the driftwood floated closer, I recognized the distinct shape of a nose as the faint sounds from earlier grew into labored wet snorts. Behind the nose, two dark eyes blinked fast, hovering just above the waterline. Even though the rest of the face was submerged, I needed no more clues.

"Ba, Lu Lu is behind us. She looks like she's drowning!" I yelled.

My father and Bảy turned to look. In one swift maneuver of their oars, they reversed the direction of the canoe. The rescue would be the first of many in the years to come. We would come to know the messy routine well. As we came closer, the black snout would heave faster, the whimpering turning more excited. While we were still a few inches apart, Lu Lu would leap out of the water, grabbing onto the edge of the canoe. I knew to slide to the opposite side, pressing against it with all my weight. With their legs spanning the width of the canoe, Bảy and my father pulled up the wet mass of fur. Once onboard, Lu Lu immediately began the assault. In big sweeping moves, she unleashed everything in her coat, mouth, and ears. By the time the torrents of water and spit stopped, we were soaked, and our canoe, filled with water, had been pushed far downstream. While Lu Lu spread out in the middle of the canoe, drying herself under the sun, we resumed the trek upstream against the currents, then across the river to get to school. In good or bad weather, every rescue guaranteed our late arrival to class.

OUR TURN

When my siblings were in the refugee camps, my father began again the search for a new escape route for the rest of our family. Unlike the planning of my siblings' escape, he had to reach outside the network of relatives to find a collaborator. He resumed taking trips away from home for days at a time. When asked where he was, I always answered that he was in Sài Gòn, checking up on my sisters and brother. In truth, I did not know his exact whereabouts but only that he was somewhere conspiring with other men to plan our escape.

These men did not meet in their homes, as any gathering of unfamiliar faces could arouse suspicion. With the authorities tipped off by prying neighbors, the participants would be taken in for questioning. Any discrepancy in their stories could unravel their plans and land all in jail. They met in illicit cafes, the only kind around. Even though they all knew the police could swoop in at any moment, meeting in public places was still deemed marginally safer than meeting in homes.

From my father's telling over the years, I could imagine what it must have been like. As cigarette smoke filled the air and the Vietnamese coffee filter dripped a steady beat, my father sized up the men sitting across from him. Could they be trusted? Would they steal his gold? Even if they were honest, did they know what they were doing?

I remember our first escape attempt. We arrived at a riverbank just as dusk turned into night. My father said that our escape boat would come for us soon. Until then, we were to hide in the bushes along the water's edge. When we got to the bushes, some people were already hiding there. While we waited, a few more joined our group.

"Stay quiet and look for the signals. As soon as you see the lights, run fast to the boat," my father whispered, pointing in the direction from which he thought the boat might arrive.

From behind the bushes, we assumed the ready-to-leap position while scanning the river for the telltale flashes of light. With the mosquitoes feasting on our skin, we waited and waited. As the minutes turned into hours past the rendezvous time, we gave up the crouching stance to sit down on the wet mud. The river before us remained a dark expanse with no sign of our escape boat. As the night stretched on, a few people started leaving.

"We should leave too. Maybe the police intercepted the boat. They'll come for us next," my mother said, repeating the same worries expressed by those who had left.

"No, we'll stay just a little longer," my father insisted.

Sometime after midnight, my father finally conceded that the boat was not coming. He said we had to leave before the sun came out to avoid detection by the local villagers. In the dark, we trudged back onto the road and headed home.

Since our whole family had been away overnight, my parents feared the police might be waiting for us back at the house. My parents had reasons to be worried. Since Cu Anh's departure, many had been asking about my brother's whereabouts. "He's studying in Sài Gòn," I was told to answer, but I could sense no one was convinced. We knew it would not take much to confirm everyone's suspicion that my brother had escaped and that we were now trying to do the same. Any villager who had seen our whole family leaving town could have tipped off the authorities. But that day when we came back to our house, no one was waiting for us inside.

Later from his contacts, my father would learn the reason why our boat never showed up. It was because it never existed. The escape plans that the organizers had painted for my father were mere words, intended to defraud. Still, he remarked that we were lucky. The con men, having taken our money, could still have alerted the police. From other sources, the police could also have discovered us hiding by the riverbank. If we had been arrested and spent time in jail, our house and land would have been confiscated.

It wasn't long before my father began to consider another escape plan. By then, my two remaining sisters had found their future spouses. Each had a different vision of her married life. My oldest sister, Chị Hai, wanted to start anew in another country with her future husband, while my second sister had decided that she would remain in Việt Nam. Unable to convince Chị Ba to change her mind, my parents finally gave her their permission and blessings to stay behind. But staying or leaving, my sisters needed to formalize their marital status before our family could attempt another escape. Within a few months of each other, in quick succession, my parents arranged for two weddings.

My sisters' weddings were rare instances of celebration outside of Tết. For each wedding, many villagers came to help, with the implicit understanding that we would return the labor in the future. Some men cleared brush, trimming and tying up low-hanging branches; some painted signs; others weaved palm and banana leaves into decorative arches. Overnight, the dirt paths surrounding our house transformed into a welcoming promenade.

The day before each wedding, the village cooks arrived, carrying enormous pots, wood stoves, and baskets brimming with food, turning our back yard into a big open kitchen. Among the women, it was easy to spot the head chef, a tiny woman issuing rapid-fire instructions to pluck chickens, chop vegetables, stir pots, all while tasting and sampling dishes that others had prepared. Bảy and I marveled at the sight of so much food. At Chị Hai's wedding, we wedged ourselves among the busy cooks, grabbing handfuls of the food they were preparing. Stashing the loot in our pockets, we ran off into the orchard to revel in what we had haphazardly seized. In a happy trance, we then greedily stuffed our mouths with what we had stolen, only to spit out everything when we realized the prized pieces of chicken gizzards were only half cooked.

On the wedding day, our family and some of the guests watched as two big canoes carrying the groom's family headed toward us. As the boat edged up the dock, people grabbed onto each other for support to get off. Every time someone moved, the boat dipped and swayed. Several villagers, guests at the wedding, ended up jumping into the water to hold the boat in place.

We all got dressed up for the occasions. Bảy and I wore the new clothes my father had bought in Sài Gòn: long, buttoned pants for both of us, a loose collared shirt for Bảy, and a red and white T-shirt with the logo "Yacht Club International" on the front for me. I had no idea what the English words meant, but the fact that they were not Vietnamese, and that perhaps the shirt had come from America, made me feel very worldly and sophisticated. My mother, her short bob neatly pinned back, wore a golden *áo dài*, while my father had on a gray suit and red tie.

I was awed to see my parents looking so nice, having grown accustomed to seeing them in the uniform of the countryside—frayed shirts over black trousers smeared with mud, rolled up to the knees. With the fancy clothes, they resembled the vibrant couple in the photographs I had found stashed away in a box. Taken before I was born, the images depicted a time when small luxuries beyond mere survival were still attainable. It was a life far from what I knew in the countryside. The photos showed my father as a young bachelor, in a white shirt, sleeves rolled up, a cigarette casually dangling from his lips; as a businessman standing in front of the Arc de Triomphe in a three-piece suit; as seasoned traveler leaning against a car, trench coat hanging from one arm. My favorite photo of my mother was taken on a family vacation. Standing by the seashore, she's holding one of my sisters in her arms while staring out into the ocean behind a pair of dark sunglasses, her white *áo dài* blowing in the wind.

Once on land, the wedding party proceeded toward our house along the paths rimmed with welcome signs and arches. Leading the procession were members of the groom's family, each holding a tray covered with a red cloth. Inside the house, the covers were taken off to reveal fruits, tea, fabric, jewelry, and the requisite of every wedding: betel leaves and areca nuts—symbols of love and marriage. For Chị Hai and Anh Trưởng's wedding, I remember a most amazing sight among the gifts—a small round cake with white frosting. I couldn't remember the last time I had eaten cake.

After the presents had been laid out on the table in front of the altar, the groom's father and mother took turns presenting each of the gifts to my parents. When they finished, a hush fell over the room. Everyone turned toward the doorway as the bride made her grand entrance. In a beautiful *áo dài* the color of amber, with her hair swept up inside a circular golden headpiece, my second sister Chị Ba looked barely recognizable to me. At the second wedding, even when I knew what to expect, I was still shocked by the transformation of Chị Hai into a stunning bride. The ceremony commenced with bride and groom lighting incense, seeking Buddha's and the ancestors' blessings for their union.

After the weddings, the questions from our neighbors became more insistent and pointed. Why were the two weddings so close to each other? Where were the rest of my siblings? Why didn't they come to the wedding? It seemed only a matter of time before the police would show up at our house demanding answers.

Our next attempt to leave Việt Nam came not long after the second wedding. The afternoon before the escape, Anh Trưởng and Chị Hai arrived from Sài Gòn. As my mother had done each time, she made a special meal to present to Buddha and our ancestors. After the adults, Bảy and I took turns. We lit incense and bowed in front of the altar. At a similar ceremony before my siblings' escape, when knowledge of storms, pirates, and kidnappings had not been part of my consciousness, I had rushed through the meditation. Now, like everyone else, I remained for a long time before the altar. In my prayers, I asked Buddha and our ancestors for their help as earnestly and as desperately as if they were standing before me.

The morning of the escape, we got ready to leave when it was still dark. Before we boarded the canoe, my parents told Bảy and me that they had some business to take care of at the last moment and could not leave the house at the same time with us. They reassured us that they would join us later, on the boat. What my brother and I did not know at the time was that our parents had no such intention. Having lost so much gold, they realized there would not be enough for other attempts if we all left together and failed. My parents had decided that they would stay behind, entrusting my and Bảy's care to Chị Hai and her new husband.

My mother kept hugging Bảy and me, reminding us to listen to my sister and brother-in-law. In the dark, I could not see my mother well, but from her voice, I sensed she was crying. I was surprised that my ever-practical mother was being so sentimental, as we would be separated for only a short time and would see each other again at the end of the day. I concluded that she was just worried. Her worries rekindled all the fears I had been trying hard to suppress. As our canoe made its way across the river, I was again consumed with thoughts of the terrible events from my siblings' journey.

That morning, my father did not ferry us to the brick factory but much farther down to a different part of town. He said he did not want to run into neighbors who might know us. Once we reached shore, he again went over the logistics for the trip with Anh Trưởng and Chị Hai. At the end, he turned to me and Bảy. Cupping my face in his hands, he reminded us to listen to our sister and brother-in-law. For a few moments, I thought I detected something different in his voice, a sadness reminding me of my mother's from before. My father then told us we did not have much time and needed to get on with the plans. In our hurried goodbyes, there was no time to explore or ask my father to explain the unease I had sensed.

It was near dusk when we arrived at a small beach in Trà Vinh, a coastal town forty miles southeast of Vĩnh Long. By the waters' edge, several canoes were idling. One of the men manning the canoes called out to us and the few others who were also waiting nearby to get on. After we boarded, he paddled the boat some distance out into the river, then stopped. He said we should wait until the "big fish" (our escape boat) had reached the designated rendezvous point, at which time someone would be dispatched to let us know how to proceed.

As more canoes gathered around us in the river, Bảy and I searched for our parents. We kept asking my sister where they could be and what could possibly have caused their delay. Chị Hai deflected all our questions. With every canoe that pulled up without my parents, the unease I had sensed earlier in the day grew heavier. I begged our sister to tell us what she knew. Finally, Chị Hai revealed to us our parents' decision and the promise she had made to take care of Bảy and me. All day my brother and I had been bickering, taking out our exhaustion and fear on each other. After the revelation, we stopped fighting.

Until now it had not occurred to me that I would ever actually be separated from my parents while they were alive. A life without them, which I had thought an irrational fear, now loomed before me, more wrenching than I had ever imagined. I begged Chị Hai to turn around, but she said we could not.

As more stars appeared in the sky, with still no word from the big fish, people became less guarded about keeping quiet. Everyone demanded to know where the big fish was and why we were waiting so long. Mosquitoes swarmed in air that was thick with heat and tension. No one had any answers. Then, seemingly out of nowhere, a small boat dashed into our circle of canoes. The man on board said that the big fish could not make it to the rendezvous point. He mentioned something about the tide being too high for it to risk the exposure. When people contested his logic, he said that was all he knew. Some people suggested that perhaps we should go to wherever the big fish was. He said it was not possible and added that the only thing we should be concerned with now was to disperse quickly to avoid being detected, since we were not far from a market that would convene in a few hours. Everyone concluded that we had been deceived. Sensing no other recourse, the canoes returned to shore. As we trudged back up the muddy beach, people openly cursed the con men. I felt only relief and joy.

In the wake of another swindle, my parents made no secret that our savings were running out. But having learned much about the underworld of *vượt biên*, of crossing the border of escape, my father decided that he would cast all our fates into one last gamble. To ensure the highest chances for success, he knew he had to be one of the organizers from the beginning. He wanted to have strong input on escape routes that minimized the chance we would encounter pirates. And he would only collaborate with someone whose family would also be escaping. A personal stake was the only collateral my father would accept.

Through an old business contact in Sài Gòn, he was put in touch with a Chinese man in his sixties who was organizing an escape for his two wives and family. For the next year, a man with white vitiligo patches on his skin and a thick Chinese accent made frequent visits to our house, where he and my father conspired through the night to plan the escape. How to procure a fishing boat and a crew? Whom to trust and bribe? What routes to take? How to recruit other passengers to fund the voyage? Each part of the complex plot required detailed planning and involved risk of exposure.

Under the watchful eyes of police and communist sympathizers, just procuring supplies for an escape was a monumental task. To prevent *vượt biên*, the government severely restricted the sale of fuel, allowing people to buy only a limited amount. As any boat caught with excess fuel was immediately suspected, storing this reserve on the boat was not possible. The same was also true with food and water. The fishermen, who were our conspirators, had to hide the limited supplies in bushes along the riverbanks until the day of the escape.

For all the organizers' planning, success was far from certain and much was beyond their control. An inadvertent slip of the tongue by anyone involved or a chance encounter with the ubiquitous police could lead to discovery. On land, failure often meant loss of money and imprisonment. At sea, the consequences were far worse. An hour's or a day's difference in the timing could result in an encounter with pirates or a storm. Triumph or tragedy was separated by a thin line of fate.

About a year into the planning, my father told Bảy and me that our family's *vượt biên* would take place in a few days. Tết, the Lunar New Year, was also approaching, and I had been especially looking forward to this year's celebrations. For the New Year of 1983, the Chinese Zodiac pig would return for the first time since I had been born. By the Vietnamese way of counting age, a newborn starts out at one, so I would be turning thirteen, having completed one full cycle. In the Western system, I was a few months past eleven years old. When I asked my father if we could delay our escape until after the New Year, he said the timing couldn't be changed. He hoped the widespread preparation for the festivities would help to draw attention away from us.

On the day of *vượt biên*, as in our prior attempts, we left our house when it was still mostly dark. While our neighbor Chú Tư ferried us across the river, instinctively I turned to scan the waters behind us. In the faint light, I spotted Lu Lu's familiar black snout bobbing up and down in the distance. That morning as our canoe pushed forward, I understood we could spare no time for any part of the messy rescue. Once we reached shore, Bảy and I told Chú Tư about Lu Lu amid our hurried farewells. He told us that he would pick up Lu Lu on his return and take care of her in our absence. A promise, we later found out, he did keep.

We boarded a bus and arrived in Sài Gòn at around noon, then took a bicycle taxi to a small café, where my father told my mother, Bảy, and me to go inside and get something to eat. He could not join us, since he had to look for medicine to buy for Bảy, who had been complaining on the bus that his stomach hurt. After lunch, we went outside to wait for my father as he had instructed. My mother said we should try to blend in with the crowd and not attract attention to ourselves. That afternoon our blending was so complete that my father had trouble finding us. When he finally did, we quickly followed him into a small alleyway where a military truck, covered with a billowy green canvas, was waiting.

"Sorry we're late. We're all here now, ready to go," my father said to the soldiers who were sitting in the front seat. It became clear that they were part of the escape plan. One of the soldiers jumped down and ran around to the back where we were waiting. He slightly lifted the canvas and signaled for us to get in.

"Hurry! Move up to the front." he said.

My father hoisted me into the truck, then my brother and mother. Inside, there were already some people. As soon as my father got in, the truck took off. It made several more stops to pick up passengers before heading away from the noises of the city. For a long time, the truck, bouncing over potholes, passed through what felt like the countryside. Though it was the middle of the day, under the canvas it was dark. We leaned away from each other, vying for air that was redolent with the smell of sweat. Outside, the wind whipped loudly against the covering of the truck. Eventually, someone near the edge poked open a tiny slit in the fabric. Fresh air and light rushed in as we all turned to take in the unexpected relief.

Suddenly the truck came to an abrupt stop, jolting everyone.

"What happened?"

"Is the escape foiled?"

"Are the police nearby?"

The questions erupted. In the chaos, someone yelled out,

"Jump down! Get down! Run!"

People near the exit in the back ripped open the canvas flaps and jumped down. Since we were much farther inside, there was no way for us to get out. While people were still pouring out of the truck, it suddenly roared back onto the road.

"Má ơi! Ba ơi!" (Mom! Dad!) The wailing burst out in the semidarkness under the canvas. The sounds, piercing and inconsolable, were unmistakable cries of children calling for the parents who were no longer there. It didn't take long for people to realize what had happened. When the truck stopped, the person who had called out the alarm to flee had assumed incorrectly that our trip had been foiled. The children's parents were among the people who jumped out, but before they could help their children get down, the truck had already taken off.

Before the incident, the adults had shushed us kids to keep quiet. Afterward, no one said anything as the children's sobs grew louder and more anguished. A few women sitting nearby tried to comfort the hysterical siblings, a brother and sister around my age, some telling them that it was good to cry, others advising them to conserve their energy by not crying so much. The hiccupped spasms eventually gave way to lingering whimpers, then finally silence.

I never found out why the driver did not turn around to pick up the distraught parents, who were running after the truck screaming for it to stop. Maybe the driver didn't know what had happened, or perhaps he did know but decided that he couldn't take the risk of returning to the attention-drawing chaos.

Around dusk, our truck turned off from the main road onto a muddy path. When it stopped, we heard the driver getting off his seat, then coming around to where we were. Flipping open the canvas, he told us to disembark. In the semidarkness, we found ourselves in the middle of a big empty field edging up to a river. A few soldiers in camouflage uniforms holding long rifles were milling around. My father said we were inside a military base in Mỹ Tho, a well-known city inside the Mekong Delta. While we stood around, more military trucks like the one that we had been in pulled up. Among the people rushing out from the covered bed of one of them were my sister Chị Hai and her husband Anh Trưởng. The stream of people continued to emerge from the truck beds.

I had not expected that there would be so many people. As it turned out, neither had my father nor the other organizers of the trip, even as they had anticipated some overcrowding. For *vượt biên* to happen, the organizers had to bribe many people. From local authorities to soldiers with military trucks to villagers at various rendezvous points, people were paid to render aid or look the other way. The organizers understood that the people they had bribed would take on additional passengers and pocket the passage fee or let their friends and relatives join without paying. What my father and the organizers did not anticipate was the extent of the corruption. In the end, the number of people they had planned for our trip had nearly doubled, from 80 to almost 160.

After everyone had arrived, we were told to go down to the riverbank and hide in the bushes until our boat showed up. In the last few rays of daylight, a huge fishing boat came into sight. It slowly headed toward us, then stopped at a distance from shore. As soon as it started flashing its lights, the throng of people immediately rushed out from the bushes, trampling over each other to the boat. Our family joined the stampede running across the beach. By the water's edge, my father picked me up and then waded in the river with me in his arms.

I looked up at a boat bigger than any I had seen, fishing nets draped all over its sides. "Quick, give me your hands," said the two men from the deck as they reached down for me. Grabbing my hands, the men pulled me up.

During the first night, our boat made its way down the Mekong River without incident. But the morning at sea would bring severe weather. Faced with the first hardship, many began to question the boat's leadership. As the storm worsened, the quiet grumblings in the beginning turned more vocal, then exploded into a near mutiny. Some were certain that the boat would not make it in the open sea and demanded that we turn around. A few people challenged the seafaring skills of our navigator by storming the helm and demanding to take over. My brother-in-law Anh Trưởng and several other passengers took it upon themselves to defend and guard the navigator so that he could continue. When it became clear that the majority had no desire to go back, the rioters quieted down

The storm passed almost as quickly as it had come on. As frightening as it was, the rain provided extra water for drinking. Spread out all around the boat were containers—buckets, pails, and plastic sheets—now all filled. Shortly after the storm, we were told that we had made it outside the reaches of the communist patrol boats. Even though we no longer had to hide and could spread out anywhere, few people did. Overwhelmed with seasickness and exhaustion, most people remained in place.

The rest of our voyage continued to be one long stupor of misery and boredom. In the beginning, there was much shouting and arguing amid the overcrowding coupled with water and food shortages. Fights broke out at the slightest provocation. Some people demanded that those who had not paid the passage fees be thrown overboard. But in the end, the more moral and compassionate voices won out, and the freeloaders were spared.

As the days passed, a despairing lethargy took over, and even the crying of children stopped. During the day, the sun bore down with unremitting intensity, searing into skin that might as well have been bare, since the clothes we had on afforded little protection. The thin fabric, worn out by repeated wetting and drying from seawater, ripped at the slightest touch. We scrambled for any available shade, draping raincoats, fishing nets, pieces of fabric, anything we could find over our heads. The night brought its own misery when the temperature dropped. The cold, made harsher by winds, seeped past the shredded clothes into our bones. We wrapped ourselves around each other for warmth.

There was little food besides *củ sắn* (jicama), a crunchy watery fruit with the taste of an unripe pear. Each day we were given a few pieces of the fruit. As punishing as the lack of food was, it eliminated the frequent need to use the bathroom. Not that many people made it to the outhouse located in the back of the boat. Too sick or exhausted, many just relieved themselves wherever they sat.

In the grip of hunger, I fantasized constantly about food, from meager meals to the sumptuous feasts at my sisters' weddings. Hot soups, steaming rice, juicy mangoes and rambutans: the images filled me with such joy that I gave myself over to the fantasies. Many times I was jolted awake by people around me, telling me to stop talking so loudly about some imaginary food. I was not the only one lost in my own world. Around me, many people talked to themselves. Some prayed; others sang. A few seemed to speak nonsense, like the girl next to me, grasping and calling out to God while looking straight at me.

By the second day, I had acclimated to the motions of the sea and could move around without falling over. I decided to venture to a raised platform on the deck where I had seen some people congregating. I saw my father near the helm and called out for him as I made my way over. He said he was so happy to see me feeling better and pulled me in to sit on his lap. It was late in the afternoon; the searing rays from earlier had mellowed to a dull heat. The ocean was not the gray foamy rage that I had last seen but a shimmering mixture of blue and green. Tiny ripples lapped outward from our boat, then folded up into the sky at the horizon. My father pointed for me to look at something in the distance. "They're dolphins," he said before I even asked. Until now, what I had experienced of the sea had only terrified me. I had no idea that the ocean could be so calm and hold such beauty. For a long time, I stayed in my father's lap, watching the most graceful swimmers leaping and twirling above the waves.

I might have felt better, but not my mother. The seasickness that had descended on all of us at the beginning tightened its hold on her. She also came down with a stomach illness that had her throwing up everything she ate or drank. My father gave her some of the antibiotics that he had bought before the trip when Bảy was complaining of a stomachache. The medicine seemed to work, and my mother was finally able to rest. While she slept, I listened for her breaths, reassuring myself that my lifeless-looking mother was still alive.

"Chanh, wake up!" My father's voice woke me as his hands frantically ran fast all over my face, neck and arms. It was our third night on the boat. Immediately I realized what was happening. Before the escape, my mother had put a few pieces of coal in my shirt pockets. She had warned me to rub the coal all over my face and arms if we encountered pirates. "Make yourself as ugly as you can," she had emphasized. The heavy lumps weighing down the front of my shirt served as a reminder of my sisters' terrifying experience with pirates during their escape two years before.

I took out the coal and joined my father in smearing it all over myself. The sharp-edged clumps scraped against my sun-peeled skin. Then I curled up on his lap, wrapping my arms around his chest. With his heart pounding against my ear, I strained to make sense of the tumult around me. Amid the shouting, someone yelled, "The ship just passed! It's not pirates! It's not pirates!" As more people called out the same message, my father's arms around me loosened. In the dim light, I looked up to see the familiar dimpled smile, only now mixed with undeniable relief.

When morning came on the third day, the boat's occupants were in rapid decline. Many, including my mother, had gotten much weaker from dehydration and illness. We had consumed almost all the water that had been collected from the storm. Thirst again dominated my thoughts, while hunger had retreated into a dull discomfort. I was fading in and out of sleep when I heard loud voices all around me, but this time they did not sound angry or fearful.

"Seagulls! Seagulls!"

I looked outside. In the distance, I could see birds circling in the air.

"We must be near land!" People shouted, hugging each other, laughing and crying.

For the rest of the morning, our boat followed the seagulls, but the ocean remained a vast expanse of blue with no signs of land. In the early afternoon, someone spotted a boat in the distance. People rushed to the side of our boat, waving and shouting for help. As we approached, we could see its occupants, who turned out to be Malaysian fishermen. Communicating through a combination of Chinese and hand signals, we told them that we were lost. Someone from our group held up the fuel containers, gesturing an exchange of fuel for their help. The fishermen seemed to understand who we were and our situation. They signaled for us to follow their boat.

We followed them for a while, then someone called out, "Land! Land! I see land!" People were yelling and pointing excitedly. My father held me up so I could see. In the distance where waves and sky merged, a long ribbon of emerald green appeared. Some people began to weep loudly. Others knelt on the floor, bowing and offering profuse thanks to Buddha, God, the heavens, and ancestors for watching over us.

Though we didn't know it at the time, the Malaysian fishermen were leading us to a refugee processing camp. While we were still some distance from land, they suddenly stopped their boat and waved for us to come closer to them. When we were near, they made gestures to us to hand over the fuel. The navigator edged our boat next to theirs and dropped down the containers. After the transfer, the fishermen pointed in the direction of land for us to proceed to without them.

As many on the boat suspected, the Malaysian government did not want any more refugees and thus the fishermen would have been in trouble if they had been caught giving us help. It was also widely known that if a boat carrying refugees was deemed seaworthy, the Malaysian authorities might force it back to the sea to seek shelter elsewhere. When our boat hit a sandbar, a few of the men began to smash the engine with whatever they could find to disable it, making it unseaworthy. With that act, they surrendered our fate to the Malaysian authorities.

My brother-in-law was among the first to jump off the boat to see how deep the water was. Finding that it only came up to his knees, he called out to everyone that it was safe and began helping people off. Many, including my mother, were too weak to walk and had to be carried. The rest of us waded in the lapping waves to get to shore.

As we gathered on the beach, a group of men in uniforms showed up. They spoke to us in English, the sound of which I recognized from a few months of fifth-grade English class in the countryside. My father and a few others stepped forward to translate. I had not known that my father could speak English. But quickly I would realize the limit of his command, as what he said sounded much like French and was accompanied by many body and hand signals. My father pointed to our boat, gesturing that the engine was broken and that we had no more fuel. Several of the Malaysian officials waded in the water to climb up onto our boat. When they came back after the inspection, they told our group to follow them.

Barely able to stay upright, we trailed behind the men along the hot sand. On land, the ground felt strange. Much to my surprise, the swaying of the ocean had become part of my bearing. Around me everyone also staggered and wobbled, holding onto anything for support.

After a while, we arrived at an outdoor structure, a covering draped over four wooden poles. A picture of a Red Crescent and Red Cross stood out against the white fabric of the tent. I had never seen the symbols before, but soon I would find them everywhere, on the packages of food, on medicine bottles, and on the clothes of people who helped us. In my mind, the Red Crescent and Red Cross would come to represent relief and the kindness of strangers.

Under the blazing sun, we scrambled for shade beneath the tent. While waiting to be processed, we were each given a small pouch of liquid, a tiny straw attached to its side. I couldn't wait to drink water. What came out of the straw, however, wasn't water but a juice so sweet that it stoked my thirst even more. Years later, in America, when I would hear my children extol the absolute pleasure of a juice box on a hot summer day, my mind would hark back to the white sandy beach of this afternoon.

We found out we were at a holding site for refugees in Merang, a town on the eastern coast of Malaysia, and we realized that we had indeed been not far from land when we first spotted the seagulls. What we had likely been doing all morning before we ran into the Malaysian fishermen was sailing parallel to the coast.

For the next few days, we stayed in the temporary camp. We were given medicine, clothes, packages of ramen, more juice boxes, and, to my relief, water. My mother regained her strength and could walk on her own by the time we had to move. On that day, several buses arrived to take us to the other side of town, where we boarded a big metal boat. Sponsored by the United Nations High Commission for Refugees (UNHCR), it would deliver us to Pulau Bidong, an island just over ten miles from shore.

My favorite photo of my mother
with one of my sisters on a
vacation long before I was born.

My father as a young man.

Bày and me in our red
kerchiefs taken at a youth
convention in Vinh Long.

At my second sister, Chi Ba's wedding
in Vinh Long. I'm wearing my Yacht
Club International shirt standing in
front of my oldest sister, Chi Hai.

My father (center) at the Golden Croissant bakery, holding one of his animal baguette creations.

My brother, Bay, preparing to deliver the Port Arthur News.

My father and me preparing the Port Arthur News for delivery on a Sunday morning.

My brother, Cu Anh, tending to our vegetable garden.

My mother and me inside our sandwich shop.

My brothers and father next to our sandwich shop.

My family in Port Arthur, TX.

Violet and me inside Thomas Jefferson High School cafeteria.

PART III: REFUGEE CAMPS

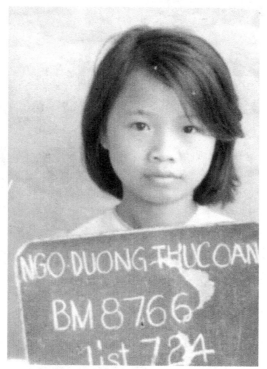

My Identification photo after our arrival in Pulau Bidong, Malaysia.

PULAU BIDONG

P ulau Bidong (the island of Bidong) consists of a single hill that descends straight into the sea. Despite being only a short distance from mainland Malaysia, it remained uninhabited until after the collapse of Sài Gòn in 1975. While residents in South Việt Nam waited to see what the new Communist government would do, the flow of refugees out of the country was only a trickle, with some ending up on Malaysian shores. As the Communist leadership in Việt Nam began to implement full-scale reforms and dole out severe punishment to those associated with the old regime, disillusionment with the government intensified; fearful South Vietnamese began to flee the country in droves. The closest and most direct routes for the refugees were through the South China Sea. Many ended up in Malaysia, Thailand, Indonesia, the Philippines; some landed as far off as Hong Kong or Singapore. By late 1977, the outflow of refugees had turned into a torrent (a portion of which was due to Việt Nam's expulsion of Vietnamese of Chinese origin).

Faced with the onslaught of boat people, as the refugees had come to be called, the Malaysian government reluctantly opened Pulau Bidong as an official refugee site in 1978. The size of a football field, the camp was located on the only level area of the island and was intended to accommodate about 4,500 people. In just one year, it swelled to 40,000 refugees. As the tide of boat people kept coming, Malaysia, like other neighboring countries, instituted a blockade around its shores and implemented the push-back policy. Any refugee boat deemed seaworthy was pushed back to sea to seek shelter elsewhere.

Amid protests from Việt Nam's neighbors over the refugee invasion and those from human rights groups over the treatment of the refugees—rampant piracy, a heartless push-back policy, overcrowded camp conditions—an international accord was brokered in the summer of 1979. Việt Nam agreed to clamp down on the exodus. It put an end to the state-enabled departures of ethnic Chinese in Việt Nam. It also implemented a series of draconian laws aimed at stopping all clandestine escapes. Anyone suspected of trying to leave the country was considered a traitor, a betrayer of the communist ideals, to be imprisoned, his or her property confiscated. The accord required Việt Nam's neighbors to ease back on the push-back policy with the guarantee that the United States and a few other Western countries would bear responsibility for resettling the refugees who continued to come. In the years that followed the signing of the accord, the flow of Vietnamese boat people dramatically decreased even as some, like our family, still risked escape despite the consequences.

On that January morning in 1983, as our group of 155 refugees set out for Pulau Bidong, the mood on the UNHCR-sponsored boat differed markedly from what it had been on our escape boat just a few days earlier. Civility and courtesy returned as people helped each other, making room for everyone to fit. Hope and excitement displaced fear and tension. My father held me up to look at the tall hill covered with trees in the distance. As we approached, I saw big coconut palm trees swaying above a white sandy beach. Children were laughing and playing in the water.

Our ferry edged up to a jetty jutting far out from the beach. As we made our way down the pier, people from all around rushed over to us, calling out names of friends and relatives they thought they recognized.

"Where are you from?" everyone seemed to want to know.

Cà Mau, Sài Gòn, Vĩnh Long, Sóc Trăng, Cần Thơ—the names of cities and towns poured forth. From our answers, people inquired about news and asked after relatives from the same hometown. We responded, then asked our own questions.

"What's it like here?"

"How long do people usually stay?"

Within a few days, it would be our turn to run to the dock to greet a different group of bewildered newcomers. Searching the crowd for familiar faces, we would shout the same questions, wanting to know where people had come from and ask about relatives and friends back home. However remote the possibility, it was one of a few ways to get news on the isolated island.

A sign that hung at the entrance welcomed us as we followed the UNHCR representatives inside to be processed. Up close, I would discover that Pulau Bidong was far from the tropical paradise that it appeared at a distance. Inside was a shantytown of ramshackle dwellings constructed from corrugated metal sheets, rice bags, boat timbers, and other discarded materials. The shacks, stacked two or even three stories high, fused into haphazard clusters. Our group walked along a dirt path that weaved past homes teeming with activities: kids playing soccer with an old coconut shell, a woman sitting on a footstool fanning a small wood fire to boil water, men playing cards. Along the path, garbage lay scattered atop open channels of brownish water. A slight breeze briefly separated the delightful scent of freshly brewed soy milk from the rest of the less than delightful odors.

We arrived at an open structure filled with long wooden desks where we would spend the rest of the afternoon filling out forms and being interviewed and photographed. At the end of the admissions process, we were given our housing assignments. I learned that the camp was divided into seven different housing zones, each with its own misery. Those located close to the beach were prone to flash flooding caused by the rain runoff coming from the hill, not an uncommon occurrence during the monsoon season. In this area, rising water would litter the grounds with garbage, including an army of roaches. People living along the hillside, on the other hand, had to endure the constant fear of sliding rocks and the uphill trudge to haul water from the wells for daily use. I was relieved to find out that our assigned hut was in a higher area of the camp. Having experienced flooding in the countryside, I didn't want to live anywhere that could expose us to it. But what I dreaded even more than rising waters was the roaches. With a paralyzing fear of these bugs, I would have volunteered to live at the very top of the hill if it meant being away from them.

After receiving our housing assignment, we walked up the hill to a two-story hut connected to similar huts, all surrounded by webs of clotheslines. None of the huts had doors—a stipulation that, we later learned, was intended to make it easier for the Malaysian camp authorities to keep watch over the refugees. Inside, it seemed almost as noisy as it was outside. We could hear our neighbors' conversations and, as I would discover, even their whispers at night.

Our family of six shared the small hut with three young men: two brothers and a cousin in their late teens and early twenties. Initially the men said little and kept mostly to themselves, but gradually they became friendlier. Over stories and card games, I grew quite fond of our housemates, particularly the oldest. Always with an English-Vietnamese dictionary in his hands, he told me he was going to be a doctor no matter what. Sometime after he had exhausted his repertoire of jokes, he mentioned that his boat had started out with many more people.

"What happened? They couldn't stand you and jumped off?" I asked.

"No," he answered with uncharacteristic solemnness. "They died."

He went on describe how his boat was lost at sea after pirates had destroyed the engine while looking for gold. When their water supply ran out, people began to die. The dead included not only children and the elderly but also many young people. While drifting, they encountered a few ships, but none, including a pirate boat, wanted anything to do with the pitiful people with nothing left to offer. When the desperate castaways had all but given up hope, they ran into a Japanese commercial fishing ship. To everyone's disbelief, the ship reversed its direction to head toward the screams for help. After providing first-aid care, food, and water, the Japanese fishermen pulled the battered boat to the Malaysian shore.

When we first arrived at Pulau Bidong, I was fascinated to hear people's accounts of their escape. Some spoke of incredible adventures, others of tragedies even more horrific than those of my siblings' boat. In the faces of some people, signs of trauma were obvious. In others, the heart-wrenching tales lurked just behind their smiles. What I heard invaded my dreams. In time, I stopped asking. I came to appreciate more fully how fortunate our journey was. Despite the thirst and hunger, our boat was spared so much.

Inside our shared hut, there was little privacy. In the back, a plastic sheet carved out a small space. Intended as a place to bathe, the enclosed area also served as a makeshift toilet when the communal latrines became off-limits after the nightly curfew. Another area that was somewhat out of view was the loft on top. The attic-like space, where my family slept at night, gave us some privacy but at a cost. Besides being hotter, it was barely big enough for all six of us to fit. A piece of cardboard became a fixed extension of our fingers; the homemade fan provided some relief from the heat and mosquitoes. But in the dark, there was something we loathed even more than being hot and itching—being chewed on by rats. Indiscriminate in their search for food, the rats sometimes appeared at night, ready to sample anything soft, including our toes and fingers.

Insects and rodents were not the only disturbances of our sleep. Every now and then we were jolted awake by a deafening thud, the sound of a coconut smashing down on the metal roofs. All over the island, coconut palm trees bearing clusters of the heavy fruits soared above the landscape. Inside each cluster, it was inevitable that one or two fruits clung on with only a most tentative hold. Any slight wind or movement could hurl down the cannonballs, each weighing as much as eight pounds. We all knew not to walk directly beneath the coconut clusters, but at times, there was no other way to get around except to run by fast.

As bad as the camp's conditions were, they had much improved since Pulau Bidong took in the first Vietnamese boat people. In the beginning, the island was just undeveloped jungle. The refugees had to construct their own housing and dig wells for water. Fear of a widespread epidemic was a fact of life in the overcrowded space with little sanitation. As each wave of refugees added a little more beyond bare subsistence, the camp came to be known as Little Sài Gòn.

By the time we arrived five years after Pulau Bidong officially opened, it had a makeshift Buddhist temple, church, hair salon, and of course, a small outdoor market—the anchor of every Vietnamese town. The bustle of Tết celebration was in full gear. Amid the squalor and scarcity, camp residents managed to recreate the spirit of the holiday. They decorated their huts red and yellow and hung pretend fireworks and empty red *lì xì* (lucky money) envelops from trees. I joined other children carrying around star-shaped lanterns, made from paper and sticks. We sang songs while banging on pots and pans. For my parents and other displaced adults, the first Tết spent outside Việt Nam must have been bittersweet. But for me, the Lunar New Year of 1983 remains one of my most festive memories.

On the island, people adapted the skills they carried over from their old life. Someone put together a few chairs and tables to open a "disco bar" where residents came to sing at night. There was even a bakery—my favorite spot around camp. Despite the lack of an oven and the scarcity of flour and eggs, an especially inventive cook managed to produce cakes. Around much of the camp, the stench of garbage might pervade, but not around her hut. A distance away, I could already detect the aroma of freshly baked goods.

Even though Pulau Bidong was sponsored by the UNHCR, it was mostly run by the refugees themselves under the guidance of the Malaysian Red Crescent Society. The task of keeping order in the camp, however, belonged to the Malaysian Police Task Force, which maintained strict control over camp security. Every night we had a curfew. From 11:30 p.m. to 6:30 a.m., we were prohibited from leaving our residences to use the latrines or for any other purpose. During the day, we had more freedom, but with a long list of restrictions, including prohibitions against harvesting coconuts, fishing in the ocean, searching for food in the forest, and trading with the locals who came by boat. Weapons or any objects that could be used as such were banned. Punishment ranged from detainment to being beaten to getting one's head shaved and possibly having one's status for resettlement downgraded.

Many of the regulations, such as the nightly curfew, greatly affected our daily life, though the one against knife possession didn't have as much of an impact as we feared. We rarely needed to use knives, since our food rations consisted mostly of ramen, dry beans, and canned meat, nothing that required cutting. For a people whose diet consisted mainly of fresh vegetables and fish, some viewed eating the preserved food day in and day out as the worst punishment. Risking punishment, they would venture deep into the forest to look for edible fruits and vegetables or swim out in the ocean to fish. Most hunted or gathered just enough for themselves and their family. Some, realizing a business opportunity, collected extra to sell at the market or to engage in forbidden trade with the locals.

Except for these busy entrepreneurs, most people did not have much to do around the island. The adults did not have to work, and kids did not have to go to school. People were suspended from their normal responsibilities, since food and shelter, however inadequate, were provided for everyone. The daily task that required the most effort was retrieving water. We stood in line at the well to draw water for washing, then at the water tap, which opened only a few hours a day, to receive our ration for drinking. After retrieving the water, we still had to haul the buckets uphill to our hut.

In our free time, Bảy and I often wandered around the island, usually ending up at the beach. Since our parents didn't want us to swim in the ocean, we mostly played on the sand. And here we were able to observe the entrepreneurs in action. Far off on the horizon, boats of different sizes lingered. They belonged to local Malaysian merchants with goods to sell. A few refugee men would ride on makeshift rafts to get to one of these boats. On the way back, the rafts would be piled high and all around with merchandise not available on the island. Apples, eggs, batteries, flashlights, shampoo, and other products were strapped on top. Canned goods and soft drinks were tied onto the sides. Buried inside the mountain of goods were the men. After battling waves to get back to shore, they still could not declare success, as the Malaysian camp police would sometimes appear out of nowhere to confiscate everything.

Many afternoons after a heavy rainstorm, instead of playing on the beach, Bảy and I would join a crowd of people hiking up the hill to a waterfall. Chị Hai and Anh Trưởng sometimes came with us, but not my parents, because of my mother's arthritic knees. Unlike Bảy and others, I never hiked barefoot. While my flip-flops did provide some protection against cuts and scrapes, they afforded little traction against the wet rocks. Trailing behind, slipping and falling often, I usually ended up staying at one of the lower levels while Bảy continued upward. Though the view was nowhere near as breathtaking as the one higher up, I still had fun playing with the other kids who also remained behind. Beneath the thin trickles cascading down the moss-covered rocks, the girls, unlike the boys, bathed with all our clothes on. But it didn't take long for the thin fabric to blend into our skin, revealing everything anyway.

When by myself, I liked to linger at the outdoor market, marveling at the fresh produce and cans of soda pop. The rules on trade must have been only loosely enforced. One time I ran into the brother and sister whose parents had jumped off the military truck when they thought the escape plans had been foiled. Like other unaccompanied minors, the siblings lived in a separate section of the camp, and I didn't see them very often. They were holding hands and laughing. The image was far different from what I remembered of the hysterical wailing only a few weeks earlier. On the island, their hardship did yield one saving grace. Unaccompanied minors usually received expedited processing for resettlement. Their stay in the camp must not have been very long, as after that day at the market I never again encountered them.

With time on their hands, my parents took to transforming our dry food rations into fresh meals. From the mung beans, they cultivated bean sprouts. The process was quite simple. All we had to do was bury the beans in wet sand. From a handful of beans, bunches of sprouts emerged in just a few days, ready to be eaten after a quick rinse. The immediacy between harvest and consumption gave the sprouts an incredible sweetness. We shared the extra with neighbors and friends, the few who did not grow their own.

From the soybeans, my parents made tofu and milk. My father took to the laborious process with the same zeal he had applied to the making of sugar in the countryside, and he ended up with about the same success. His tofu had a chewy texture while his milk retained a strong unpleasant smell of raw soybeans. We all begged him to give up and let us buy from people who knew what they were doing. Around the island, tender tofu and aromatic soy milk could be found inside the many residents' huts. Unlike soda or coffee, they cost only a few cents or could be traded for dry soybeans. Craving the same flavors himself, my father eventually gave in to our request.

Despite its widespread availability, I didn't want soy milk. What I wanted was a soda pop. The orange beverage, poured from a can, was served in a clear plastic bag, as there were no disposable cups. A straw protruded from the top, around which the bag was tied shut with a rubber band. Inside, a few cubes of ice floated in the froth. On a hot day, the cool drink had the effect of a magic potion. It not only quenched my thirst but also lifted my mood, vanquishing all my annoyances.

On flimsy tables around the market, cans of soda pop teetered on top of each other to form the shape of a pyramid. To have one, all I needed were some coins, and I knew exactly where to get them. I strode up to my father, often in deep conversation with friends, and without asking, I reached deep down in his pants pockets.

"What are you doing?" My father asked each time, even as I suspected he already knew the reason.

"I just wanted some money to buy an orange soda."

"Ah ... what a little trouble maker you are," he mumbled, feigning annoyance while reaching into the same pockets. By some sleight of hand, he always managed to find the coins that had eluded me. I grabbed them and ran off. I liked knowing that whatever belonged to my father also belonged to me. As I grew older, this would extend beyond coins to include his disappointments and sadness. I would feel his troubles as if they were my own.

Around camp, the adults might be free of responsibilities but not of worries. The worry that consumed everyone, even children, was getting off the island. To do so, we first had to be informed that another country wanted us. The only way to receive such news was through the PA system, the lifeblood of the camp. At the slightest crackling of the microphone, everyone either stayed put while shushing each other to be quiet or rushed to the nearest loudspeaker. Delivering messages of our fates, the voice that boomed out from above us might as well have been that of God.

With our heads tilting upward toward the speaker, we listened for our names to be included in or excluded from the many lists: mail, interview, reinterview, health testing, health retesting. Inclusion in the interview list meant a country was expressing interest. The health testing list signified progress in the long process. Retesting, on the other hand, foretold possible weeks or months of delay. The mail list could mean a letter from Việt Nam, now mythologized in everyone's mind as the abandoned homeland to which we assumed we could never go back. Or it could mean a letter from abroad, sometimes with a money order inside. Ours would come on occasion from my siblings already in America. With the money, we could afford certain luxuries: my orange soda, the fresh fish at the market, the flashlight—a godsend at night.

"Are you on the list?" was the question we all asked each other around camp. "The list" could only refer to the departure roster that contained the names of everyone scheduled to depart the island on a particular date. The wait for this day was only months for people classified as political refugees or with family from a Western country who could act as sponsors. But for those deemed economic migrants with no relatives abroad, the wait could be years. After being denied asylum by one country after another, many of the rejected became desperate. Given over to hopelessness, a few even took their own lives, a tragic irony given all that they had had to endure to arrive on the island in the first place.

A few months after our arrival on Pulau Bidong, the interview list for resettlement included some people from our boat. From then on, my father joined the small crowd of people who seemed to reside during the day beneath the intercom. Within a short time, he would hear our names among those scheduled to be interviewed with the US delegation.

129

When we first arrived on the island, I had assumed it as a given that one day we would join my siblings in the United States. However, entry into the United States was not guaranteed. Throughout the multipart interview process spread out over weeks, my parents were quite nervous. At home, they practiced answering questions that they thought we might be asked. Their anxiety bled over to me as I kept hearing more stories of people with relatives in the United States who, for various reasons, were denied entry into the country and had to seek asylum elsewhere. I didn't know much about these other places, only that they were not America—the mystical land I had often thought about and where our family would be reunited. Because my father was not a soldier in the South Vietnamese army, it was not clear whether our family would be categorized with the political or the economic refugees.

At the last interview, we finally received the news that we all had so much wanted to hear: our application for asylum in the United States had been approved. After completing numerous health tests, primarily for tuberculosis and hepatitis, our family finally made that most desired of lists—the departure list for America.

Five months after our arrival to its shore, we left Pulau Bidong. On the day of our departure, the big metal boat that had delivered us to the island returned. A goodbye ballad, sung by one of the refugees, streamed out from the intercom. As the poignant melodies echoed across camp, friends followed us to the beach to say goodbye. Over on the mainland, a bus was waiting to take us across Malaysia to another refugee camp—a transit camp called Sungei Besi.

SUNGEI BESI

Our second camp was located outside Kuala Lumpur, the capital city of Malaysia. In Sungei Besi, as in Pulau Bidong, the refugees were walled off from the surrounding Malaysian society. This time, we weren't separated by the sea but by barbed-wire fences surrounding the camp. The refugees were forbidden to leave or to interact with anyone on the outside lest they decide to disappear among the locals and make their home in Malaysia.

People, however, still found ways to trade. Most days around dusk, Chinese-Malaysian merchants could be seen lingering on the other side of the fence, offering pork, coffee, cigarettes, and other goods not available inside the camp. Under the watchful eyes of the camp security force, a few camp residents would sidle up to our side of the fence. As we had done in Pulau Bidong, my brother and I would sometimes watch the traders from afar, holding our breaths for the inevitable chase and, every so often, an arrest.

In the new camp, our daily routine became much more regimented, revolving mostly around waiting in line, not only for water but also for food. Three times each day, we stood in line to receive our meals. Each came with a piece of fruit, my favorite part. A wedge of watermelon at a lunch would etch in my memory as the hallmark of our stay in Sungei Besi, but not a positive one.

Soon after eating it, I began to feel sick. At first I wasn't so worried about the stomachache that had me spending the rest of the afternoon at the communal latrine. But by nighttime, I felt much worse. Consumed by thirst, I kept drinking but was unable to keep anything in. I soiled through all my clothes, then my mother's and sister's. No matter how many blankets my mother wrapped me in, I could not keep warm. As the night blended into the next day, it hurt just to breathe. Fading in and out of sleep, I kept seeing Lượm, my friend from the countryside, in a loop of vivid dreams. During moments of alertness, I was seized by fear that I would share her fate. Emerging from the long stupor a few days later, I realized I was spared—though not by merciful spirits but by antibiotics and electrolytes that my friend never had.

131

As Sungei Besi was intended only as a transit camp, our stay was brief. We had more medical screenings and immunizations and some English classes. After less than two months, we left the fenced compound for the Philippines, our last stop before coming to America.

PHILIPPINES REFUGEE PROCESSING CENTER

T he flight from Kuala Lumpur to Manila, two capital cities separated by 1,500 miles of ocean, was my first trip in an airplane. In postwar Việt Nam, the sighting of an airplane in the sky was cause for great excitement because it was such a rare occurrence. At the first sound of the distinctive rumble, my friends and I would drop what we were doing to gaze upward, searching for its origin. Calling out, "Máy bay! Máy bay!" (Flying machine! Flying machine!) to alert others, we scrambled toward any spot with a better view. As the airplane drifted across the sky, I wondered what it was like inside. Was it something so fantastical as to defy imagination or something resembling the inside of a bus and thus also filled with people pushing up against each other and cages crammed with livestock?

Inside the airplane at the Kuala Lumpur Airport, I was amazed to discover a clean, orderly space filled with rows of seats, much nicer than any bus in which I had ever traveled. No livestock was in sight. Every seat, padded with a soft cushion, had its own light coming from above and a little table in front that could be folded and tucked away. Ensconced in my own seat and not on my mother's lap as I often had been on the bus, I had no one pushing or leaning into me.

Soon the engine began to roar, becoming louder as the plane raced down the runway then took off into the air. It seemed miraculous that such an enormous object carrying such a heavy load could lift off from the ground at all, much less with such grace. Soon after takeoff, I felt the familiar lurching in my stomach that often accompanied me on bumpy bus rides. To my relief, the feelings subsided when the plane stabilized. I stayed transfixed by my window, looking down at the ant-like bustle of the city below as it became less recognizable and then disappeared altogether. The drone of airplane noises soon lulled me to sleep.

After our plane landed in Manila, we boarded a bus for a three-hour trip to our last refugee camp. Nestled in the foothills near the mountains of Bataan, the Philippines Refugee Processing Center (PRPC) opened its doors in 1980, under an agreement between the United Nations High Commission for Refugees

133

(UNHCR) and the Philippine government. Designated as a second-asylum camp, the PRPC took in only those who had already gone through a first-asylum camp like Pulau Bidong or similar ones in Thailand, Hong Kong, and Indonesia. Everyone who arrived had been accepted for resettlement by another country, mainly the United States and a few other English-speaking countries.

As its name suggested, the main function of the PRPC was to process the refugees before they headed off to their resettlement country. Initially, the processing involved final tuberculosis testing and wrapping up of paperwork. Gradually the camp expanded its role to help the refugees adjust to their new lives. By the time we arrived at the PRPC in 1983, three years after it opened, the camp had come to house the world's biggest school for English as a Second Language (ESL), with a multitude of cultural-orientation programs geared toward life in America.

The PRPC was not what I had expected in a refugee camp. There was no fence separating us from the outside. We were free to interact with the local Filipinos from the nearby town of Morong who came in to trade. With a large outdoor market, school, hospital, library, Buddhist temple, and church, the camp felt like a city. Multinational UNHCR Aid workers and Filipino camp staff mingled among camp residents—Vietnamese, Cambodians, and Laotians. People seemed more relaxed and hopeful. The mood felt lighter than in our previous camps.

The PRPC was divided into different neighborhoods. Inside each were rows of connecting one-room huts with concrete floors and iron roofs. For the first time, our family of six had our own space, which came with a small wooden bed, a table, and some chairs. Our food ration included fresh produce, a much welcome relief. Twice a week, we and our neighbors gathered to divide up our group's allotment of vegetables, chicken, eggs, and sometimes fish. The division was simpler for bigger units like our family than for one person, receiving two stalks of bok choy, one small fish, or a single chicken wing. I often wondered what someone would do with such tiny portions. Some people always complained no matter what they received, while others were still cheerful even when they happened to be the last to choose and ended up with only the leftovers.

While the overall camp conditions had improved, certain things stayed the same. Alcohol of any kind was still banned. Our hut still had no doors. From the entrance, we could see through the small space to the mountains in the back. The ventilation only did so much to lessen the heat trapped by the iron roof of our hut. For most of the day, the stifling heat was worse inside than outside. We still had to wait in line to collect tap water and to use the communal latrines, which were squat holes inside a dark enclosed space. At night, we still had a curfew starting at 9 p.m., when all the power around the camp was shut off. Rushing to use the latrine before the lights were turned off and then running home to beat the curfew remained the height of my daily stresses.

In the PRPC, a typical day for Bảy and me was more structured, revolving around classes. Everyone, young or old, was required to learn English and American culture, and the adults also had to perform community service. For many adults, it had been years since they had been inside a classroom. For a few lifetime farmers and fishermen, it was their first time ever.

All the English teachers around camp were Filipino. We learned by repeating phrases that our teachers said we would need to know as soon as we arrived in America. "Could you help me find my classroom?" "Excuse me, where's the cafeteria?" In a room full of kids about my age, I twisted and curled my tongue, mimicking our teacher. No matter my efforts, the sounds I produced resembled little of what I heard. I could do Vietnamese tones—all five, even six like a Northerner—but I just couldn't make the sounds that my teacher did. I wanted to somehow communicate that to her.

As Vietnamese is a tonal language, a sound can have different meanings with slight shifts in pitch. The letters "ma" could mean: ghost (*ma*), mother (*má*), which (*mà*), tomb (*mả*), horse (*mã*), rice seedling (*mạ*). What the Vietnamese language doesn't have are the beginning and ending consonants that are so abundant in English. The most dreaded English words for a Vietnamese speaker are multisyllabic words, with beginning and ending hard sounds and, as if those were not enough, a combination of complex sounds in the middle. "Wednesday," "selfish," "plumbers," the words wreaked havoc on my tongue.

Besides pronunciation, English also has little in common with Vietnamese in its grammar structure. What is a verb tense? Why are there so many different tenses? Why does a verb have to change when the same action is performed by a different person or at a different time? We asked our teacher these and other questions regarding concepts that had no equivalent in our native speech. Often it was difficult to even articulate our confusion.

The refugee camp was not the first place I had heard English. "Nanateee, ah na tu," said my fifth-grade teacher in Vĩnh Long. He spoke slowly while tapping at the numbers in the year 1-9-8-2 on the blackboard. I remember being surprised that a Vietnamese person could speak English.

"Nurse," he called out. It was the word we were supposed to practice at home. "Remember to curl up your tongue in the middle then pronounce the *s* at the end." At home, no matter how hard I tried, I could not bend my tongue the way he had suggested. I finally decided that I would pronounce "nurse" like *nước*, the Vietnamese word for water, where the ending *c* is silent. I was sure that a little sound like *s* at the end or *ur* in the middle could not matter that much.

A year later, in the PRPC, I would learn from my Filipino teacher how much all those sounds mattered. But surrounded by kids who spoke Vietnamese, I did not feel the urgency to learn English. Talking to each other only in English, as our teacher insisted, often felt like pretend conversations. It did not seem real that within a short time I would have to use the strange language exclusively to make myself understood in America.

As much as my friends and I struggled with the English lessons, we really enjoyed the cultural trainings. We learned what to expect at school, how to buy food at a supermarket, how to put coins into a vending machine—something I had never heard of. It seemed unbelievable that there was a contraption with an endless supply of candies that could drop down with a few coins and a push of a button.

During a lesson about meals, our teacher showed us photos of some typical American foods: hot dogs, hamburgers, pizza. From the grainy pictures, we could barely make out the mysterious foods. Still, they looked appealing, in part because we were always a little hungry.

"But what is the one food that people always have at every meal?" someone asked. It was a question that was on everyone's mind. Our teacher explained that there was no fixture at a typical American meal. The closest might be bread, but Americans did not have the same feelings about bread as Vietnamese did about rice. We found her explanation most puzzling.

One time, our teacher promised to bring a breakfast food called cereal for us to taste. The idea of our teacher sharing food with the entire class was as novel as the concept of eating in class. When the day arrived, the little round wheels, dry and tasteless, underwhelmed us all. In America, I would find out that our teacher was right: cereal tasted much better with fresh cow milk.

One day our class had a visiting teacher from America, a young man in his twenties. We listened with rapt attention to the visitor's description of life in the United States. He told us about holidays like July 4th, when there are always fireworks, and Halloween, when people give candy to children who show up at their front door. My friends and I were in awe that people in America would have so much candy and could be so generous with food.

The visitor also showed us photos of what a house in America looked like. We were surprised to learn that in each house there were so many rooms—the living room, the dining room, the parlor room, the rec room; most had no Vietnamese translation. From the absence of mosquito nets in the bedrooms, I concluded that maybe America had no bugs at all—no mosquitoes, no flies, and none of the creatures I most dreaded, cockroaches. At the end of his talk, the visitor said we could ask him anything we wanted to know. At first the questions were about school, television, food. But soon they would progress into our fears and hopes for the future. "Will people in America be nice to us? Will they accept us?" "Will we be OK?" We all wanted to know.

In the PRPC, besides learning about American culture, we became acquainted with another culture. During the day, local Filipinos from nearby towns often wandered into our camp to trade. Carrying bundles suspended from poles, they walked from hut to hut calling out the ubiquitous greeting, "Hello my friend!"

"Do you have something for me?" they asked in English. Rice, plastic, charcoal or any supply we had extra, they wanted in exchange for fresh fish and produce.

"My friend" was the title the Filipino traders used for everyone, young or old, man or woman. I immediately took to the expression, as it offered an ease that I was not used to. In Vietnamese, there are many pronouns for "you" and "I." Depending on the context and the relationship to the person with whom one is speaking, *anh, chị, em, con, cháo, bác, tôi, mình, ta, chú, thím, cô, cậu*, and others can mean "you" or "I." The designations also serve as titles that must be included before every adult's name. A speaker's choice of pronoun immediately sets the tone of the conversation, revealing his or her perception of the other person's status and age and of their relationship. This decision requires a consideration that I, like most children, tended to gloss over, since it demanded a subtle understanding of various relationships that I did not yet quite grasp.

"Chanh, the woman you were speaking to is older than me so don't call her *Cô* [Miss/Aunty],"my mother reminded me. "*Cô* is for a woman younger than your mom. You should call her Bác." I couldn't tell that the woman was older than my mother. Even if I could, the title *Bác* still might not have been appropriate, since age was not the only determining factor regarding what to call someone. *Thím*, *Mợ*, and *Dì* were also pronouns for females around my mother's age. Each signified a different kind of relationship and level of intimacy.

Besides the actual physical age, there is also the honorary age to keep in mind in certain circumstances. This was the case of my relationship with a daughter of one of my father's good friends. To my great discomfort, she always addressed me as *chị* (older sister) and referred to herself as *em* (younger sister), even though she was several years older. My mother explained that since my father was older than her father, she was younger than me in rank.

"Show respect by always addressing the person at the start of the conversation" was another favorite in my mother's repertoire of advice. Not doing so meant talking to no one or as she put it, "talking to the air." With each reminder, I became more attuned to the nuances of the Vietnamese language. In time, like other children before me, I learned to parse the web of relationships. I came to understand that my identity was not fixed but tied to others around me. Mastering the Vietnamese language, above all else, demands an acknowledgment of this fluid concept of the self.

"Hello, my friend," I called out to the Filipino merchants at the market. As I tried out my stilted English, frustration often filled long pauses while my mind churned to conjugate verbs and recall vocabulary. In the maze of decisions, I was at least spared which pronouns to use. With only "you" and "I," the choice was simple, and no one felt slighted.

Our stay at the PRPC lasted seven months for my parents, Bảy, and me but a few months longer for my sister Chị Hai and her husband Anh Trưởng due to a mix-up in their paperwork. On the day of our departure, my parents, Bảy, and I boarded a big bus that took us back to the airport in Manila for the flight to our new home on the other side of the world. It had been more than a year since we left Việt Nam.

PART IV: AMERICA

My father in front of our sandwich shop in Port Arthur, Texas

FIRST IMPRESSIONS

The bumpy ride to the airport in Manila brought on familiar queasiness. My mother had taken along a tin can and had an uncanny sense for knowing the exact moment I needed it. Looking out the open window and finding relief in the fresh breeze, I watched green hills surrounding the PRPC pass by and fade from view. As we approached the airport, the quiet of the countryside gave way to the bustle of the towns surrounding Manila.

On the flight to America, I was drawn to the startling patterns of blue and green beneath my window. But most surprising were the neatly folded bags tucked in the seat pocket I found while rummaging around.

"They're for you to use if you feel sick anytime during the flight. You throw them away when you're done," my father explained. I hadn't remembered seeing them on our flight from Kuala Lumpur to the Philippines. Relieved to discover such a convenient solution for motion sickness, I was so surprised that the nice bag was made for just a single use. Many other items on the flight were also designed to be used only once, then thrown away: napkins, plastic utensils, and containers of food. Unsure if I could get these fancy items in America, I saved all of mine, then asked my brother and parents for theirs to take with me.

After what felt like days, we finally emerged from the plane into a brightly lit area lined with shops and people hurrying about. "Welcome to Houston!" the sign above us read. Around the airport, every sight and sound felt strange and wonderful. Speakers broadcast music and announcements in foreign languages, while well-dressed people pushed luggage in wheeled carts past shops stacked high with fancy merchandise. Everything seemed so clean and orderly. There was no pushing or shoving, something I expected in any crowd of people. Noticeably absent too was the loud bustle of voices. The cultural lessons at the refugee camps had never mentioned that American people spoke so quietly. Sensing the abnormal volume of our conversation, we hushed each other and softened our speech.

We joined the crowd of people walking past elevators, water fountains, and vending machines, the magical contraptions that deliver instant relief of thirst and hunger. Things that I once just imagined were now real and wonderful. In shops stocked with a dizzying assortment of candies and cookies, I recognized an old friend: a brown package dotted with brightly colored candies. I knew my parents would not stop for M&Ms, but I now was certain what my first purchase in America would be.

A small girl about three years old walked a few steps ahead of me. Her hair was the color of gold. She was holding her mother's hand while clutching a doll to her chest. The sight mesmerized me. Silly as it may sound, until Pulau Bidong I had assumed that hair could only be black, white, or a mixture of both. The person who disabused me of this notion was a UNHCR representative who interviewed us when we first arrived on the island. She was the first Caucasian I had ever met up close. Her features differed markedly from my own and those of people around me. But most striking was her hair. The strands resembled threads of corn silk. Around camp I would encounter a few other people with the same pale skin and golden hair. As UNHCR workers, they lived separate from us and spoke to each other in a language I could not follow. Everything about them seemed so alien that I couldn't imagine them as having once been children. In the airport terminal now stood a small version of the UNHCR representative. The little girl, pulling on her mother's shirt and demanding to be carried, acted like any tired black-haired child.

The connection I felt to the girl did not extend to the adults around us, with skin of different shades, both lighter and darker than ours. Everyone also seemed much taller and bigger. In the sea of people, few looked like us. Until then, that had never been the case. It had not occurred to me that my black hair in the airport was as uncommon as the UNHCR representative's blond hair in the refugee camp. I did not realize it then, but from that moment on, being Vietnamese would, more than any other trait, come to define who I was in America.

Down the long terminal, I spotted my siblings waving excitedly to us. We all took off running, then fell into a collective embrace when we reached each other. For a long time, we stayed clutching each other. My parents did not say much; their silence paid homage to three years of separation. But my siblings were effusive, jokingly referring to Bảy and me as wild urchins who needed to be tamed.

Outside the airport terminal, we stepped into crisp, chilly air, the tail end of a Texas winter. My mother's nephew Anh Hưng and his wife were also at the airport to greet us. The couple had arrived in the United States as college students in the early 1970s with the intention of returning to Việt Nam. But in 1975, after South Việt Nam collapsed, they remained in America. Trained as chemical engineers, the newlyweds settled in Port Arthur, a small town in southeast Texas, near an oil refinery where they worked. In 1981, when my siblings and three young cousins were in refugee camps, Anh Hưng and his wife sponsored their immigration.

The ninety-mile car trip from the Houston airport to our new home in Port Arthur was a most welcome contrast from the noisy bus rides I had known where I often sat on my mother's lap. With the car's windows rolled up, I could barely hear the traffic outside. For the first time, I had my own seat inside a vehicle. This demarcation between personal and communal spaces in America deeply appealed to me.

When we exited the highway, Anh Hưng said that we were entering Port Arthur. We drove along a shaded road lined by big, tall trees. Beautiful houses of different architectural styles stood behind what resembled enormous green rugs. Cu Anh pointed out that he cut *cỏ* for some of these homes. I realized that *cỏ* referred to the lush lawn, not to weeds as I had thought. My brother's after-school job, which I had first read about in Việt Nam from his letters home, began to make more sense.

Emerging from the shaded neighborhood, we drove along mostly treeless streets flanked by homes much smaller and more run down than the ones we had just encountered. We then turned into a gravel driveway flanked by a yard that was a mixture of dirt and uneven patches of grass. A house with faded green paint stood to the side.

"Welcome to your new home!" my cousin announced.

I couldn't wait to see the inside of a house in America. While everyone was outside talking, I ran up to the porch, added my shoes to the pile outside the door, and slipped inside. Behind the door, I felt as if I had entered a fortress, sealed in by walls and tight-shut windows, the crisp chill from outside replaced by a heavy heat. In the open huts back in the refugee camps and in Việt Nam, I hadn't experienced such a distinct difference between inside and outside air. A few steps from the entrance, I felt a soft caress beneath my feet. I looked down to discover that the floor was not barren but covered. Carpet, I remembered. The visiting American teacher in the Philippines had shown us a picture. In the land of monsoon rain, the idea of a permanent floor covering had seemed absurd, as unappealing as it was inconceivable. "How can you hang the carpet out to dry if it's stuck to the floor?" we asked. "Wouldn't it stay muddy and wet all the time?" The teacher's answers led me to assume that carpet must be a feature found only in homes of rich Americans equipped with some elaborate system for cleaning and keeping dry. I was thrilled to see it inside our house.

In the back, two rooms shared a wall. The neater room, I guessed, must belong to my two sisters and the other, with books and clothes strewn on the floor, to my brother and the three male cousins. I ran over and sat down on a mattress. The thick padding felt as soft and luxurious as I had imagined from the photos. Next door to the bedrooms was the kitchen. This kitchen was not a small, walled-off alcove outside, it was a whole room inside the house filled with cabinets, a sink, a refrigerator and a stove with many cooking ranges. Still there was space left for a table and some chairs.

People started streaming in from the outside. The space that had felt enormous when I was alone seemed to shrink. My parents thanked Anh Hưng and his wife, who owned the house, for letting us stay until we found a place to rent. Until then, the ten of us—our family of seven and my three cousins—would share the 1,000-square-foot home.

With a strict budget, finding a house to rent would turn out to be much harder than my parents had thought. One landlord after another would tell my father that a house had already been rented out. Days later, he would come across the same listing in the newspaper. Returning to inquire, he would hear, "You have too many people." "There are too many kids." A few landlords didn't hide their reservations about having Vietnamese immigrants as tenants in their house or anywhere in their neighborhood.

To improve our odds, my parents began telling prospective landlords that they had only three children, who were almost grown and would soon be out of the house. Sometime after, my father saw a listing for a three-bedroom house, a rarity, as most within our budget were smaller. He went with my cousin, Anh Hưng, to check out the property. Right away, they realized that the landlord had also done some fudging of his own. The rental—advertised as a spacious ranch house in a quiet neighborhood—turned out to be a small fixer-upper on a busy street, opposite a twenty-four-hour convenience store. Its third bedroom, the feature that appealed so much to my parents, was little more than a minimally fixed-up attached garage. The landlord, however, didn't seem to care that we were Vietnamese. What seemed to concern him most was whether my father could pay the $300 monthly rent, due the first of every month. When my father assured him that this would not be a problem, he agreed to rent to us.

On the day we moved in, before we even finished unpacking, my father insisted that our whole family walk the few steps over to the landlord's house to introduce ourselves. On the back porch, an overweight man in his late fifties was sitting at a table, his face flushed and his breathing a series of heavy wheezes. He was tinkering with some broken appliance, the parts spread out in front of him. What drew my attention was the chair he was sitting in. It was not a regular chair but a wheelchair. Later I would find out that he used to own a roofing company and had fallen from a roof. He could still walk, but only a short distance, mostly to get in and out of the car. Physically, he might have looked debilitated, but everything about his manners hinted at an air of being in charge.

Back at the house before coming over, my father had stressed that we needed to be extra friendly when we met the landlord. It was likely that he would be upset, as he only expected five of us. I realized that Bảy and I were the unwanted add-ons.

145

The man in the wheelchair looked up when he heard us approach. I smiled brightly and noticed my siblings all did the same. He didn't smile back. As he stared at us, the initial look of surprise changed into one of undisguised annoyance. Abruptly, he turned his wheelchair to face the screen door.

"Loretta, come out! The tenants are here," he yelled into the door. Actually, this is what I now think he might have said. Back then it sounded something like,

"Latarata, gout tetenen he!"

Amid the garble of sounds, I could only pick out one or two words resembling English. I looked to my sisters and brother for help in translating the rest. Their expressions revealed their own bafflement.

Over the years, people have often asked me when I first realized I could speak English well. The moment is as hard to pin down as when I first crossed the threshold into adulthood. However, if I had to pinpoint an instant, I would say it was the first time I truly understood what our landlord had said instead of just pretending and guessing. The gruff Texan had a way of speaking that was not familiar to our hesitant ears. His words did not come one after another but rather spilled out in one jumble, with a few seeming to be still stuck in his throat. The incoherence was exacerbated by the voice, a heavy gravelly-sounding baritone, resulting, apparently, from the ever-present cigarette wedged between his stained fingers.

"Hello," we said, still smiling.

"Hello," he grumbled as he returned to staring at us, his eyes going from my father down to me. In the mounting tension, we all stopped smiling and turned our heads toward the screen door, pinning hope for rescue on whomever he was calling.

Finally, we heard footsteps. A sprightly woman who we presumed was his wife burst through, smiling. Loretta was many things he was not—thin, small, and friendly.

"So sorry for making y'all wait," our landlady said while handing her husband a glass of ice tea. In one gulp, he finished the drink, then deposited the empty glass in her waiting open palm.

"Well, hello there! Welcome! Welcome!" she continued. Her enunciation, with the strong Texas lilt, was surprisingly clear. In a few short weeks, I had learned to recognize the drawn-out legato of Texan English that was the opposite of the choppy cadence of my Filipino teachers' English in refugee camp.

The drink seemed to have soothed our landlord somewhat, as he gestured for us to sit down. While we sat around the table, our landlady told us about herself and her husband and about the neighborhood. She did not seem to mind that we were Vietnamese or notice that there were more of us than promised. In the middle of her chatter, her husband's garbled jumble suddenly returned. My father looked over at my brother and sisters for help, but they just shook their heads. While we might not have understood what he said, it was obvious that his annoyance had been brewing.

Clamping his hands on the wheels of his chair, our landlord backed away from the table, then rolled fast to the other side of the porch, where his anger erupted into a long rant. When it ended, he slumped back in his chair, breathing heavily. His wife, who had followed him, pulled out a napkin from her pocket and dabbed his forehead with it. Leaning down, she whispered something to him, then returned to us. She told one of my sisters to relay to my parents that her husband was angry because he felt deceived. He thought there were only five adult tenants, not seven and no teenagers. We left him no choice by revealing this fact only after we had already moved in.

On the other side of the porch, our landlord continued rolling back and forth in his wheelchair. He paused to light a cigarette, then took several long drags while conspicuously avoided looking over to our side.

"Welcome, anyway. My name is Loretta. My husband's is Walter," our landlady said. But we never called our landlords those names. I could barely make out that tiny *l* sound wedged in the middle of "Walter." Most likely, my parents didn't even hear it. From then on, we would copy my father and address him as Mr. Water. Mister because it was unthinkable for any of us, including my parents, to refer to an adult, no matter that he was not Vietnamese, without a title. *Anh, Chú, Bắc, Ông* were but a few of the designations for an older man in Vietnamese. In English, there was only *mister*. As for Loretta, we also never called her by the name with which she had introduced herself. Her name was three unfamiliar sounds too many, and unlike *Walter*, *Loretta* had no approximation to a common English word. We took to calling her Mrs. Water.

"Thank you, Mrs. Water, Mr. Water," my father said, then nodded to us to do the same.

One by one, we stood up from the table and repeated what my father said. Mrs. Water smiled back, but Mr. Water just grunted, steadfastly hanging on to his annoyance from the other side of the porch.

We arrived in Texas just as the winter of 1984 was fading out. Accustomed to the heat of the tropics, we never felt warm enough. When people around us had shed their outerwear, we doubled up on the worn socks brought over by Mrs. Water and kept on our thick coats, donated by a local charity. In the mornings, I put on even more layers, mesmerized by the wisps of breath vapor rising from my lips like incense smoke.

For me, a crisp, cool smell would come to represent the scent of America. But in Texas it usually came not from the cold air of winter but rather from air conditioning. Even when it was still chilly outside, the cool blast rushed out of the opened door of every place we entered—the grocery store where we marveled at the shelves of food, the government offices where my parents filled out forms for aid, and the health clinic where we received more vaccinations. At the clinic, I was amazed to see the nurse discard a perfectly good needle after she extracted it from my arm, only to select a new one for the next shot. I thought back to the courtyard of our school in the countryside, where I once stood in line with my classmates to receive our shots, and the one needle that went from my arm into the pot of boiling water to be reused. Perhaps more than any other discovery, the discarding of a needle after only one use would demonstrate most vividly for me the contrast in wealth between Việt Nam and America.

Of the places where I encountered the scent of cool air, I associate it most strongly with Tyrrell Elementary School. I enrolled in the school a few days after arriving in Port Arthur. Every morning, in a fifth-grade classroom filled with books, posters, and cups overflowing with pens and pencils, we stood at attention to recite the pledges, one to the United States, and the other to the state of Texas.

I copied the kids around me, placing my hand over my chest and repeating what I thought I heard. "One nation, underlined." It wasn't until many months later that I realized there could be more than one English phrase or word that began with the prefix "under."

I soon settled into a routine, albeit one with many small discomforts. In class, I was often distracted by the terrible sensation of my feet being bound in my shoes. The refugee camp in the Philippines was the first place I had worn closed-toed shoes with socks. The footwear felt like casts around my feet, and soon I reverted to wearing sandals. In America, my parents insisted that I wear close-toed shoes to school because that's what Americans did.

"What are you again?" I heard this question several times a day in school.

"Vietnamese."

"You're Viennese? What's that?" This response I heard just as often. I had no idea what Viennese was. At home, I looked up the word in the dictionary and learned that it was person from Vienna, a city in Europe. The definition shed only some light. Back then my knowledge of geography outside Việt Nam was almost nonexistent. I was certain, however, that I was not Viennese. The kids at school would not be the only ones referring to me as Viennese. I would hear it from other non-Vietnamese, including adults. It occurred to me that perhaps their substitution of "Viennese" for "Vietnamese" was like our approximation of "water" for "Walter." The pronunciation was just easier for the tongue. After all, didn't everyone in America know about Việt Nam? There had been a great war only ten years prior.

One morning shortly after I enrolled in school, my teacher signaled for me to come to her desk.

"Can you put together $1.30?" she asked, pointing to a pile of coins lying scattered on the table.

I was familiar with American money but not enough to distinguish the coins without close inspection. But aware that the teacher was watching and waiting, I quickly did what she asked. She looked at the coins I had chosen, then asked me to pick out another sum. We went back and forth a few more times. After the last trial, she motioned me to follow her outside the class. We walked down the long corridor, then turned into a classroom.

Inside, the kids were noticeably younger. The posters on the walls confirmed a possibility I had dreaded back in refugee camp when my father told me of an adjustment he had made in my history. I was inside a third-grade class.

When my parents filled out our paperwork in Pulau Bidong, they declared Bảy and me two years younger than we were. Anticipating the loss of time in refugee camps, they hoped the age reduction would ease our adjustment to school in America. Being in a lower grade would give us time to catch up. When my father first mentioned the age change, I immediately thought of the possibility that I might be pushed back too many grades. On the first day at Tyrrell, I was relieved to find out that I was placed in fifth grade, the level at which I had left off in the countryside. Now there was the possibility of going back further.

A few feet from me inside the third-grade classroom, the teachers were discussing my fate. I rushed over and wedged myself in between, knowing I had to make my case before it was too late. In the past, when confronted with the chasm between my thoughts and ability to express them in English—an expanse filled with fear of being laughed at while not being understood—I had either stayed quiet or spoken only the minimum. The possibility of getting stuck in third grade—a catastrophic disaster, it seemed to me at the time—summoned in me an unknown reserve. I found myself speaking as freely to the teachers as if I were speaking Vietnamese.

What came out was indeed mostly Vietnamese, mixed with body language and whatever English words I managed to remember. I pleaded my case, listing all the reasons why I didn't want to be in third grade. When my tirade ended, my teacher, who had never heard me speak more than a few words, smiled to the other teacher. Taking my hand in hers, she led me out of the classroom, down the corridor, and back to our old classroom. More than relief at being back in the fifth grade, I was amazed to discover that my limited, mangled English actually worked. I could use it to communicate more than just simple thoughts. The discovery helped me shed my fear of speaking English in public.

Our town had two elementary schools. My father had chosen Tyrrell because it was close enough for me to ride my bike. While Lee Elementary had some Vietnamese students, Tyrrell had only one other besides me. Upon our first encounter, the other Vietnamese student, a fluent English speaker, made clear that she did not want to translate or be any kind of conduit between cultures for me. I would have welcomed her help, as the simulated classrooms and pretend cafeterias in the Philippines had prepared me for only so much.

"Your cubby is the blue one over there," my teacher said. I walked over to a wall of lockers, except I did not recognize a cubby painted the color she mentioned. In Vietnamese, the word *xanh* describes both green and blue. The specificity of whether something is *xanh da trời* (sky *xanh*) or *xanh lá cây* (leaf *xanh*) is used only as needed. Until I learned English, I had not thought of blue and green as two separate colors, but more like shades of one, leaning strongly toward green. I became aware of the distinction in refugee camps, but I had not thought much about it back then. It was only in America that I realized we even perceived colors differently from everyone else. I hesitantly decided which locker was blue and therefore mine.

Around Tyrrell, everything felt unfamiliar, including what I thought I knew well, such as handwriting. In Việt Nam, I had not used pencils but only ink-dipped pens to write. I was taught to press the pen tip only lightly so as not to tear the paper. "Don't make the letters so big. Write small!" my teachers in the countryside of Việt Nam often chided, reminding us to make the most use of precious paper. In America, my teacher was telling me the opposite, "Press the pencil down harder. Don't write so small. Make the loops rounder and bigger."

The way we learned was also different. In Việt Nam, a typical history lesson would have our teacher lecture or read from a book for us to record in a notebook. At home we would memorize the lesson to recite verbatim for a test. The practice is called *trả bài*, which literally means giving back the lesson. During class, the teacher rarely asked our opinions, and we never thought to challenge what she said.

Around the classroom at Tyrrell, lively discussions were the norm. During a lesson about Texas pioneers, our teacher asked if anyone in the class had a Native American ancestor. A few kids waved their arms in the air, calling out for the teacher's attention. Even this act of seeking permission to speak in class was different. In Việt Nam, we would place our elbow on the table, forearm erect, fingers together, then wait in silence. Discussions rarely strayed into anything personal, which was the opposite of what our teacher in America encouraged. A boy went into detail about his great-grandfather, the Indian chief. When his stories digressed into those about vacations and pets, the teacher still listened cheerfully and even joined in with her own personal anecdotes.

The cafeteria, the auditorium, the playground, all became part of my classroom in American culture. I was thrilled to discover individual food trays, the crisp, white paper for writing, and folders to organize the abundant paper. But most amazing was the water fountain, the instant deliverer of cool relief. Thirst, an annoyance I had assumed was a given at school, was no more. When not overwhelmed by my surroundings, I observed in awe. I spent only two months at Tyrrell Elementary School before the summer arrived. These two months would seem idyllic when I entered middle school.

ACCLIMATION

I n America, my parents began looking for work as soon as we were settled. During the day, they spent hours at the Immigration and Refugee Resettlement office combing through job postings. At night, they searched for help-wanted ads in the newspaper. They applied for every position that they thought might not require much spoken English: bagging groceries, collecting shopping carts, cleaning offices. "We'll call you back," my parents would often hear after handing over the application. For days, weeks, even months they waited, but none of those jobs materialized. In time, my parents would come to suspect that "We'll call you back" implied a goodbye more than a promise. The list of English phrases whose meanings seemed to differ from what the words implied also included "How are you?" which we learned was more a greeting than an actual inquiry about our health.

My parents sensed that their language skills were not the only obstacles to their finding work. Even though my father's heavily French-accented English might be hard to understand, it was adequate for the jobs he sought. And although my mother had only started her English lessons in refugee camps, she was a motivated and studious learner and had progressed enough to speak and understand basic English. Their age and the sentiments of a small Texas town, my parents believed, also conspired to make finding employment difficult.

With other relatives, also recent immigrants to America, unable to find jobs, my cousin Anh Hưng and his wife came up with a plan to tap into the pool of available labor. They decided to open a French bakery, following in the footsteps of another relative in Washington State. Anh Hưng asked my father to be the lead in the kitchen. At age fifty-eight, my father would put on yet a different professional hat, that of a pastry chef.

Anh Hưng sent my father to the bakery in Washington for a week to learn the art of French baking. My father came back full of praise for the wonderful climate of the Pacific Northwest and the ubiquitous cherry trees with ruby red fruits, which we had never tasted before. On a day off, my father had gone cherry picking with some of the people from the bakery.

"You guys would love the sweet-sour taste. Too bad there are no cherry trees here in Texas," my father said.

"Do you think you still remember how to climb trees?" he added, flashing his familiar mischievous smile and turning specifically to me. Perhaps he meant nothing by it, but every reference to our past always struck me as some sort of reminder, a vague admonition to remember our roots.

The Golden Croissant opened in 1985 with my father as its head pastry chef and my mother as its all-around food preparer. My father would leave our house for work in the hours of the morning that were closer to midnight than dawn. By 4 a.m., he and another baker were already steeped in dough. In a few hours, croissants, éclairs, and muffins would have to be ready for customers to stop by on their way to work. Around this time, my father would take a break to drive home to pick up my mother and return to the bakery with her.

In his work, my father found an outlet for his artistic talent. With a few quick scribbles, the constant doodler could sketch whatever animal or flower I requested. As a baker, instead of pen and paper, my father would work with dough and dried fruits. Every holiday provided yet another opportunity for him to try out a different creation: turkeys with massive wattles, bunnies with chubby cheeks, Santa Clauses with enormous tummies. He could form the dough into almost any shape that the customer requested. If he had not made something before, he would look at a picture, then zoom in on the traits that defined the object. Impressed by the menagerie of animal baguettes, a reporter from the *Port Arthur News* wrote an article about the Vietnamese-owned business and its quirky baker.

My father's work shift ended at 11 a.m., but he often stayed until the late afternoon. It wasn't work that kept him beyond his shift, it was his desire to be with my mother and go home together. By the time my parents left the bakery at around 4 p.m., my father had been at work for more than twelve hours. Six days a week, this was his schedule. During these long hours, the dream of having his own business returned.

It did not take long after we moved in for Mr. Water to confirm what he had suspected when he first glared at the seven of us: our resources were scant. His obvious anxiety that we might miss a rent payment or destroy his house seemed to explain some of his gruffness. But his anxiety was misplaced. While we could afford little besides rent in the eight years that we lived next door, we were never late with our rent payment. Meeting our financial obligations mattered a great deal to my parents.

The sense of obligation also extended to the monthly bill that came from the US government for the cost of our plane tickets to America. Spread out over many years, the installments did not amount to much. My father mentioned that we could choose not to pay by claiming hardship, thereby postponing the debt indefinitely. But he was adamant that we not take that option, often reminding us that the US government had already done much for our family. Paying back for the plane tickets was something we should do.

Soon after we moved in, I somehow inherited the job of being the primary interface between our family and the Waters. On the first of every month, my father handed me an envelope with a $300 check inside. It was my job to run across the yard to place the rent payment in a very specific place. Not against the back door, not in the mailbox, but "in their hands," my father said each time.

After a few deliveries, I came to a decision. No matter how the rest of my family addressed our landlords, I was going to do it the way Mrs. Water had introduced herself to us at our first meeting. Standing on the back porch, I tapped on the screen door. The longer I waited, the more certain I was of my decision. The greetings were ready on my lips: *Hello, Walter. Good afternoon, Loretta.*

The door swung open. Looking up at me from the wheelchair was a deeply lined face, bespeaking many more decades of living than my thirteen years. No matter how much I had rehearsed, I could not bring myself to call someone my father's age by his first name.

"Hi, Mr. Water," I ended up saying while quickly handing over the envelope.

If *Water* was one or two degrees of distortion from *Walter*, his pronunciation of our names was orders of magnitude from the original sounds. There were too many of us along with too many strange sounds to associate with the faces. Mrs. Water said we were the first Oriental tenants they had. Their references to us as "Oriental" reminded me of kung fu movie dialogue and seemed anachronistic to me even given my tenuous grasp of American culture. After repeated reminders of our names, Mr. Water devised a mnemonic device for some of us. His memory cue most likely originated from my name. "Oanh" was close enough to "one." But then, he came up with Two for my brother-in-law Trưởng, and Three for my sister Thuy (Chị Tư's official name). At first, I couldn't tell which one of us he was referring to, but from context, I could mostly guess. The rest of my siblings did not have names and were known only as the younger brother, the oldest sister, the sister with the short hair, and so on. The closest approximation of our names he reserved for my parents, making them sound like Bond villains: Mr. and Mrs. No.

Our yards were separated by a narrow patch of shared grass and a wire fence. My brothers and I often hung out on the back stoop to escape the stifling heat inside our house. Given the cost, our AC was seldom used even during the hottest months. From where my brothers and I were, we could not help but hear Mr. and Mrs. Water's comings and goings.

"Loretta!" we would hear moments after Mr. Water's car pulled up into the driveway. By the time the car door opened, Mrs. Water was already waiting nearby with the wheelchair. Fumbling with a cane, Mr. Water maneuvered to hoist himself out of the car, a drawn-out procedure that had him struggling for breath. As the minutes dragged on, Mrs. Water remained close by, watching anxiously but doing little. Perhaps she knew better than to offer too much unsolicited assistance.

"I don't need any help!" was a phrase we heard almost as often as her name.

For all of Mr. Water's outbursts, his devotion to his wife was obvious to us early on. On another rent delivery mission, I happened to catch Mr. Water as he pulled into the driveway. The car shimmered, beads of water trickling down the sides.

"I have her car washed and filled up every week. Been doing that for years," he told me, a rare smile stretching across his face.

Mr. and Mrs. Water were around my parents' age, but their three children were all grown and no longer lived at home. Like my parents, they were often together. He would be tinkering with some broken appliance while she stayed by his side, ever ready with tools and cold drinks.

In the time that we were their tenants, I was the primary deliverer not only of rent but also of messages whenever something in our house broke.

"Chanh, go over and tell Mr. Water that the washing machine stopped working," my father said.

"Ba, why me? Why not someone else?"

"Well, because you're pretty brave," he said, smiling. The compliment rang hollow since I never thought of myself as brave, but I loved hearing my father say it, and I suspected he knew it as well.

The circumstances might differ each time I ran over when something broke, but the question my father wanted me to include was always the same: "Who pay?" Of the trips next door, I did not mind the rent drop-off, since it required little beyond the greetings. But I dreaded the "Who pay?" missions. I had to use my limited English to explain mechanical complications that I did not fully understand. There was often much back and forth and guessing on my part. Since Mrs. Water deferred most home-maintenance questions to her husband, I ended up talking primarily with Mr. Water. Long after I could converse fairly well with other people, I still had a hard time understanding his speech. Fearful that his anger might erupt at my next request to repeat something, I sometimes just filled in the gaps with what I thought might make sense.

Over time, I detected a pattern in Mr. Water's response to the "Who pay?" question. If something broke and he thought we were responsible, then we would pay. If we were clearly not at fault, then, despite some initial resistance, he would pay, though not for a new appliance but only for parts that my brothers would use to fix or replace what was broken. But often the question of responsibility was not so clear-cut, as in the toilet that clogged one too many times. Was it because it was old and prone to clogging when there was a lot of rain, as we reasoned? Or was it because of overuse from too many people, as he countered?

While talking to Mr. Water, even in a straightforward situation, I kept expecting his wrath, as I never felt I could make myself adequately understood. He always wanted to know more than what I knew how to explain. Sensing his agitation rising, I would grow more flustered, my English sounding increasingly like Vietnamese. In mid conversation, he sometimes abruptly put up his hand. I understood the none-too-subtle signal that he had had enough of my explanation.

"I just have to see for myself what happened," he said, clamping his hands over the wheels to roll his chair fast toward our house. It was my cue to rush ahead to alert everyone of his arrival.

At our house, he would often find my brothers hunching over the scattered parts of the disassembled washing machine, sink, or toilet. After we moved in, many appliances took turns either expiring dramatically—like the washing machine that stopped with a scream in mid-spin—or just quietly giving up, as when we found the refrigerator contents had spoiled.

What Mr. Water hadn't expected when he first growled at us in our first meeting were my brothers' skills for reviving dying appliances. The future engineers loved opening up mechanical gadgets to diagnose problems. Inside, the jumble of gears conversed with them in a language they understood. Feeling their way around, they would patch up the troubled spots to bring an ailing appliance back to life, at least for a while longer. While my brothers might have lacked formal training in fixing things, they had plenty of field experience. As far back as I could remember, they always loved to tinker with anything mechanical. In the countryside, they would make toys from discarded materials found around us. Finding a stray wheel, piece of wood, strip of metal, they transformed the parts into scale models of self-propelling or explosive devices, never dolls or anything cuddly I might like. Amid rags and tools, my father hovered nearby, ready with advice.

"Bảy, you need to check to see if it has enough oil."

"Cu Anh, don't turn the handle too hard."

If instructions were not executed to his satisfaction, my father would reword the advice, growing visibly more irritated. At times his counsel was helpful, but often I could tell it was not appreciated by my brothers.

"OK, OK, Ba. We understand," they sometimes cut in before my father finished talking. The backtalk rarely went further. For two Vietnamese boys imbued with outsize teenage confidence, contradicting one's father still had its limits.

In America my siblings and I all had jobs outside school. My third sister, Chị Tư, worked at the Goodwill clothing store, where she bought most of my clothes. My fourth sister, Chị Năm, worked at McDonald's during the night shift, closing out the restaurant at midnight. Sometimes, when her manager was in a generous mood, Chị Năm would come home with hamburgers, chicken nuggets, apple pies, and other leftovers that would have been discarded. My brothers and I delivered newspapers. I was responsible for folding the newspapers and putting them into pouches for my brothers to distribute by bicycle.

Every day after school, I was greeted by stacks of newspapers in our garage, delivered earlier by the newspaper company. After ten or fifteen blissful minutes immersing myself in the world of Garfield, Cathy, Beetle Bailey, and other comic-strip friends, I set out to work. It didn't take long for my fingers to warm into the automatic motions of prepping a newspaper for delivery, bending the sides of the paper together, then wrapping a rubber band around the folded paper or, if it was wet outside, sliding it into a plastic bag. By that time it had been a while since lunch, so I began to think about the food in a square pan that had Garfield's heart all aflutter. What is lasagna? My mind conjured up different possibilities that made me even hungrier. Soon I would drift on to other thoughts, only to find myself wondering about this mysterious food again the next day.

There was still daylight when my job ended, but for my brothers, this was often not the case. As our newspaper routes expanded, it took them increasingly longer to make their deliveries. Rain, winds, broken bicycle chains, flat tires, and a host of other factors all added minutes, at times hours, to their job. The more problems my brothers faced on their delivery routes, the more I had to contend with the fallout from customers over the phone. Calling our house to complain that their paper was wet, torn, or, most often, missing, some apologized profusely, but most did not hide their irritation.

In the absence of visual cues, phone conversations were already torturous exercises in deduction. But I especially dreaded these complaint calls, which required my constant repeating of a few phrases.

"I'm sorry, could you please say that again?" The request was usually the fastest, least painful way to get the information.

"Could you say it more slowly?" The appeal asked a bit more from the customer, but it was still tolerable.

"I'm sorry, I still don't understand what you said after ...? Could you spell that word for me?" The last-ditch effort tested the patience of even the most sympathetic customer. As the letters of the alphabet began drifting out from the receiver, I quickly scribbled them down on a notepad. Midway into the word, invariably came my response, "Ah ... so that's how you say it!" No matter how many times the scenario was repeated, each instance took me through the same wave of embarrassment followed by anxiety, then exhilaration for having discovered the correct pronunciation of another tricky word. Before hanging up, many customers made clear their displeasure at having to work so hard to convey their displeasure.

Of the phone calls over the years, there was one that kept me pondering long after. A customer called to say that her dog had disappeared around the time that my brother was seen in her neighborhood. "Does your brother know where my dog might be?" she wanted to know. The question was simple enough, but there was something in her tone, along with a reference to the ample size of my brother's newspaper sack, that made me uncomfortable. Did she imply that my brother had kidnapped her dog, alluding to a certain stereotype regarding Asians and dog eating? I couldn't be sure if my self-consciousness had distorted the customer's tone and added the allusion, or if I had misread the situation entirely and her question was nothing more than a plea from a desperate dog owner seeking information from any source. I called my sisters over to help, but they, too, were baffled.

Despite the rain, cold, heat, falls, dog chases, and near-accidents with cars, my brothers did not seem to mind their job. On beautiful afternoons, they sometimes remarked how much they enjoyed riding their bikes. There was, however, one aspect of the job they really disliked: collecting payment. Toward the end of each month, they had to knock on every customer's door to ask for the $5.50 subscription fee. Of that amount, our take was $1.50; the rest belonged to the newspaper company. Most customers were happy to pay. A few even included a tip and asked them to come inside for cookies and milk. However, every month, there were the inevitable nonpayers, citing bad service or their financial distress. Some didn't even come to the door despite repeated knockings, even though they could clearly be seen through the windows. Cancellation of their subscription was an inadequate solution as we, not the newspaper company, still had to absorb the loss for that month.

The *Port Arthur News* was a weekday afternoon paper, but on weekends it was published in the morning, which meant there was no sleeping in for any of us, including my father. On Sunday, his one day off from the bakery, he still got up early to help us fold newspapers. Technically, he did get to sleep in, since 4 a.m. was still later than his normal wake-up time for work at the bakery.

It was still dark when we headed out to the garage. Inside, it was piled high with newspapers. Beneath a small lightbulb dangling from the ceiling, we squatted on the concrete floor, each hunching over our own stack of newspapers. Mine came up almost to my chest, as Sunday papers were much thicker than those from the rest of the week. Half asleep, I went through the motions of bending in the sides of the paper, then slipping the folded paper into a plastic bag. Flinging the bag onto the surrounding pile, I then reached for the next paper in the stack and continued the process. When my fingers scraped at the cold floor, I got up to retrieve another stack of newspapers, then sat down to resume folding.

A few feet from me, my father was going through the same motions. But his newspaper folding sounds were dwarfed by his breathing, a series of uneven, strained breaths. The decades of smoking, a habit he had given up not long ago in refugee camp, had apparently caused enough damage. Unlike my mother, whose health was often on my mind, my father was rarely sick. It occurred to me that in America my father was now getting old.

When there was enough sunlight, my brothers began heading out on their bikes, two pouches stuffed full of newspapers hanging down from each of their back seats. After they left, my father and I continued folding and sorting. When all of the pouches were set up for the different delivery routes, we went back into the house. My father usually returned to bed, but I never did. My much-awaited part of the week had arrived.

In the rare quiet, I could do whatever I wanted. What I wanted most was to have the TV all to myself. But first, I had to resolve the urgent matter of my growling stomach. Standing in front of the refrigerator, I dreamed of steaming ramen and hot fried rice. With ease I could bring these fantasies to life. Yet week after week, despite the same internal debate, I ended up with a cold breakfast only because it required little waiting. As Scooby Doo and the gang unraveled mysteries and Papa Smurf delivered his wisdom, I sat transfixed in front of the warm glow, devouring my feast of cut-up ham splattered with Sriracha hot sauce.

While watching TV, I was as fascinated by the commercials as I was by the shows themselves. Both depicted a world that bore little resemblance to my own—of kids in their own bedrooms, families going on vacations, and parents cheering at sports games. Neither my siblings and I nor any of our friends played sports at school, and our parents, like those of our friends, had never come to school or met our teachers. The only trips our family took were to Pleasure Island, a man-made island on the other side of town where we dug for clams and fished for crabs with pieces of chicken tied to a string. The few toys we had around the house, we either bought at garage sales or found on the streets. "I don't wanna grow up. I'm a Toys R Us kid," I sang along with the commercial, even though the depiction of an enormous store filled with kids crying out for "more games, more toys, oh boy!" seemed as surreal to me as the Smurfs' mushroom houses.

Through our newspaper delivery job, my brothers and I would discover a toy store of our own. The Port Arthur News Company had a rewards system for incentivizing its newspaper deliverers. Keeping track of the customers' phone calls, the company awarded points based on how many complaints the newspaper deliverer received. At the beginning of each month, a manager, a middle-aged man who could talk at length about any aspect of the newspaper business, would come to our house. After collecting payment, he would show us our complaints report, including the number of points we had earned. After discussing ways for improvement, he would hand us a pamphlet. Beaming from the glossy pages were board games, toys, and sports equipment. The cost was not in dollars but in points.

Such happy times occurred much more frequently when the number of newspapers my brothers took on had not spiraled out of control. The increase happened gradually whenever a newspaper deliverer quit and the manager turned to my brothers, already experienced and known for not turning down work. In less than two years, the 150 papers we had started out with grew to almost 500. In the winter months, my brothers often finished their deliveries in the dark. Customers called our house nonstop, with the very reasonable request of receiving what was supposed to be an afternoon newspaper before eating their supper.

At our newspaper delivery peak, it was clear that my brothers needed to scale back. Customers' grievances, however, were not the only driving factor. Cu Anh had just started eleventh grade and had begun to think beyond high school. My father was adamant that getting into a good college, above everything else, should be his main priority. Yielding to my father, my brothers substantially reduced their work. After the reduction, my father still thought that Cu Anh did not have enough time for school and insisted that my brothers stop delivering newspapers altogether, which they soon did.

By this time, my father, the eternal entrepreneur, had decided to try his luck in America to once again be his own boss. As it turned out, helping my parents in their new adventure would end up taking more of my time than folding newspapers ever did.

From a few newspaper customers, my brothers found a job that paid much better and took much less time: cutting grass. For Cu Anh, it was a return to his earlier occupation. Using the customers' own lawn mowers, they earned $10 a yard every two weeks. Mr. Water also asked my brothers to mow his grass. His payment was not in money but in exchange for the use of his lawn mower for our own yard.

For Mr. Water and paying customers, my brothers took care to keep the grass lines parallel to each other and to hug the flowerbeds just so. For our lawn, they didn't take the same care. The uneven grass lines made clear my older brother's attitude toward grass as *cỏ*, or weeds to be rid of. In place of the manicured lawns, he would rather have vegetable patches providing food or wildflower gardens requiring little maintenance.

In our free time, my brothers and I liked to hang out in our yard, playing badminton or volleyball, a game we all loved and had discovered for the first time in America. Our fun was often thwarted by the fire-ant mounds scattered throughout the grass. Since we usually walked around barefoot, using poison for the ants didn't seem to be a good choice. Instead, we opted to pour scalding water over the mounds. The no-cost, readily available method worked, but only for a time, as eventually the colony always reformed, at which time we would dump more hot water. One day while cooking on our barbecue grill, Cu Anh came up with another method that he thought would solve the ongoing nuisance once and for all.

On the weekends, after he finished grilling, Cu Anh would spread the smoldering charcoal on top of the ant mounds, starting in the more distant ends of the yard, far from Mr. Water's side. At first, no one noticed the blackened spots. But as the extermination by fire spread, they became harder to miss. Certain that it was only a matter of time before Mr. Water found out, Bảy and I begged Cu Anh to stop. But he didn't seem to share my fear of Mr. Water and only agreed when my father intervened. But this, however, did not happen soon enough.

One afternoon, my brothers and I had just started a game of volleyball when Mr. Water eased his car into the driveway. When the car engine was turned off, I heard what sounded vaguely like an argument between Mr. and Mrs. Water. My brothers and I kept playing, as it was not out of the ordinary for Mr. Water to grumble about something while his wife tried to calm him.

"Come here!" I suddenly heard. The baritone booming with anger didn't sound like it came from the other side of our fence but from somewhere near. I stopped playing to look around and realized that the voice was indeed only a few yards from us. At the edge of our driveway stood Mrs. Water next to Mr. Water in his wheelchair.

"Come here," he repeated.

As we slowly made our way across the grass toward the Waters, I caught a glimpse of the blackened patches. With certainty, I knew the reason for their unexpected visit.

"Hi, Mr. Water. Hi, Mrs. Water," I said, hoping the overfriendliness might soften his wrath.

"What are those?" Mr. Water shouted while we were still a few feet away. Picking up the cane hanging on the side of his wheel chair, he pointed to the burned spots.

Before we could answer, he continued yelling.

"Look, I don't know what y'all were thinking. But here in America, YOU DON'T BURN GRASS! YOU CUT IT! YOU UNDERSTAND?" The rising volume had the effect of separating his words, and for the first time, I was able to understand most of what he said.

After the tirade, Mr. Water collapsed backward into his wheelchair. The beads of sweat rolled down his face and onto his shirt. As if the outburst had depleted all his energy, he said nothing and just glared at us. My brothers and I turned to look to the ground. The silence, punctuated by his heavy breathing, dragged on until I heard the familiar Texas twang.

"Walter, they're just kids. Don't be so angry at them."

Mrs. Water's intervention seemed to work. When Mr. Water resumed talking, I could sense a shift in his tone.

"Look, I think your mom and dad are good folks. Maybe they don't know what you kids are up to. I sure hope they didn't tell y'all it's OK to burn grass. If you do it again, I'm gonna kick you all out. You understand?" He enunciated each word slowly while leaning forward in his chair and glancing from one of us to another.

"Yes, sir," we mumbled.

"From now on, you take care of the grass, OK?" Mr. Water added before he turned his wheelchair around. Cu Anh nodded, but I could tell he was really thinking, *What's the big deal? It's just grass.*

After that, while we didn't exactly lavish attention on our lawn, my brother stopped dumping charcoal or even hot water over the anthills. In time, new grass grew over the burned patches. Our yard and the Waters' still looked different. On their side, the lawn was a lush green carpet with neatly kept flowerbeds. On our side, the yard was more uneven, with blotches of a sun-scorched brown.

We also had flowers but of a different sort. Smaller and less ornate than those next door, our yellow blossoms dotted the vines in our vegetable garden. Far away from the Waters' house, my parents had carved out a small part of our yard for growing food. Hanging down from the trellis that my brothers had built over the garden were loofahs, bottle-shaped gourds, and bitter melons. At the beginning of each planting season, the precious seeds were carefully doled out and shared among friends and relatives. More than just food, the tropical fruits and vegetables grown from these seeds were a reminder of a home half a world away.

After the grass-torching incident with Mr. Water, the détente between our families was again tested when my sister and brother-in-law finally joined us in America from the Philippines. With their arrival, Mr. Water's rental house now held nine people. As my father had done with us, he insisted that Chị Hai and Anh Trưởng accompany him to the Waters' house to introduce themselves. When my father asked if anyone else wanted to come along, none of us volunteered. Finally, my third sister Chị Tư, good daughter that she was, agreed to do it. From the back stoop, the rest of us watched the entourage cross over to the Waters' porch. With barely suppressed laughter, we rushed back inside the house at the familiar creaking of their screen door.

As Chị Tư recounted later, Mr. Water was less than thrilled with the additional two tenants, but nowhere as angry as he had been at our first meeting. When they were leaving, Mr. Water asked if my parents were expecting anyone else to come and live at the house.

"Yes," Chị Hai answered, "a baby in a few months." Before Mr. Water's wrath could erupt, my father reassured him that Chị Hai and her family would not be staying long.

True to my father's promise, my sister and brother-in-law left Mr. Water's house soon after the baby was born, a few months after their arrival in America. Taking my father's advice, they moved to Houston, a much bigger city with many more opportunities. During the day while Anh Trưởng searched for work, Chị Hai stayed home with the baby. At night they combed through want ads, studying maps and bus routes. After a series of temporary jobs, Anh Trưởng found steady work at an auto repair garage helping other mechanics. He was grateful for the job, showing up early and staying past his shift to learn the trade.

One morning Anh Trưởng gave a customer, who had dropped off her car for repair, a ride to her workplace. On the way, she asked about his background.

Among other tidbits, Anh Trưởng mentioned that he had studied chemistry in Việt Nam. He had forgotten about their conversation until the customer returned a few days later to pick up her car. She handed him an application for a lab technician position at the university where she worked and said he should apply.

A college degree is a must, the application specified. Even though Anh Trưởng had graduated from college, he had no proof of having done so. Even if he could obtain a copy of his college degree, he wasn't certain if one from a Vietnamese university would be recognized in America. Still, he filled out the application. Just as my father, freed from a French POW camp, had encountered a most timely mentor when he was a penniless veteran in Sài Gòn, Anh Trưởng would find his benefactor in a young professor who was setting up his research lab. Having come of age in America during the Việt Nam War, the lab director identified with the Vietnamese immigrant. Taking Anh Trưởng at his word, the professor offered him the job as his lab assistant.

The stable income enabled Chị Hai to stop working part-time and pursue her own dream. After passing her TOEFL (Test of English as a Foreign Language) exam, she enrolled at the University of Houston, putting her two-year-old in daycare whenever she had class. Four years later, the mother-daughter pair had a dual graduation: daughter from kindergarten into first grade and mother from nursing school into the workforce.

Five months after we arrived in America, I started middle school. Thomas Edison Middle School was much bigger than Tyrrell Elementary. More than size, the two schools differed significantly in the makeup of the student populations. Whereas the kids at Tyrrell were fascinated by the lone clueless Vietnamese immigrant, the kids at Edison were jaded from having seen too many. Sheer numbers, perhaps even more than familiarity, bred contempt.

"Go back to where you came from!" "Go back to China!" kids shouted along the hallways or snickered underneath their breath. They hurled the invective almost as an automatic response to any perceived slight. I often wondered why the place we were told to go back to was always China, since our school only had a few Chinese kids. The reason emerged as I began to grasp how others perceived us. In America, we were seen only in the broadest strokes. In Việt Nam and in refugee camps, the question of my name was almost always followed by an inquiry about my *quê* (countryside or place of family origin). So, although I was born in Sài Gòn, I was quick to add that my father was born in Huế and my mother's family came from Long An, a province not far from Vĩnh Long.

In America, the details of our background no longer mattered. Anyone who looked like us was considered Asian, and for many Americans, Asian could only mean Chinese. It was not only the outer layers of our identity that got peeled off. What I had always considered to be the core—my name—also came loose. A typical Vietnamese name is usually made up of three parts: the family name, or last name, followed by a gender indicator (*Thị* for female, *Văn* for male) and then often a two-word first name. My name, Ngô Dương Thục Oanh, is a bit unusual because in place of the female gender indicator, my parents had substituted *Dương*, my mother's last name. *Oanh* refers to the Oriole, an enchanting bird with contrasting plumage, and *Thục* means well-mannered. Taken together, Ngô Dương Thục Oanh has a melodic cadence. From the rise and fall of its sounds, I have always imagined a graceful bird gliding over fields and waters.

In America, Ngô Dương Thục Oanh became simply Oanh Ngo. The contracted name—stripped bare of its tonal marks, with the order inverted—peered out at me from the pages like a stranger. Coming from my own lips, it sounded like an unwelcome alias. Coming from a native English speaker, it emerged as a jumble of tortured sounds, unrecognizable even when I was expecting it. My time at Tyrrell had prepared me for the ways my name could be mispronounced. The first day in middle school, with a different teacher for each class, I would put this knowledge to good use.

As the teacher took attendance, calling out names, she approached those whose last names began with the letter "n." The school day was almost over, and I had already gone through the roll call with other teachers. I knew what was about to come. The teacher would pause, pick up the roll sheet from the table, bring it closer to her face, then squint her eyes. The longer her hesitation, the more likely this was my cue to intervene.

"That's me!" I would call out. A pause followed by a puzzled look had become a placeholder for my name until I slogged through the explanation of how it should be pronounced. There were two versions. The short one was, "It's pronounced just like W-a-n and N-o." I spelled out the letters. The bastardization that I volunteered had strayed so far from my name as to render it meaningless. But with everyone staring, the quick explanation had to suffice.

In other settings, if the person was interested, I would offer the long version. "Oanh is pronounced like *Ahhn*, with the *O* in front. And Ngo: pretend that you're saying 'bingo,' but keep the first syllable silent and only say the second. Make the *n* and the *g* sounds come out together." After a few attempts, most came close to pronouncing Oanh, but rarely did I encounter a native English speaker who could manage the *ng* sound combination.

I too had a terrible time with others' names. Each name was another vocabulary word with only a visual association that had to be committed to memory at that moment. The nicknames added yet another layer of confusion. "This is John, but he wants to be called Jack," the gym teacher said, introducing my partner for square dancing. There was also Charles, who went by Chuck, sitting next to me in my math class. Unable to reproduce the slight distinction between *Chuck* and *Jack*, I ended up calling both boys Jack.

After a while, I began asking kids, at least those who were willing, to write down their names. *Sean, Shaun, Shawn*: the mix of letters seemed to follow even fewer rules than the already rule-defying typical English words. Having encountered only the *nh* letter combination in Vietnamese, I had to resist the impulse to rearrange the letters in John to make it *Jonh*. It occurred to me that Oanh must have the same pull for native English speakers. The ubiquitous misspelling of my name, putting the *h* before the *n*, now had an explanation.

Names were not my only source of confusion. Endowed with a subpar sense of direction, I was often lost as I made my way around Edison Middle School. My disoriented state, along with my mismatched clothes and homegrown haircut, left little doubt of my status. I was not just an immigrant but the lowest in the hierarchy of immigrants: the fresh-off-the-boat kind. Of the lingering glances cast my way, I could not tell looks of pity from looks of sympathy. I wanted neither.

A few weeks into sixth grade, a boy began to take a particular interest in me. His was not the flattering kind but the kind that would transform school into a place of misery. In our first encounter, I did not even catch what he looked like. What I saw before my folders and books went flying, then crashing onto the floor was a blur of a red sleeve swiping across my arm. There was no question in my mind that the act was deliberate, even as the reason eluded me.

I dropped to the ground to gather the spilled content. As the tide of students parted around me, I thought I heard footsteps coming back toward me. When they came closer, instead of veering, they seemed to head straight to where I was. A pair of black sneakers suddenly emerged. In the next instant, I saw them on top of one of my books, the heels pressing and twisting hard on the open pages.

"Hey, stop it!" I yelled out, but the shoes had already turned to join the crowd. From the back, I recognized the black sneakers and the red sleeve. They belonged to a boy. He was laughing while hurrying down the hallway, his fingers sliding along the wall of lockers.

A few days later, the book toss happened again. I immediately thought of running to Bảy, in eighth grade and his last year at Edison. But I had no idea where my brother was. Unlike the small courtyard of our school in the countryside, where we were mostly within sight of each other, the hallways of Edison were vast. Even if I managed to find my brother, the boy would be long gone. Anger overwhelmed fear as I ran after the black sneakers, stepping over books and papers.

"Hey, you!" I said, grabbing the back of the boy's shirt. My heart pounded. I had no idea what to expect or what I was going to do next. The boy turned around. When he saw me, he burst out with the same raucous laugh as before.

"It's not funny. Don't do it again!" the words spewed out to my surprise. The boy continued to laugh as he walked off, leaving little doubt that my threat carried no weight even if my mangled pronunciation was clear enough to be understood.

After the confrontation, the book toss took place with more regularity. Like a specter, the boy seemed to appear out of nowhere at a few spots around school. Detecting a pattern, I began to mix up my routes to and from my classes. Always on alert, I quickly turned and headed off in another direction if I spied him from afar. But every so often I still felt the familiar jolt on my arm. Before I could tighten my grip, the books and papers were already flying.

"Cần giúp không?" (Do you need help?) a voice called out above my head. I was again on the ground, gathering books and papers. I had always waved away offers

170

of help. With tears barely held back, I had wanted no witness. But this time felt different. In just three words, I sensed a genuine kindness. I looked up, expecting to see someone with hair and eyes like mine. Instead, smiling down at me was a girl with light brown hair and big hazel eyes. Is she someone sent down from above to rescue me? The thought flickered through my mind. I didn't know how else to make sense of the Vietnamese words that had just graced her lips. Without waiting for my answer, she crouched down next to me, reaching for the stray papers and stuffing them into a folder. "Hi, my name is Violet," she said. From that day on, Violet and I became inseparable.

Violet's mother was from Việt Nam. Her parents met at an army base in Sài Gòn in the late 1960s. There was something about the quiet young woman who did laundry and shined shoes that deeply appealed to the American serviceman. She could speak only a few words of English, but as they got to know each other, the young soldier knew he wanted to marry her. His sergeant strongly advised against the marriage, warning of the high cost and mountain of paperwork involved. Determined to bring his bride home, Violet's father saved up and waded through the bureaucracy. Her parents got married just before her father's tour in Việt Nam ended.

In America, the newlyweds had two daughters in quick succession. The family lived in California inside an air force base for a few months, then moved to Montana to be near family. In the land of snow, the marriage began to flounder. When Violet was six, their parents divorced. Her father remained in Montana while her mother relocated with their two daughters to Texas, a place with a more tropical feel and a Vietnamese community.

Amid all the changes, there was one constant in the girls' upbringing—their deep Christian faith. Even as her parents settled into new relationships, Violet always trusted that God would find a way to bring them back together. She held out hope through first grade, second, then third. By then, both parents had gotten remarried. But by fourth grade, her prayers were answered when her parents left their spouses to remarry each other. There was no doubt in Violet's mind that the reunion could not have happened without divine help.

When we met two years later, in sixth grade, Violet was high on God, and she wanted me to soar with her. She told me about Jesus and other stories from the Bible, all of which I had never heard before. Each time she saw me, she gave me more pamphlets and brochures from her church. Please read and think about it, she begged me.

Sometime after we met, Violet and I were waiting in front of the school for the bell to ring. Suddenly she turned to me and hugged me tight. When she pulled back, I saw that her eyes were red. She started to speak excitedly of a day coming up soon that she had been anticipating for so long.

"Oanhnie, everything will change so fast," she said. She went on to describe a day filled with fantastical happenings. I listened with rising interest, as it did not resemble any American holiday I knew. Then Violet became quiet, turning subdued before she continued.

"I love you so much. I want us to be together always. I don't want you to be left behind," she said.

"Violet, where are you going? Why would I be left behind? When is this day going to happen?" I blurted out, on the verge of tears myself.

That morning was the first time I heard about the Rapture. But it would not be the last time that Violet beseeched me to join her in it.

Not long after I met Violet, two young men came to our house one afternoon. I was in the kitchen with my mother when the doorbell rang. As we rarely had visitors, I leaped to answer it. Smiling through the slit in the door were two young men wearing matching short-sleeved white shirts and dark pants. Only the color of their ties was different. With every strand of hair in place, the men resembled younger versions of the anchormen on the evening news programs that we obsessively watched to learn English.

"Can I help you?" I asked, expecting the crisp diction of Peter Jennings in response.

"Xin cho chúng tôi vào nhà," they responded ("Please, may we come in?").

Of the five Vietnamese tones I knew well, the men missed a few in their pronunciation of the request, but what they said was clear enough to be understood. Unlike Violet, who upon closer inspection did have some Vietnamese features, the men had none. How did they learn to speak Vietnamese? And more importantly, why? In the mystery, my thirteen-year-old heart blossomed.

"Dạ, được," (Yes, of course), I answered, taking off the chain lock to open the door. It occurred to me that I should have checked with my mother, but they were already inside.

"Chào Bác," the men greeted my mother who had come in from the kitchen. They had chosen the appropriate designation (*Bác*) for my mother, an older but not too old female. My mother looked as shocked as I was.

She pointed to the couch and gestured for the men to sit down. From their briefcase, they took out two small black books and handed them to us. With a cadence suggestive of rote memorization, they spoke of God, sprinkling their talk with words I recognized as Vietnamese but had never heard before. By speaking a language that tugged at my heart, the men managed to reach me in a way that they never could have had they spoken English. As it was so difficult for me to learn English, I imagined that it could not have been easy for them to learn Vietnamese. Whereas I had no choice, they chose to learn a new language. The thought was as incomprehensible as it was alluring. My ears strained to listen to their voices while my eyes were drawn to the light hair on their arms, the blue of one man's eyes and the catlike green of the other's. My gaze soon became so focused that I stopped trying to figure out what they were saying. The singsong flow of Vietnamese words floated around me, detached of any meaning. The two elders from the Church of Jesus Christ of Latter-Day Saints were my first crushes in America.

The men suddenly got up from the couch. So distracted, I hadn't realized they had gotten to the end of their talk. They thanked us for inviting them into our house and handed us some pamphlets. The brochures in Vietnamese made clearer in writing what the men had said but still left me confused. What I was certain of was that, like Violet, the men wanted me to join them in their beliefs.

Before Violet and the missionaries, I had not thought that religion was something I could choose or change. Like many of our relatives, we considered ourselves Buddhists even though we only worshipped at home at the ancestral altar. The only formal Buddhist education I had was from Cô Năm in Sài Gòn when I was seven, before we left for the countryside. But what she taught me about karma and the ways to live a worthy life never left me. In my mind, Buddha and the ancestors fused together. I imagined them residing somewhere in the heavens, watching over me but always judging. For my deeds, I would be punished or rewarded in the afterlife and perhaps the next.

The first Christians I had met were the family who shared a housing unit with us in Sungei Besi refugee camp. We were awoken every morning when they rose in the dark to attend mass. Back then I assumed it was something all Christians had to do each day. The family never spoke about their faith, and I never thought to ask.

In America, I learned much about Christianity from Violet and her family. The concepts of salvation and eternal life deeply appealed to me and were unlike any Buddhist beliefs I knew. At Violet's urging, I went to church with her family a few times. The people whom Violet introduced me to seemed to possess the same certainty of purpose that she exuded and that I craved. But in the end, I could not make the leap to join my friend. I just did not believe enough to abandon my own faith, conceived long ago inside the incense-filled room and woven deeper into me each time I knelt in front of our family altar.

More than religion, Violet's family offered a glimpse of an America that I imagined non-immigrants inhabited. It didn't matter that Violet's mother was also an immigrant. The fact that Violet was native born and her father was American was enough for her family to be the final authority in all things Americana.

I attended my first birthday party at Violet's house, took my first swing at a piñata, then stared in disbelief at the shower of candies that came down, all for the taking. I went bowling with her church group. Violet helped me pick out my bowling shoes and ball. I watched her sister get ready for a date. Her father teased her about the boy and her mother helped her with her hair. In our house, the subject of dating never came up, and from my older siblings, I understood that I was not to date during high school. At times I longed for such freedom and for such an easy-going relationship with my parents.

I also spent my first Thanksgiving with Violet's family. In school, we had learned about the festive holiday in which everyone could participate. Among the dishes overflowing the dining table, I was fascinated by the centerpiece—an enormous golden turkey. I wondered how we were going to eat the bird whole.

At a Vietnamese meal, meat is always cut into small pieces, the preparation taking place in the kitchen, far from the guests. The mystery was solved when we sat down at the table and Violet's father picked up an oversized knife and fork. With everyone watching, he began slicing into the crisp golden skin. Thick pieces of meat fell on top of each other, filling up the plate.

I couldn't wait to taste home-cooked turkey and was about to reach for the food when I felt a light touch on my leg. Turning to me, Violet whispered, "We have to say grace first," then quickly added, as she bowed her head, "just do what I do." Violet's father began to speak, offering thanks to God for myriad blessings, including my presence.

After that first Thanksgiving with Violet's family, I would spend the future ones at our house. The holiday of thanks was the rare event in which the adults felt they belonged. Celebrating America's immigrant roots, the occasion held a special appeal to the refugees struggling to find a footing in their new home. Over time, Thanksgiving in our house would take on many aspects of Tết celebration, revolving around family gathering and food. From afar, my siblings would return home for the feast that featured not only turkey, stuffing, and mashed potatoes but also spring rolls, papaya salad, and noodle soup.

As I became more familiar with life in America, my impression of Violet's family as typical Americans began to fade. There were signs that they veered closer to the immigrant life I knew than what I saw on TV's *The Cosby Show* or *Growing Pains*. Both Violet's parents worked for the hospital in town but not as doctors or lawyers like the parents on the TV shows. Her mother was the housekeeper inside the hospital, and her father was the groundskeeper on the outside. For a short time, until Violet's family moved to a nicer home, they lived in a townhouse shared with another Vietnamese family. When it rained, I knew to help Violet hustle for pots and pans to catch dripping water. Even our family's cars looked similar; both were heaps of rusted metal, leaking oil and spewing clouds of smoke. When her ride pulled up after school, Violet often did the same thing I did, hopping in quickly, then crouching down in the back so as not to be seen.

The impression I had of Violet from our first encounter, however, endured over time. After school, Violet was often busy running errands for friends from church, delivering meals to sick neighbors, or serving as a candy striper at the hospital (which, she explained to my disappointment, involved no candies). Once Violet mentioned that she had babysat the night before. When I asked what she was going to do with her newfound wealth, she said that she had declined the parents' payment. As they did not have much, she was just glad she was able to help.

My father was a firm believer in the power of music in learning English. Heeding his advice, I signed up for chorus when I started sixth grade, but as soon as the music teacher picked up her baton, I regretted my decision. She said we would warm up with a song that everyone knew, "Twinkle, Twinkle, Little Star." I stood silent as the kids belted out a tune I had never heard before. In the following weeks, we would move on to other songs that everyone also seemed to know. "You know Dasher and Dancer and Prancer and Vixen. You know Comet and Cupid and Donner and Blixen," the kids sang. But I didn't know any of them or even what a reindeer was.

My anxiety was bearable until the teacher began asking different students to stand up and sing alone. One day she finally called on me, but it was not to sing. She wanted me to see her after class.

"I know you just came to America," she said. "I think it's great that you signed up for chorus. But don't worry, I won't call on you to sing unless you raise your hand." Handing me a thick folder, she said that the song lyrics she had compiled were mine to keep.

In my scant knowledge of American culture, Christmas carols were the most puzzling. In *Winter Wonderland*, I thought Parson Brown was *person brown*, a Hispanic snowman. I loved the melody even as I had no idea why it was important to mention skin color in a song about snow and sleigh bells or why this unusual snowman would want to know if I was married. In the reindeer song, I had sung, "You'll go down in HIS-STO-RY," mimicking the kids around me. With the folder of lyrics, I realized what we had been singing was not two separate words, *his* and *story*, but only one word, *history*. The word had been split into three syllables, in fact, pronounced in the way that my Filipino English teachers had drilled into us never to do.

At home, I pored over all the words that I had been miming in class. With time to absorb the information, I finally understood the story of Santa and the young caribou with the red nose who defied his bullying peers to become so famous.

As I became familiar with the tunes, I gradually shed my fear of singing in class. My teacher was delighted in my transformation and one time even asked if I wanted to sing by myself. But my newfound confidence extended only so far, and I declined her offer. Music turned out, as my father had predicted, to be a wonderfully effective way to learn English. Decades later, whenever I sing our national anthem, I can still see the lyrics streaming across the well-worn page from long ago.

The class that helped me even more with English was my ESL (English as a Second Language) class. Our teacher was familiar with all the quirky errors that Vietnamese speakers often made: mixing up tenses, disregarding plurals, dropping ending sounds. "There's no cow in because," she often said, aware of our tendency to sound out English words as we would in Vietnamese. Homing in on our mistakes, she insisted that we speak to each other only in English. She asked about our lives outside school, then used this knowledge to help ease our transition. She realized, for example, that Vietnamese cuisine didn't use dairy, and so for classroom celebrations, instead of pizza she would always get us fried chicken. She reminded us that other immigrant kids before us had encountered as much difficulty, but they persevered and eventually adjusted, and so would we if we kept learning.

When I entered seventh grade, I began hearing mention around our house of a test called the SAT. According to my father, doing well on this test was the key out of *tất cả mọi chuyện* (the total of all problems) for my brothers and me. *Tất cả mọi chuyện* was my father's shorthand for our circumstances in America. The way out, as I understood it, had little to do with the answer to the question I was often asked at school, "What do you want to be when you grow up?" What I wanted didn't really matter. What mattered was that I had to be able to support myself. This meant a professional career, one that could only be obtained by having a college education.

In Việt Nam, my father had been consumed with finding us an escape route. In America, I recognized the same determination in his efforts to help my siblings and me to get into college and to pay for it. An avid reader, he sought out information regarding college admission requirements, loans, and scholarships. He advised my sisters Chị Tư and Chị Năm, already in college in the neighboring town, on how to apply for grants and work-study programs. For my brothers and me, he concluded that good grades in school and high SAT scores were the key. It was around this time that he insisted that my brothers and I phase out the paper routes to concentrate on our studies.

I wanted the key for getting out of *tất cả mọi chuyện* that my father had mentioned, except I didn't know exactly what the SAT was. I would discover the answer inside a thick book that he had brought home for Cu Anh, a junior in high school. On the outside cover, the letters *S A T* stood out prominently in red ink. Looking inside, I was amazed to discover what I had been looking for but had been unable to articulate. Until then, I had learned English mostly by rote, memorizing phrases of dialogue or song lyrics exactly as I had read or heard them. What I had learned only touched upon the surface of grammar. With so many vagaries unexplained, the English language often seemed like a mystery, one I had come to assume I could never fully understand.

Laid out before me now in the big SAT book were pages upon pages devoted to English grammar. As if someone had shone a brilliant light into a dark cavern, I could make out the maze. There was a whole chapter devoted to verb tenses, from the basic to the complex. The illumination even extended to the most confounding of all: the perfect-progressive tense. For the first time, I understood why it was correct to say, "I've been working my whole life," but not, "I've been knowing you my whole time." Stative vs. dynamic verbs, mood, voice, case—I reveled in the unearthed secrets.

The SAT book also contained lists of vocabulary words, the chosen few from the sea of many. I wanted to know them all. "Argot: slang or jargon" appeared on the top right column of a page. Only I had no idea what either "jargon" or "slang" meant. The accompanying sample sentence—"In the argot of the underworld, he was taken for a ride" —only added to my confusion, because I didn't know what "underworld," or "taken for a ride" meant, either. I turned to the dictionary for help, digressing increasingly further from where I had started. But in the end, as always, I was glad, because from just one word, I came to know many others. Encountering any of them later while reading something, I would feel a rush of excitement, as if I had run into an old friend at an unexpected place.

For many adults in America, the SAT might evoke less-than-fond memories, but for me, it occupies a singular place. In preparing for the college-admission test, I fell in love with the English language, from its vast vocabulary to the precision of its meaning to the versatility of its sentence construction and even to the way it sounds. I came to embrace fully a language that I had once found so maddening.

By the time I entered eighth grade, I had graduated from ESL to regular English class. In two years, my command of English, along with knowledge of American culture, had improved significantly. I had shed the thick accent and bewildered looks of a fresh-off-the-boat immigrant. On the first day of school, I was looking forward to meeting new teachers and seeing which friends were in my classes. My excitement evaporated when I arrived in math class. I instantly recognized the laugh ingrained in my memory with images of flying books. Until then, I had not had any classes with the boy who had caused me such misery back in sixth grade.

He was already in his seat when I entered the classroom. An empty desk next to his turned out, as luck would have it, to be my seat assignment. Joking around with other kids, he didn't seem to notice when I sat down. Throughout the period, I avoided looking in his direction. At the end of class as we were packing up, I heard:

"Hey, what did she say our homework is?"

I turned to look at him. For once, our faces were at the same level, and I wasn't on the ground looking up.

"You don't remember what you did?" I asked in crisp, clear English.

"No, what'd I do?" he said. His surprise was evident.

I didn't know what to make of his answer. He had to remember.

"You knocked my books on the floor when I was in sixth grade. You kept doing it after I told you to stop," I said, drawing out each word with anger long suppressed.

"No, I didn't! I don't know what you're talking about," he said. The surprise in his voice rose to match his conviction.

"Well, you did! And I don't know what the homework is. You'll have to ask someone else." It did occur to me that such hostility on my part could exact more torment. But my worry turned out to be groundless, as the boy never bothered me again, at least not in the way that I had feared. The bother came from his endless requests for my help with math problems. For a long time, I either ignored his questions or pretended I didn't know the answers.

Back in sixth grade, I was certain that the boy had spent his days outside school mapping out my routes and planning my despair. Two years later, I realized that I had been mistaken. The boy had not cared enough about me to do any of that. Most likely he was just bored when he saw me in the hallways. Knocking books from the arms of a befuddled girl provided momentary humor, a relief from boredom. I was just one of many hapless kids who were easy pickings and whose faces he instantly forgot. He had no memory of my torment, as it meant nothing to him.

As the school year went on, the laugh, the raucous howl of indifference, continued to make me wince, but my anger did start to cool. I sometimes answered his questions when they did not require much effort on my part. Being civil felt much lighter than being annoyed. It also seemed pointless to hang on to a grudge when the bully did not even remember.

A DREAM RETURNED

T he dream of having his own business returned to my father during his long hours at the bakery. He envisioned a sandwich stand, much like the *bánh mì* carts found at every street corner in pre-Communist Sài Gòn, featuring the quintessential Vietnamese sandwich. It didn't seem to concern my father that outside the small Vietnamese community in our town, few had ever tasted or even knew what a bánh mì sandwich was. Layers of roast meat inside a crispy French baguette smothered with liver pâté and homemade mayonnaise, topped off with pickled carrots, cilantro, slices of cucumbers, fresh chili peppers, and a few dashes of soy sauce—the sandwich had long been a popular food staple of the masses in Việt Nam.

The hybrid of flavors from the East and the West had its roots in the French colonialism of Việt Nam. In a culture known for being wildly adaptive to foreign culinary influences, the simple baguette that the French had filled with only ham, cheese, or butter grew into a smorgasbord of flavors eaten for breakfast or a midday snack. It grew in popularity from the 1920s to the 1950s, when it really took off. Having seen how popular the sandwich was in Việt Nam, my father had a hunch it could hold the same appeal for the American public. Unlike other Vietnamese food, the bánh mì sandwich had many ingredients familiar to Americans. He believed this would make its crossover to America more likely.

"I'm going to give MacDonald's a run for its money," my father joked. In his David-versus-Goliath declaration, I sensed a fierce determination.

While my father described his vision for the sandwich shop, I only imagined the daily grind of owning a restaurant. Having spent time at the bakery as well as listening to my parents' conversations, I understood that much was involved in owning a food business. Apart from preparing and serving food, there was the restocking of supplies, preparation for the next day, and continual vigilance over every detail. There would be little down time for my parents to spend with us.

More than fancy clothes, birthday parties, or vacations, what I wanted in America was for my parents to have a more regular "9-to-5" job, work that would pay enough while allowing time at home. That, for me, was the American dream. Owning a restaurant was the antithesis. Everyone in the family would be involved, even though my parents would bear the brunt of the work. If the shop turned out to be a success, as my father hoped, the extra work would consume my parents even more, and I would see them even less.

"Ba, please don't do it! Can you please just find a regular job?" I pleaded, appealing to my father any chance I could. I didn't have to convince my mother, as it was clear that she did not share my father's enthusiasm for starting a business. "We're too old for all the headache," I often heard her grumble. Despite her reservations, I suspected that in the end she would yield to my father. Knowing that he was set on a dream, it was inconceivable that she would do anything but help him make it happen.

Somewhere in their long marriage, my parents seemed to have morphed into one being, sharing the same dreams and worries. In response to daily stresses, they had their squabbles, but my father almost always gave in to my mother for home-life details. In many ways, the undisputed head of our household was the archetypical Vietnamese patriarch—reserved, prideful, authoritarian. But unlike some men of his generation, particularly successful men, my father remained devoted to his bride from long ago. In return, my mother trusted my father completely, deferring to him for every major decision in their lives.

The move to America, much like the transition to the countryside of Việt Nam, was hardest on my mother. Unlike my father, who had traveled widely inside and outside Việt Nam, she was a homebody without much desire for travel or adventure. What my mother had was a steely resolve and a survivalist sense of pragmatism. This combination of will and practicality enabled her to adapt to farm life in the countryside and the equally challenging circumstances in our new home in America.

But perhaps what sustained my mother most throughout all the turbulence was my father's devotion. I sensed early on that my mother was the most important person in my father's life. When she cooked, he lingered in the kitchen. When she sewed, he read nearby. In America, they often studied English together. My mother's preferred reading material was the daily *Dear Abby* advice column, which offered both English and cultural lessons. As they dissected the meaning of an unfamiliar word or American custom, she would make gentle fun of his peculiar French-accented pronunciation, and he would tease her about her guilelessness.

One afternoon after my father picked me up from school, we went home along a different route. He then turned into the parking lot of Howard's, our town's most popular supermarket. As we drove past the main entrance, my father waved to the owner, who was outside greeting customers. "Hello, Mr. Ngo," Mr. Howard called out. I couldn't think of a reason why Mr. Howard would know my father by name. My father continued toward the back of the parking lot to an area I hadn't known existed. Our car eased to a stop in front of two enormous metal bins piled high with empty cardboard boxes, broken crates, and other discarded items.

"Do you see it?" My father asked, pointing in the direction of the garbage.

I looked around to search for what my father might have in mind. Behind the metal bins, I spotted a shed, dusty with swaths of paint peeled off and slightly smaller than our one-car garage. For months, my father's vision for his business had vaguely swirled in my mind. Now I could visualize it.

"Ba, is that what you have in mind for the bánh mì shop?" I asked.

"What do you do think?" He turned away from me, and I only saw the back of his head, partially covered by a faded baseball cap. Yet I could clearly envision the hope on his face awaiting my affirmation. I realized that the time for protest had passed.

"It's good, a little run down, but I think you can fix it up," I said. Inside the vortex of love, loyalty, and resentment, I remained quiet during our ride home. I didn't bother to ask my father what I so much wanted to know: how in the world did he manage to find an abandoned shack in the back of a supermarket parking lot that fit so well for the purpose he had mind?

That night, my father gathered all of us in the living room to announce the news that the sandwich shop was a go. He said that the owner of Howard's Supermarket had agreed to let him fix up the shed however he wanted. For $100 a month, he could place the renovated shop on the other side of the front parking lot, facing the supermarket. None of us was surprised that my mother had already known about the plans. Still seeming wary, she nevertheless reminded us how much it meant for my father to be his own boss and urged everyone to give our total support to the patriarch who had sacrificed so much for the family.

The next few months were a flurry of activity as we transformed the beat-up shack into a sandwich shop. At the time, my parents were still working at the Golden Croissant Bakery, and my brothers and I still had a few paper routes. In the spare time outside work and school, we all prepared to get the shop ready, doing everything on our own and hiring a professional only as a last resort.

It quickly became apparent that the process wasn't going to be easy or fast. There were countless trips to City Hall to get approval for work to be done around the shop. I sometimes accompanied my father on these missions, during which we often found out that it was not enough for things just to work. "It's not up to code," we heard from one inspector after another. The perfectly functioning sink had to be replaced because it was not deep enough; the bathroom, with its big window, still needed a vent; the plumbing had to be reconfigured to accommodate a grease trap.

My father's vision materialized more fully when the renovations were finished and the appliances began to arrive. The arrival of the cash register completed the transformation inside the small space infused with the smell of fresh paint and hope. We took turns pressing and testing the array of buttons. In the beginning this contraption seemed to have a mind of its own, discharging its drawer forcefully at random intervals. The cash register took up most of the space on a side counter. Its size mirrored my father's hopes for the future of his business.

While my parents were intimately familiar with bánh mì sandwich varieties, from the overstuffed hoagies in Sài Gòn to the more sparing baguettes elsewhere, they knew little about the other sandwich on our menu—the hamburger. My father set out to learn as much as he could.

One weekend, he came home with take-out bags from Burger King, Sonic, Wendy's, and McDonald's. We helped him take apart each hamburger to inspect its components. My father wanted our thoughts on every detail, from the thickness of the meat patty to the crispness of the lettuce and the softness of the buns. After the discussion came my favorite part—the taste test. We were surprised to discover that each hamburger, despite having essentially the same ingredients, had a distinctive flavor. Wendy's, with its well-seasoned beef and buttery buns, prevailed as the focus group's favorite. McDonald's, despite our familiarity, came in last. While we offered our opinions, my father took notes, nudging us to elaborate even more.

"Maybe we can add our own touches," he commented amid the empty wrappings. Whatever touches my father had in mind, I had a suspicion *nước mắm* (fish sauce) would find its way into the ingredients as it had with other American dishes we had attempted at home. None of us, including my mother, thought tinkering with the hamburger was a good idea. Given our unanimous opposition, my father agreed to leave the classic American sandwich as it was.

The final transformation on the outside of the shop occurred when my brothers hung our single professionally painted sign with the name of the business: "Budget Sandwiches." My father had seen the word "Budget" on the sides of a truck. He thought the name would appeal to budget-conscious customers looking for a quick, tasty meal. It had not occurred to my father, or to any of us, that what might be a great name for a car-rental company might not sound so appealing for a food place. But like other cultural subtleties, the linguistic nuance, at the time, lay beyond our grasp.

Budget Sandwiches debuted in the spring of 1987. For the grand opening, my father hoped to see a diverse crowd, drawn in by bánh mì's affordable price. For Vietnamese customers, the hot baguette offered a familiar taste of the old homeland. For non-Vietnamese, the sandwich with familiar ingredients presented a culinary adventure that wasn't too exotic. My father was betting that anyone who tried the sandwich would leave our shop thrilled with their find, eager to spread the word to his or her friends. In time, the line of customers waiting outside our stand would grow even longer. "Cheap, tasty, convenient. What is there not like in a bánh mì sandwich?" my father wondered aloud.

But reality did not match my father's vision. Our opening day turned out not to be so grand, with far fewer customers than he had anticipated. Most were Vietnamese. The few non-Vietnamese customers we had chose a hot dog or hamburger over the bánh mì sandwich after tasting the free sample that we offered. At the end of the day, our total revenue came out to $56. After accounting for rent and other expenses, our profit was about half of that amount.

In the following days and weeks, we did not fare much better. Our daily revenue hovered around $60. The bulk of our customers continued to be Vietnamese. Each day we used the cash register less, as we realized that it was just easier to figure out the small calculations in our heads. The emblem of my father's hope—the giant with the awesome computing power—sat idle, serving mainly as a cash box. The Golden Arches down the street had nothing to fear.

After Budget Sandwiches opened, my parents' days took on a different routine. In the morning, they would leave for work together. As my mother never learned to drive, my father was her chauffeur. At the shop, their day would be punctuated by moments of hectic service mixed with long stretches of down time. In the lull after the lunch rush, my father would close the shop to take my mother home, then return to the shop by himself.

In my mother's absence, my father always maintained that he could manage the occasional pile-up of orders on his own. When I offered to come to the shop after school, he always insisted that I stay home to do homework and only show up at closing time to help clean up. But guilt tugged and prodded me to come to the shop much earlier most days. He didn't send me away and in fact only seemed to confirm my suspicion that he needed the relief.

In my new after-school job, I traded newspaper ink-stained hands for bánh mì jalapeño-stung fingers. I didn't bother to hide my resentment that we were now in the restaurant business, something that I had never wanted and lobbied against. Doing homework, talking on the phone with friends, or watching shoppers around the supermarket parking lot, I preferred them all to preparing and serving food. I knew we needed customers, yet I resented their demands. I viewed every order as an annoying disruption. A small order was still tolerable, but a big order meant a frenzy to prepare food, followed by another to restock supplies.

Cilantro, mayonnaise, roast meat—most of our ingredients had a short shelf life. How much to stock was never clear. Too much resulted in perishable ingredients getting discarded when there was a lull in customers. Too little led to unmet demand during unexpected spikes in business. We never seemed to be able to find the right balance.

At times, I just preferred that the customers stay away.

"I think there's someone heading toward us," my father announced one day. It was twenty minutes before closing time. The floor had already been swept, the meat slicer with its fearsome blade washed clean. My father still sounded hopeful. I stopped what I was doing to look out at the figure heading toward us in the fading light. I was also filled with hope, but of the opposite kind from my father's.

"Ba, he turned the other way," I said. "I'm going to flip the sign over, OK?"

My father glanced at the clock, then at me. Letting out a small chuckle, he nodded. Before long, I would stop informing my father altogether. If I saw anyone heading toward us while we were cleaning up, I would quickly turn the sign over to CLOSED. Over time, I noticed my father's enthusiasm for customers who came at the end of the day also waned. Our initial closing time of 8 p.m. moved up to 7:30, then 7.

At night, the work from the shop followed us home and seemed to have no end. In between homework, my siblings and I would take turns shredding carrots, whipping mayonnaise, slicing up old baguettes to make toast. My mother would stand by the stove roasting meat, making meatballs, preparing food that she could not make in the small confines of the shop. When not helping my mother, my father would be at the kitchen table paying bills or going over inventory. Each day ground into the next in the continuous scramble to eke out a living. So relentless was the struggle that at times, in exhaustion, my mother would wonder aloud which was harder: running Budget or escaping Việt Nam. A hyperbole we all understood for a sentiment we all shared.

To increase our revenue, my father realized we needed to draw in more customers. As any paid advertising was beyond our budget, he had my brothers paint the promotions onto the menu boards leaning against the shop. My father applied every advertising gimmick he observed—two for the price of one; buy two, get one free; free soda with every order. I learned to distinguish the difference between half-price and two-for-the-price-of-one deals. In both cases, the discount was the same, but for the customer, the half-price discount was better, as he or she had the option of buying just one item. For the owner, the two-for-the-price-of-one offer was preferable because it guaranteed the sale of two products.

Hoping to expand our reach beyond the Vietnamese base, my parents added other items to the menu that were considered more mainstream: fried rice, French fries, and Chinese eggrolls. While the latter two came frozen in a package and only needed to be refried, fried rice had to be made from scratch. At $5 per order, it was the most labor intensive. Hunching over a hot skillet, I had to work fast to stir the mound of rice so that the grains wouldn't clump together. While my arms ached, the rising steam added even more misery to the hot and humid Gulf Coast summer. As it was already difficult preparing one portion, it was even more arduous to combine multiple orders. I came to detest the item that was our most profitable. Out of my father's earshot, I sometimes said we were out of rice as soon as someone expressed an interest.

While the promotions and new menu items did attract more customers, most of our business continued to come from the Vietnamese community, mainly the fishermen. Many Vietnamese immigrants along the Gulf Coast had taken up shrimp fishing because was work that required little English or capital. It also allowed extended families to pool their savings to buy their own boats and work together. Staying out at sea for weeks at a time, the fishermen needed to stock up on supplies. Many would order ten or twenty of our bánh mì to take with them to eat on the first few days of the trip.

So dependent on the fishermen, our business cycle would come to mimic theirs. Oddly, our daily revenue would follow a pattern that vaguely matched the Fahrenheit degree temperature outside. Summer was the height of shrimping activities and thus the busiest time for our shop. The column of sold items extended all the way to the bottom of the page on the clipboard where my father kept tally of all our sales. In the summer, our daily revenue usually hovered around $80–$90, occasionally breaking $100.

In the winter, shrimping season came to a close. As the fishermen stayed inland to take on other work, the column of sales rarely reached past the middle of the tally sheet. Our daily revenue dropped to about $40-$50, at times dipping to $30, even $20. Some days, we barely made enough to cover expenses to keep the shop open. The dismal earnings in the first winter came as a shock but never changed much over the years. We learned to just wait out the cold weather until the fishermen returned when we might earn enough to have some savings.

Despite the American public's indifference to the bánh mì sandwich, my father never lost faith that it would catch on. With unflagging zeal, he continued to steer non-Vietnamese customers who came to our shop to give his proud creation a try. For all his efforts, the bánh mì sandwich never made the successful crossover to the mainstream in the time that our family owned the sandwich shop.

As it turned out, the entrepreneur betting on his hunch wasn't wrong; he was just ahead of his time. In the years since, as Vietnamese immigrants across America set up other bánh mì shops, the sandwich finally gained traction in the age of celebrity chefs and food blogs. The eye-catching baguette, not too exotic yet tasty and affordable, appealed to young Americans looking for a culinary adventure. If my father were alive today, he would be so pleased to witness the phenomenal popularity of the bánh mì sandwich in countless cities across his adopted homeland.

By high school, I had shed much of my resentment for working at the shop. I no longer hid whenever kids or teachers I knew approached the store. At school,

I gamely took down requests from pranksters who thought it was hilarious to place orders with me in class. At the shop, I had figured out a system for studying while doing work. On the walls near where I had to stand in place to wash dishes, peel carrots, or whip mayonnaise, I would tape notes from my classes or English vocabulary lists.

My culinary skills had also improved. Preparing food no longer seemed like conducting an experiment with wildly unpredictable results. Instead of a curdled mess of separated oil and egg yolk, I could count on producing light, fluffy mayonnaise; in place of soggy rice and eggs, I could end up with perfectly crisp fried rice. I had internalized the protocol for assembling the bánh mì sandwich: Warm up the bread just enough for the outside to be crispy but the inside still soft. Spread a generous dollop of mayonnaise and pâté on the warm bread. Sprinkle a few dashes of soy sauce. Add roast meat. Top with pickled carrots, cucumber slices, jalapeño peppers, and cilantro, in this exact order to make the sandwich pretty.

With my budding expertise, I grew more comfortable being at the shop by myself. When I was younger and easily flustered, customers sometimes offered to come inside to help. "No, thanks, I'm fine," I said each time. Some kept insisting despite my explanation that it was against health regulations, not to mention odd, for customers to be in the kitchen preparing their own food. A few ended up cancelling their orders and said that they would come back only when one of my parents was around.

I acquired my skillset just in time to put the skills to full use. For two weeks in the summer before I entered tenth grade, my brother and I had to run the sandwich shop for my parents. They were out of commission because of my mother's knees.

In Việt Nam, my mother was already struggling with knee pain. She had found relief in various folk medicines, acupuncture, and *dầu xanh*, the analgesic green oil considered by many Vietnamese to be the panacea for all kinds of aches and pains. In America, her arthritis worsened. Many mornings, she needed my help getting out of bed. Sprinkling a few drops of *dầu xanh* onto my palms, I gently rubbed her stiff, swollen knees. As the *dầu xanh* seeped into her skin, the heat from the oil thawed her knees back to life. To lighten her mood, I would recount stories from Việt Nam or talk about my friends and school. But my mother, the ever-curious English learner, preferred another topic. She often asked me to explain an English word or phrase that she had encountered somewhere.

In the beginning some of the words she asked me seemed obscure. "Antiquated," I discovered, meant "old," but I suspected that neither of us would need it in our daily conversations. "Packing heat" was not the most natural way for a small Vietnamese woman to say "carrying a gun." In these lessons, I shared with my mother the nuances of the English language, rarely emphasized in books, that had caused me to stumble. Sesame has three syllables and is not pronounced like "see, same." The *o* in *oven* is pronounced like *ə* and not like *ō* as in *open*. In my mind, certain English words and phrases are forever linked with the wintergreen scent of *dầu xanh*, the radiating warmth from my mother's knees, and the softness of her skin.

One morning, about five years after we arrived in America, my mother woke up with pain much worse than usual. No amount of stretching or massaging seemed to help. At the health clinic in town, she was told that she needed to have her left knee replaced. Because we had no private medical insurance, my father applied for her to have the surgery at the University of Texas Medical Branch, a nonprofit teaching hospital in Galveston known for treating patients with no place else to go. To our relief, my mother's application was approved. The operation, only a few weeks away, would require her to be in Galveston for two weeks.

When my father said he would stay with my mother, Bảy immediately volunteered to keep the shop open with me. By this time, all my other siblings had left home. While I understood that our family could not afford the loss of income for a full two weeks in the busy summer season, I had little desire to manage the shop with only my brother for such a long time. Being more experienced than Bảy, I would have to shoulder a majority of the daily responsibilities. But seeing no alternative, I did not protest Bảy's offer.

In the short time before the operation, my parents did everything they could to prepare us. My father, concerned with the shop's security above all else, made Bảy practice boarding up the windows and made me practice locking up each night. At home, my mother showed me how to roast meat, in case we had so much business that we ran out of the food she had prepared.

On the day of the surgery, my parents left the house when it was still dark. After seeing them off, I went back to bed only to hover on the edges of sleep. In my parents' absence, it felt as if I was back in the countryside of Việt Nam on a night when my father was away planning our escape, and everything seemed vaguely ominous. I grabbed my pillow and ran to Bảy's room, but found him asleep in the living room. I squeezed in on the other end of the couch. For the next few hours, with my brother's snoring a most calming salve, I joined my cartoon friends on TV in their adventures.

We opened the shop at 8 a.m. Bảy removed the burglar-prevention planks off the sliding windows, a small one on the side and two bigger ones in the front, then leaned them outside the shop to display our menu. I set up everything inside, including putting together the meat slicer. After what felt like our own grand opening, we waited for customers. In the lulls, we played cards, listened to music, and argued. Time seemed to stretch on without end.

Before my parents left, they had emphasized that they only wanted us to maintain things and not attempt anything extra. Still, I wanted the shop to thrive under our watch. All morning, I had been reminding customers of the buy-five-bánh-mì-get-one-free deal. "Buy two more, and you can get one free," I nudged a customer who had placed an order for three. When he responded that he couldn't possibly eat all six, I suggested that I could keep the vegetables for the extra bánh mì separate. This way, he could save whatever he didn't eat and warm the bread when he wanted. In the past, my father had mentioned the promotion only when the order was for four sandwiches or more; I was now pointing it out to every customer.

After the lunch rush, the light but steady stream of customers came to a complete halt. I understood why my father would close the shop at around this time to drive my mother home. Following his routine, I told Bảy to go home and come back around 4 p.m. In Bảy's absence, boredom became stupefying. Looking around the shop for things to do, I thought of an idea when I spotted the phone book on top of the refrigerator. Taking down the yellow tome, I opened the directory to reveal columns of Nguyens, Phams, and Trans, the Vietnamese last-name equivalents to the American Smiths and Joneses.

I rehearsed the sales pitch in my head, then began dialing. "A lo," I heard. My mind suddenly went blank. Forced to improvise, I gushed about our bánh mì and the great promotions we were offering. With each subsequent call, I became less nervous. Some people listened to the end, then politely declined; others hung up within seconds; a few asked for directions to our shop.

I was still making calls when Bảy returned but decided to call it quits to walk over to Howards Supermarket even though I didn't need anything. I thought of all the times I had been upset with my father for leaving just as I showed up. Until that day, I had never been inside the shop for so many hours. I finally understood the urge to get away from the smells of roasted meat and refried oil inside the tiny space. When we closed at 7 p.m., it felt as if I had lived at the shop for the whole summer.

At night, my father called to tell us that my mother's surgery had gone well. He quickly switched to asking about our day. I had anticipated the question that was the fuel for my phone solicitations and sales pitches. I had wanted to tell my father, "We did great. You won't believe how much we made." Instead, I answered simply, "We only made $76."

"Good, good," my father said. His voice seemed lighter. Unsure how he would feel, I decided not to tell him about the phone calls, which drew in two customers and added $6 to our revenue. Before hanging up, my father asked if I had remembered to lock up. Of course, I answered.

"Chanh, thức dậy!" (Chanh, wake up!), a voice said. It sounded different. I realized that it was Bảy's voice, not my father's. Within a short time, my brother and I were back at the Budget hut. Standing on the cylinder block, a makeshift stepping-stone by the side door, I dug inside my purse for the key. To my growing panic, there was none. I then remembered the stop we had made at the dumpster on the way home the previous evening and realized that I must have accidentally thrown it out along with the garbage. Paying for a locksmith was out of the question, and Bảy, however handy he might be, couldn't possibly pick a lock. The only way to get inside had to be through the bigger front windows, which we would have to force open by breaking the clasps holding them in place. But first, I had to tell my brother what had happened.

"What do you mean you threw away the key?" Bảy repeated yet again. He had just finished removing the last plank from the front windows and was still standing on the raised wooden platform where customers stood to place their orders.

"Bảy, I don't know. Can you please just help me get inside?" I no longer bothered holding back my tears. As long as I had known my brother, they had never failed to elicit his sympathy.

"Fine, we'll try breaking the window clasps," he said, moving over to make room for me on the platform. With our hands firmly planted on the window, we pushed our weight against the glass while sliding it to the side. At first, the window creaked slightly but didn't budge. Suddenly, we heard a loud snap; the window zoomed to the right, taking our arms with it. The scent of bánh mì escaped into the open air.

Bảy hoisted himself off the platform and through the window into the shop. I ran around to the side door and waited for him to open the lock from the inside. The door swung open with an intensity I hadn't expected. My brother glared down at me, as angry as I had ever seen him.

"Chanh, the door wasn't even locked!" he yelled, pointing to the key sticking out from the lock on the inside.

It seemed impossible that I could have forgotten to lock up the previous night, a step that I had assumed was automatic. But there was the key hanging from the lock. My decision to forgo sleep to watch TV the previous morning seemed in hindsight to be not such a good idea. I jumped up from the cylinder block into the shop, rushing after Bảy to the cash register. The giant contraption looked intact, with no obvious sign of forced entry. Everything else around the shop also seemed to be in place. Bảy turned to look at me while shaking his head and smiling with relief.

For the rest of the time that my brother and I were in charge, I lost the desire to break sales records or do anything out of the ordinary to impress my parents. As we eased into a routine, each day felt less long but still left us thoroughly exhausted. When my parents came home after two weeks, I was beyond thrilled, filled with a newfound appreciation for what it took to make a living. My mother, with a new knee, slowly regained her mobility, as my father, in his rightful place, took command of the shop.

REAL-LIFE CLASSROOM

udget Sandwiches was a real-life classroom for all of us, especially my parents. American customs and culture, which they had known only in books, came to life. At the shop, my shy mother was forced to speak English to customers and the occasional telemarketers. "I am not interesting!" she would proclaim over the phone. For my mother and native Vietnamese speakers, "interesting" and "interested," like "boring" and "bored," were interchangeable.

As much as my mother struggled with English, she valued being able to speak for herself. "I don't want you to interpret for me forever," she often told me. In her free time, she liked to scribble into or speak aloud from a densely annotated notebook of English words and phrases. Twice a week, at night, she attended an adult ESL class held at my middle school. Whenever I could, I would come with her to class. I generally liked the slow-paced, nurturing atmosphere of any kind of ESL class, but I particularly enjoyed the adult ESL classes. It felt inspiring to learn English alongside exhausted adults who seemed to have an even harder time than I did.

Attending class with my mother also gave us an opportunity to be together. By the time we arrived in America, we were about the same height, but my feelings toward her remained as they were in Việt Nam. In both places, I loved being with my mother, even when she was just doing chores. In the countryside, I sat next to her while she sliced banana trunks for the pigs, and I swam near the ripples of grease as she rinsed dishes in the pond surrounding our thatched hut. In America, I was her sous chef when she cooked and her needle threader when she sewed. When not feeling well, I still asked her to apply *cạo gió*, the scraping off of bad winds that I never cared for. I just wanted her company.

At the sandwich shop, it was not only my mother's English but also my father's that needed deciphering. Even though his command of written English was quite good, his oral skills were a different matter. Many people had trouble understanding his odd accent, a combination of French and Vietnamese intonation, and his habit of interjecting random French words into conversations. Each day at the shop was one long language-immersion class for my parents.

They were not the only ones who had trouble communicating. A few of our customers were Mexican and spoke even less English than my parents did, so at times the communication barriers went both ways. For a long time, an older man would come to our shop during lunchtime to order a hot dog and a Popsicle. My parents always wondered about the combination, since the man had such trouble keeping up with the ices while eating his lunch. When asked, I told my father I wasn't aware of the pairing of hot dogs and Popsicles, like hamburgers and french fries, but wasn't entirely sure. One day the customer showed up at our shop with a newspaper advertisement. When placing his order, the man pointed at an image while making a hand signal for something to drink. My parents finally understood that the man wanted a Pepsi-Cola, not a Popsicle. They had never heard the soda referred to by its full name.

About a year after our shop opened, my father and I were introduced to an American tradition in a way that would leave a lasting impression on my entire family. It was a beautiful spring afternoon. I was doing homework when the phone rang.

"You want fifty sandwich?" I heard my father say in English.

"Buy-five-get-one-free deal, yes, we still have." The excitement in his voice was palpable as he took the largest order we had ever had.

My father was still beaming when he hung up the phone. The fact that the order came from a customer who spoke English was even more important than its size. It seemed that our bánh mì sandwich was on its way to making the crossover to the mainstream public that my father had hoped.

We took out the extra bag of baguettes from the freezer. While I washed more cilantro and whipped up another batch of mayonnaise, my father cut up jalapeño peppers and sliced the roast pork that my mother had just made the day before. With the prep done, we assumed our positions. I was the starter, cutting the bread and warming it up in the toaster oven seven at a time, the most it could hold. After spreading the mayonnaise and the pâté and sprinkling a few dashes of soy sauce, I handed over the warm baguettes for my father to add the meat, carrots, cucumber slices, jalapeños, cilantro, and a touch of black pepper.

"Who do you think it could be?" we asked each other as we worked.

"Maybe people finally figured out how good bánh mì sandwiches are."

"About time," we joked.

Finally, it was done: ten bags, five sandwiches in each. Giddy with anticipation, we waited for the mysterious customer. After half an hour, then an hour, the sandwiches began to lose their crispness. I opened my notebook and resumed my homework from two hours earlier. In the margin, I saw the date—April 1. My chest tightened as I glanced up at my father, who was rearranging the ten bags just so while looking outside expectantly.

"Ba, you know what we're going to have for breakfast, lunch, and dinner for the next few days," I started, knowing that no humor could soften the rest of what I was about to say.

We never found out who placed the order. From the incident, we learned to ask for contact information anytime an order came over the phone. If anything seemed suspicious, we would call back to confirm. Over the years, our family has joked about our various cultural mix-ups in America, but even with time, the April Fools prank never lost its sting.

Other traditions unfolding around the supermarket parking lot were much sweeter. The sea of red, white, and blue on the Fourth of July, the turkeys of Thanksgiving, the decorations at Christmas, and the sound of bagpipes on St. Patrick's Day—I loved them all. For each occasion, I helped my parents decorate our stand to match what we observed around us. Of the festivities, I looked forward most of all to the spring carnival. For days, roller coasters, Ferris wheels, and booths filled with games took over most of the parking lot of Howards Supermarket.

A few years after Budget Sandwiches opened, a man came by and introduced himself as the operator of a traveling carnival that would soon take place over a few days on the supermarket parking lot. He asked if he could hook up his water line to ours for his workers to use while the carnival was going on. My father agreed and offered to charge him only for the actual cost of the water. Along with his payment, the effusively grateful operator included several rolls of tickets to the carnival and said that we could have even more if we ran out. He only requested that we not give away the tickets. I did mostly as he asked, though I did share them with my best friend, Violet.

More than the rides and games, the carnival provided the one opportunity out of the year when I felt rich. With wads of tickets filling my pockets and more stashed back at the shop, I didn't have to think about money. While waiting for Violet to ride yet another nausea-inducing roller coaster, I raced around to the different game booths. Whack-a-mole, dart, ring toss, each offered a chance to win a toy I'd always wanted: a stuffed animal. In our small town of Port Arthur, this was the most excitement we had all year.

PUSH AND PULL

I n America, we were reunited with relatives, many I had not seen since our family left Sài Gòn for the countryside in 1978. Once or twice a year, our extended families would get together at our house for *đám giỗ*, the anniversary of the death of our deceased grandparents. My parents would close the sandwich shop early to host the gatherings filled with *chú, bác, cậu, dượng, thím, dì, mợ, cô*—aunts and uncles from both sides of the family. The titles I called the relatives conveyed the precise nature of their relationship to me, whether the aunt or uncle was maternal, paternal, younger, older, a blood relative, or related by marriage. *Mợ*, for example, refers to the wife of one's mother's brother, whereas *thím* refers to the wife of one's father's younger brother. *Cô* is for one's father's younger sister, *bác* for his older sister, and *dì* for one's mother's sister, older or younger.

When other kids and I came up to offer our greetings, a few relatives freely offered their observations on how we looked or should behave.

"You're too fat."

"You're too thin."

"Your skin could use some deep scrubbing."

Insults or advice? Often it was impossible to tell. Yet so common was such commentary that we all knew just to smile politely and brush off the sting.

Food plays a major role at *đám giỗ* as it does at every Vietnamese gathering. Preparations for the special meal had all the women in the kitchen all afternoon. Any girl deemed old enough was expected to help. The dishes for *đám giỗ* might vary among families, but a few, such as *gỏi* (salad), *cháo* (congee), and *xôi* (sticky rice), remained constant. In America, the recipes were altered to accommodate readily available ingredients. Cabbage replaced green papayas in salad; chicken stood in for more expensive seafood in congee.

A *đám giỗ* feast could not be complete without *chả giò*, a dish synonymous with special occasions. Every Vietnamese family has its own recipe for the fried eggrolls. Besides the basic ingredients of minced pork, carrots, and glass noodles,

199

my mother also added cat-eared mushrooms and taro root. Growing up, I had always thought ours the best, but as an adult I realized that many of my Vietnamese friends thought the same of their mothers' *chả giò*.

After my mother finished preparing the eggroll filling, we gathered around the table to roll *chả giò*, with the novice copying the more experienced. I watched in amazement at the fast, graceful movements of my aunts' fingers. By the time I had finished my one misshapen eggroll, they had several perfectly shaped ones on their plates.

While the women worked, they shared stories of their struggle to adjust in America. In their jobs as cleaners, assembly line workers, and dishwashers, many expressed a deep sense of alienation. Stymied by language and culture, they found the struggle to interact with the outside world as exhausting as work itself. Everything required an explanation—where they came from, the lunch they took to work, even the clothes they wore.

Outside the house, the women stopped wearing *đồ bộ*. The matching blouse and pants, ubiquitous on the streets in Việt Nam, were considered pajamas in America. They learned to wear long-sleeved shirts to cover up the red marks from *cạo gió*, the scratching off of wind. A co-worker at an eggroll assembly plant where one of my aunts worked had asked her if the red lines were bruises from domestic abuse. The women shared with each other practices considered endearing among Vietnamese that they should avoid in America: holding hands while walking, standing close when talking, and offering comfort by squeezing shoulders and arms or caressing a face during a conversation. These were considered an invasion of one's space in America.

Many mentioned that the adjustment was even harder for their husbands. Once the unquestioned authority in the family, the men found their identities shaken. With the wife working, the husband was no longer the sole provider. With the children more knowledgeable, the father lost his status as the all-knowing patriarch.

In the beginning, we all, young and old, struggled to find our footing in our new homeland. After a few *đám giỗ*, I noticed that kids had made enormous progress, but not the adults. Like my parents, my uncles and aunts also turned to their children for help to navigate the cultural maze. It was obvious that they too disliked being so dependent on their children. Even as the parents wanted their kids to acclimate and adjust, it seemed that the more their children succeeded, the further the parents and children grew apart and the deeper the alienation became.

Because my father's English was better than that of many older immigrants, these problems didn't present as much friction in our family as in others around me. But cultural gaps persisted. When my brother and I randomly joked that we could do whatever we wanted—watch any TV show, say anything, eat any food—because "it's a free country," my father would respond with anger at the disrespect and laziness he felt the expression implied.

"Mỹ hóa" (Americanized), my parents would sometimes say to me and my siblings. Meant as an accusation that we had forgotten our roots, the label was tossed out for any conduct not deemed Vietnamese—dating in high school, talking back disrespectfully to adults, staying out late. At times its use seemed gratuitous, as when I declined my mother's offer to put fish sauce on spaghetti or when I used a plate instead of a small rice bowl for dinner. Warranted or not, the criticism stung each time.

Unable to find steady bearings in their new home, many adults openly yearned for the past, a time before the date that was ingrained in our minds, *Ba Mươi Tháng Tư* (April 30, the day in 1975 when Sài Gòn fell to the Communists). For every Vietnamese family I knew, the day stood out as a colossal wedge in the timeline of events, where life was split into distinct "before" and "after" periods. The severed sections of their lifetimes resembled little of each other. In Việt Nam, I had heard my parents say, "Before '75, he was a corporal," to refer to an uncle who became a cycle rickshaw peddler after his release from reeducation camp, and "Before '75, he was a teacher," to refer to a neighbor who sold yogurt illegally from a cart in postwar Việt Nam. In America, I would hear, "Before '75, he was a policeman, a lawyer, a pilot..." to refer to relatives and friends now janitors, convenience store clerks, and assembly workers. "Before '75," and "after '75" — the phrases had become prerequisite to the description of every Vietnamese adult, including my parents.

The displaced refugees sought comfort reminiscing about the abandoned home on the other side of the world. A few times a year, they found it in a Vietnamese musical variety show called "Paris by Night." Recorded in the eponymous city, the program was intended for the Vietnamese population in

France, but its reach quickly expanded across the ocean to the more populous Vietnamese community in America. After a few years, production of the show was even moved to California, following the Vietnamese diaspora's center of mass. My parents always knew when each "Paris by Night" videotape was coming out. Money might be tight, but somehow they always managed the $15 to buy it. Except for the new songs of immigrants yearning for home, much of the music was from before 1975. Banned under Communist rule, many songs had not been heard for more than a decade. Still it usually took only a few notes for my parents and siblings to recognize and exclaim in exuberance the long-forgotten tune suddenly recalled.

More than music, what reminded my parents of Việt Nam were the letters from my second sister Chị Ba, who had opted to stay behind when we left. At the end of each day, my father eagerly checked the mailbox for a light blue envelope, the hallmark of international mail. When a letter arrived, my parents would read and reread the news regarding a grandson they had never met and a daughter they missed terribly.

Around me, every Vietnamese adult seemed to hover on the periphery of fitting in. I often wondered if it was possible for an adult who looked like me to be accepted as fully American. I would find my answer inside our living room.

"Good evening. I'm Connie Chung," she intoned behind the anchor's desk. With a dark mane touching her shoulders and a voice combining authority and calmness, Connie Chung was the weekend news anchor for NBC News. She looked to me like she could be my mother, but there she was on national TV, informing Americans about what they needed to know. I traced the movements of her lips, deep red against porcelain skin, mimicking them and repeating what I heard. No matter my attempts, my voice trailed hers as an imperfect echo.

Until I heard her name, I had thought that the pairing of an American first name and an Asian last name could only be a jarring collision of sounds. A few of my Vietnamese friends had started to call themselves Anna, David, Cathy, to the barely-concealed chagrin of those around them. I once heard my teacher point out the absurdity of such a union.

"Larry Nguyen," the announcer called out, announcing the winner in a math contest.

"Larry Nguyen, now that's something you don't hear every day," the coach, chuckling, whispered to another teacher. He was a devoted coach and teacher who took under his tutelage many Vietnamese students. His comment nevertheless reinforced my suspicion that no matter what cloak we put over ourselves, we would never be fully accepted as American. By merely uttering her name, Connie Chung dismissed this notion.

From school and books, I learned that a person's race should not matter. Yet around me, race seemed to dominate not only how people perceived us but also how we perceived them. In the abstract, I knew that friendship among people from different races, like success for Asians in America, was possible. But I had limited personal experience with non-Vietnamese people. Connie Chung was the first to show that Asian Americans could prosper in America. At the supermarket, Connie smiled from the covers of magazines lining the shelves at checkout lines. The public not only accepted Connie but also seemed enthralled with her. And so was I. I often found myself thinking about her life and what it was like beyond the anchor's desk. Any slight change to her farewell of "Thank you and good night. See you next weekend," had me speculating the kind of day she might have had.

One afternoon in the dead of winter, when sandwich shop customers seemed as rare as Texas snow, I had finished my homework with hours left until closing time. Sitting by the glass sliding window and looking out to the quiet supermarket parking lot, I had an idea. I picked out a crisp new sheet of paper and penned my first and only fan letter.

"Dear Ms. Chung,

I wanted to tell you what an impact you've made in my life. I came to America a few years ago. I've learned English and much about the world from watching you on TV. I just wanted to say thank you very much."

For a long time, I kept the letter, as I did not know where to send it. One day I happened to see the address for NBC News in a magazine at the library. I mailed the letter with little idea of whether it would get to its intended recipient. Weeks later, a big manila envelope arrived in our mailbox. My heart danced as I tore open the package bearing the Peacock logo of NBC News. Inside was an autographed picture of Connie Chung along with a note wishing me luck and encouraging me to do good work in school.

In my junior year, one of my teachers nominated me to a local TV station for a segment called "Student of the Week." I received the news in a phone call one afternoon as I was about to head out to work at the sandwich shop.

"Congratulations! You were chosen for being a good student and for having overcome a lot of hardship," said the caller, who had identified herself as a TV reporter.

Hardship—the word dampened my excitement. In my mind, hardship was just another way to say that we were poor, a fact I knew well. But until we came to America, I had never thought of us as that. In the impoverished countryside of Việt Nam, I had not felt poor, because compared with everyone else, we always had more. When I could have only one bowl of rice at mealtimes, I knew many who had gone without food. Even though I had only a few outfits, some of my classmates wore one nice shirt throughout the year. Back then, I always felt slightly embarrassed for my riches.

In America, even though we had a lot more food and clothes, I would learn what it was like to be on the other side. When we first arrived, we were on welfare. We also received food stamps, which lasted a while longer. In the beginning, I didn't understand that the paper vouchers that we used at the supermarket, the free lunch that I received at school, and the clothes that I wore represented the generosity of the US government and the community. But they were also prominent markers of our poverty. The recognition of our new status made me embarrassed and altered my perception of how others viewed us.

In high school, I cringed each time I took out my free-lunch card. Many times, I ended up skipping lunch. I would have packed food from home, but didn't realize it was an option, since I didn't know anyone who did. When I found out that the Goodwill store, where my sister bought most of my clothes, was a secondhand retail shop, I became paranoid that a girl would come up to me at school to proclaim for all to hear that my outfit had once belonged to her. I stopped wearing used clothes and cycled through the few outfits I had left.

Doing with less and without did not upset me. What I minded was for the world to know.

"On the day of the interview, a cameraman and I will follow you around to see what your day is like," the reporter continued.

"Will you just come to my school? Or do you need to come to my house also?" I asked. At school, amid the sea of similar backpacks and identical lockers, I could blend in. At home, it would be much harder to disguise our circumstances.

"I think the viewers would want to see where you live and what your home routine is like," the reporter added. Met with silence, she quickly said, "It'll be fine! Don't worry!"

Her cheer did quell my anxiety and made me think that perhaps our house could be made presentable enough. I knew with certainty, however, that the camera lens could not extend to the sandwich shop. In my mind, it was the emblem of our hardship. Outside, the hodgepodge menu stenciled in mangled English—French Fry - $1.50, Fry Rice - $5.00—was peeling off. Inside, the small air conditioner, in a perpetual duel with the toaster oven, heaved loudly. For most of the year, the air, smelling of reheated oil and roasted meat, felt hot and uncomfortable. I also didn't want the reporter to interview my parents, putting on display their hesitant English and clothes redolent of sweat and grease.

"I hope it's all right that it'll be just me at the house. My parents will be at work," I volunteered.

"I understand that your parents own a sandwich shop and you help out a lot. Maybe we can also go there and talk to your parents," she suggested.

"I don't think it's a good idea. My parents don't speak much English. They're kind of shy and wouldn't want people around," I answered.

The falsehood in my statement filled me with shame. My parents, who had been actively learning English and conversing with customers for almost five years, would have been fine expressing themselves. Even my introverted mother would likely have welcomed the chance to show off the language skills she had worked so hard to acquire. My father, the dapper dresser, would have been thrilled to jettison his work clothes for something stylish to be in the limelight. Being on TV would have given my parents the rare opportunity to experience for themselves a bit of the American dream for which they had gambled everything, instead of just living in service of that dream for their children. Besides talking about our academic success, my father could show off Budget Sandwiches, his proud creation. Beyond pride, the interview would have provided much-needed publicity for our shop. But as I held the phone in my hand, all I could think of were the tiny shack of the sandwich shop, the grimy clothes, the awkward pauses in my parents' English that would necessitate my coming to their rescue.

"It will be just me at my house. My parents wouldn't want so many people inside the shop," I reiterated.

"That's all right with me. But you should check with your parents. If they change their mind, please let me know," the reporter said before hanging up. But I never checked with my parents. Instead, I simply asked my mother to remain at the store with my father the afternoon of my interview. As with other things going on in my life in school at the time, my parents never asked to participate but just accepted whatever I told them.

Days before, my mother and I dusted and swept thoroughly inside the house. We also tidied up the outside while my father mowed and trimmed the lawn. The day finally arrived. As I exited my bus when it arrived at school, two adults came over to greet me: a man wielding an oversized camera and a stylishly dressed woman with a notepad in her hand. For the next few hours, the cameraman and reporter followed me around school. They talked to my teachers and sat in on my classes. When school let out, the reporter said she would meet me back at our house.

"Your house is lovely!" the reporter exclaimed when I opened the door. I now believe she certainly meant what she said. But at the time, so distorted in my view of how others saw us, I was sure her exuberance masked some sort of pity. Inside our house, the reporter kept tugging her shirt collar. It occurred to me that I should have turned on the air conditioner. To save money, we generally relied just on fans to cool the house. Only in the previous year had we begun to use the air conditioner, but only at night. So accustomed to our house being hot during the day, I had not thought until then that there could be another option.

"I'll turn on the AC," I sheepishly offered.

With a simple flip of a switch, cool air started blowing in. The reporter and I took our seats around the kitchen table while the cameraman set up his equipment. A teapot, swaddled in a home-sewn jacket to keep it warm, sat in the middle of the table. I realized that a cool beverage would have been more appropriate, but not offering tea to an honored guest felt so unnatural that I yielded to the entrenched notion of Vietnamese hospitality. I poured the hot jasmine tea, made earlier by my mother, into three cups.

Between sips of tea, the reporter signaled for the cameraman to begin. She asked about my life in and out of school. My answers led to inquiries about my growing up in Việt Nam, our escape on the boat, the refugee camps, and our early days in America. In observing the reporter observing me, I caught glimpses of how she perceived me and my family. What I detected was a view much more charitable than my own. Of our family circumstances in America, the reporter only saw parents and children working hard. Of my unusual choice of refreshment inside our hot kitchen, she didn't find anything embarrassing.

Toward the end of our interview, with the camera still rolling, I noticed out of the corner of my eye something scurrying on the ceiling. I turned my head slightly, so as not to cause alarm, and glanced upward. My fear was confirmed. Hanging upside down, not far from where we were sitting, was an enormous cockroach, its antennae wagging from side to side.

Snakes, spiders, mice—I don't particularly care for them, but they do not send me fleeing. Roaches, even the dead ones, do. For as long as I can remember, I have had a phobia of these insects. In the wet, muggy climate of Vĩnh Long and refugee camps, I didn't encounter many, even though they thrived in such environment. Perhaps the lack of bright artificial light made them hard to detect at night, and during the day they probably just blended in with the surrounding nature.

Port Arthur was the first place where I encountered roaches that could fly. My presumption about America and its lack of bugs, from the American visitor to our refugee camp in the Philippines, added more shock to the first sighting. The Texas tree roach, befitting its name, lived mostly outdoors. But attracted to light, water, and food, they often wandered into homes, wedging themselves through any openings. Insecticide placed around the perimeter of our house proved to be an effective deterrent. Occasionally, some still managed to come inside. More than anyone in our family, I lived in a stupefying fear of these creatures. If I saw one inside our house, I would run to anyone nearby, begging him or her to get rid of it. If no one else was home, there was the faithful can of Raid Insecticide spray. Deploying the foul-smelling poison required a sustained proximity to a creature I so feared that often I remained frozen long after I finished the deed.

I glanced over at the reporter and cameraman, relieved that neither seemed to notice the enormous brown mass moving above their heads. But relief was fleeting as I became certain from the roach's flared-up wings that it would take off flying at any moment. If it landed on me, any trace of composure I had left would be obliterated.

If there was shorthand for our poverty, a cockroach was it. For everyone watching TV to observe such a sight inside our house was already more than I could bear. For the world to witness it along with my breakdown was a thought so disturbing that I could no longer think straight.

"Are you OK?" the reporter asked in the middle of another question.

"Actually, no. I don't feel so well all of a sudden. Is it OK if the interview ends here?" I answered as I stood up.

"I'm sorry to hear that. Is there anything I can do to help?" She said while nodding toward the cameraman to wrap up. I wanted to let the reporter know that my sudden agitation had nothing to do with her. More than that, I wanted to tell her: "Yes! Yes! You could help me. See that thing hanging down from the ceiling over there? If I turn away, could you please get it off? And could you please not include it in the TV footage?"

"Could we just step outside for some fresh air? I think that would help me a lot," I heard myself say instead. The words sounded as if they were spoken by someone else. I hadn't realized that my mind had settled on the request that made little sense. Outside, the temperature was nearing triple digits, and waves of heat could be seen undulating in the windless air. Without waiting for the reporter's response, I rushed to the front door.

In the mad dash, I thought I had heard a swish in the air behind me. As my hand touched the doorknob, I turned around to look back. On the floor next to the cameraman's tripod was the cockroach. My sudden movement must have jolted it to fly down.

I leaned back against the door, instinctively covering my face with both hands. I had no more plans. In the darkness, I heard:

"Oh man, I hate these. When it's hot like this, they come in from the outside looking for water."

Between my fingers, I saw the cameraman stomping his foot on the floor. He pulled out a napkin from inside his pants pocket and bent down to scoop up the squished bug. He then walked over to the trash can and threw away what was in his hand.

The Student of the Week segment aired some weeks later. In the TV footage, there was no mention of a flying cockroach or a crumpled napkin. But in my mind, those memories, along with the glaring absence of my parents, loomed with such dominance as to displace much else from that day.

When does a new place feel like home? I realized Port Arthur had begun to feel that way when I wrote an essay for my junior-year English class with the theme "Why Am I Golden Triangle Proud?" Until then it hadn't occurred to me that I belonged in our town. The sense of being an outsider, imprinted from our early days, had not yet abated even as I began to adapt.

The Golden Triangle—composed of Port Arthur and its neighboring towns, Beaumont and Orange—held a substantial Vietnamese community. The resettlement of so many Southeast Asian refugees along the Gulf Coast happened by chance, a result of the US immigration policy of scattering immigrants across America. Finding a climate similar to Việt Nam, many decided to stay where they were assigned and found work in the fishing and shrimping industry.

Until the arrival of the first Vietnamese refugees in the mid-1970s, the Golden Triangle had little exposure to Asians outside the coverage of the Việt Nam War on TV. Many locals did not take well to the newcomers. In Texas' Galveston Bay, just over an hour's drive from Port Arthur, members of the KKK white supremacists set fire to several Vietnamese-owned fishing boats and held cross burnings and rallies intended to drive away the new arrivals. It took a lawsuit filed on behalf of the Vietnamese fishermen in 1981 to finally put an end to the years-long campaign of terror.

By the time we arrived in Port Arthur in 1984, the overt hostility was mostly gone. Even so, a sense of division lingered. This mistrust was in many ways reminiscent of what our family experienced in the countryside of Việt Nam after we were forced to leave Sài Gòn. Both there and here, the locals viewed newcomers as a threat to their way of life and as competition for scarce resources. But unlike the homogenous Vietnamese village where an outsider would never be fully accepted, the Golden Triangle eventually weaved the latest group of arrivals into its fabric as it had the Germans, Africans, Mexicans, French, and other previous immigrants. The Vietnamese immigrants ultimately grew and flourished, drawing others to the area. Within a decade of the first refugees' arrival, the rich culture of the Golden Triangle had come to include us.

In absorbing the newcomers, the Golden Triangle was exceptional compared to a village in Việt Nam and in many countries around the world, but it was unexceptional as a microcosm of America. In a land of immigrants, a sense of belonging was possible, it just needed time. This was the conclusion of my essay, which was published in the *Port Arthur News*, the very newspaper my brothers and I used to deliver when we first arrived in our town.

Four years after we moved into Mr. Water's house, our family shrank to just my parents, Bảy, and me. My two sisters, having graduated from Lamar University in Beaumont, had moved away for their jobs, and Cu Anh had left home for Texas A&M University. I went from sharing a bed with my sisters to having my own bed, then my own room. Mr. Water finally had the number of tenants he had initially wanted.

By this time, we all had become proficient enough in English that even my parents could recognize and laugh at the distortion we had made of the name "Walter." Still we continued to refer to our landlords as Mr. and Mrs. Water. Neither ever corrected us. For me, the mispronunciation was a wince-inducing reminder of our early days. But like a nickname coined in childhood, the error had come to represent an understanding between our families. Calling our landlords by any other name felt like a rejection of our immigrant roots.

Fortunately, I no longer needed to use the names as often as I did when we first moved into our house. Except for the monthly rent delivery, I rarely had to cross the yard to ask the "Who pay?" question. Things inside our house just didn't break down as much as before. Perhaps my brothers had already fixed everything, or as Mr. Water liked to remind us: fewer people meant fewer repairs. When something did break, we often just took care of it ourselves without telling Mr. Water.

Occasionally I still had to cross the yard to report some one-off problem. I remember one incident clearly. It was a few weeks before Bảy would leave home for college. All summer, he had been fixing things around the house, changing oil in our cars, cleaning out the storage shed. One morning, I was in the kitchen making breakfast when I heard footsteps trampling around the attic. When they reached where I was standing, they suddenly stopped. A squeaky noise emerged slowly at first, then exploded in a loud crash as pieces of plaster and dust fell all over me and my pot of ramen.

"I'm fine!" I heard Bảy's voice. I looked up to find his feet dangling not far over my head. The ceiling was an open hole.

"Chanh, go ask Mr. Water what we should do and who pay,'" my father said when I called him at the sandwich shop.

I knocked on the Waters' screen door and waited, not sure how to explain what had happened.

"Why did your brother go up there?" Mr. Water cut in before I even finished.

"He was checking out the heater," I answered.

"How did he manage to fall through the ceiling?"

"I don't know. Maybe it's just old?" I said, ready for the wrath to erupt. But that morning, it never did.

"Tell your brother I'm coming over in a minute," Mr. Water grumbled, displaying no hint of anger.

For all his grousing, it was clear that Mr. Water had softened considerably toward our family. He brought over his tools when he saw my father or brothers tinkering with the car. He gave my parents a ride to the sandwich shop when our car could not be revived. He cut out coupons that he thought we could use and asked us to save for him cigarette coupons. My father had given up smoking a few years earlier in order to pass the health screenings in refugee camps.

Inside our kitchen that summer morning, Mr. Water seemed more concerned for his tenant, covered in white dust and plaster, than for his house with a gaping hole in the ceiling. Only after asking Bảy several times if he was all right did Mr. Water start talking about "who pay" and what needed to be done.

A few weeks after he had put the ceiling back in one piece, Bảy left home for the first time—to the University of Texas at Austin. Inside a house filled with his upkeeps, I missed my know-it-all best friend from childhood. Surrounded by cans of Raid, I yearned for those times when I had heard, "Chanh, don't look for a second!" I knew what the warning entailed. Immediately I would clamp my hands over my already-shut eyes while a rolled-up newspaper smashed repeatedly against a surface. The sounds soon turned to those of newspaper crumpling. I kept my face covered, waiting for Bảy to scoop up what needed no mention. Only when I heard his footsteps heading away did I open my eyes.

The cans of Raid were not the only memory triggers. The squeaky door, the difficult math problem, the abandoned volleyball net all made me pause. "That's not how you do it. Let me show you," my brother would say, pushing me aside. The bossy comment used to annoy me even when I needed the help. As I lay on the bathroom floor trying to unclog the sink, how I wished to hear it again. For so long, I had taken for granted that the unsolicited offer, like our time together, had no expiration date. A few times a year, I would find in our mailbox a letter for me bearing an Austin return address. Inside, I would find a $20 bill folded in a sheet of paper. "Chanh, do whatever you want with it." The curt directive was sometimes the only writing on the page.

It was another first of the month as I stood outside the Waters' door with the rent envelope. "In their hands, not under the door," my father's words echoed. I thought of all the times I had waited in this same spot. The past count was many, but the future one was a single digit. With only a few months remaining of high school, I would soon join my siblings in leaving home. Listening for the sounds coming from the other side of the door, I heard the creaking of wheels. I knew that the rent delivery would be fast. Even though Mr. Water no longer scared me, I still didn't know what to say to him beyond the greetings.

"Hi, Mr. Water," I said while handing over the rent.

"Tell your mom and dad to come see me when they get home from work. You come with them too, OK?" I heard as I turned to leave. I spun around, retracing the few steps back.

"Mr. Water, you can just tell me," I said.

"No, no, I want to talk to them myself," Mr. Water responded.

The stroll with my parents across the yard later that evening felt like a march to the principal's office to be informed of some offense I didn't know I had committed. I couldn't think of any reason why Mr. Water would want to speak face-to-face with my parents.

On a small round table on their back porch, Mrs. Water had set up a pitcher of pink lemonade with five glasses. In the seven years that we had been neighbors, this would be the first time my parents and the Waters had sat at a table to share a beverage.

"Sit down, please sit down," Mrs. Water said, her normal exuberance much subdued.

After we had sat and taken a sip of the lemonade, Mr. Water began to speak. Enunciating each word slowly—something I had never witnessed—he told us that he had recently found out that he was very sick. His doctor would not confirm how much time he had left, but he suspected that it was not long.

"Mr. No and Mrs. No, did you understand what I said?" he bypassed me to speak directly my parents. They nodded.

"I want you to buy the house. Y'all been good neighbors. I want Loretta to be near good folks after I pass. You can have it for what I bought it, minus the rent you've paid me."

I glanced at my parents. The stunned expression on their faces made clear that they didn't need my help translating. For me also, the news of Mr. Water's illness came as a shock, but not his warmth toward my parents. Not long after we moved in, Mr. Water was over at our house watching my brothers take apart yet another appliance. "Mr. No, it's not easy, huh?" Mr. Water said to my father while shaking his head. I could tell that he was not referring to the broken washing machine, but rather to my parents having to start over at their age in America. "Your father is a good man," Mr. Water said as he turned to me.

However much empathy my parents may have felt for Mr. Water, they couldn't grant him his wish. It had always been their dream to retire to Houston to be near my oldest sister and her family after I finished high school. My parents had already been trying to find a buyer for the sandwich shop.

Mr. Water died a few months later. His was the first funeral I attended in America. Inside the cold chapel, I was struck by the quiet somberness. The muted sobs from people dressed in black contrasted with the loud wailings of the funerals I remembered in Sài Gòn, where white-clad mourners passed by our house in the days before South Việt Nam collapsed.

"Chanh, go over and see how Mrs. Water is doing," my mother said some time after the funeral.

I knocked on the familiar screen door and waited. For the first time, I had no rent payment to hand over or house repair questions to pose. When Mrs. Water saw me, she hugged me for a long time, then invited me to come inside. On the other side of the door, the house was much smaller and more ordinary than I had imagined.

We sat down at the kitchen table. Mr. Water's folded wheelchair leaned against the wall next to us. Mrs. Water talked about life without her husband and the loneliness she experienced. She pointed to the car in the driveway, then the refrigerator and dishwasher in the kitchen—new purchases Mr. Water had insisted on when he knew he was dying. He didn't want her to have to cope with household repairs for at least a while. She shared stories of their married life and gave me updates on her grown children. She wanted to know what my siblings were doing. She asked about school and my parents.

"You know, Walter might have yelled at y'all sometimes, but he always thought you were good kids. He missed your brothers when they moved away," she said. I hadn't known that.

Our conversation continued much past the time I had thought the visit would end. That afternoon, our talk had nothing to do with the house—with questions of "what broke?" and "who pay?"—and everything to do with the people living in it. For the first time, I felt our worlds overlap even as I realized nothing had changed except our understanding of each other.

EPILOGUE

I arrived at Rice University in the fall of 1991. The campus is an oasis of green with stately archways and pillars inside the bustling metropolis of Houston. In the afternoons after classes were done, I often took the longer route back to my dorm along the tree-lined paths. Beyond the hedges, as any place outside Rice was known, the heat might feel oppressive. But underneath the canopy of live oaks and magnolia trees that blanketed much of the campus, it had dissipated into an intermittent breeze. With no chores waiting, I was in no hurry, my steps a slow amble beneath the shade.

A few rays of sunlight broke through the thicket of leaves to bounce around my feet. My thoughts turned to the sandwich shop and then naturally to my father. In my mind the two are inseparable. I wondered if he had a hard time managing the dinner hours without me, whether it took him long to clean up and set up for the next day, and if, while grocery shopping, he mistook parsley for cilantro yet again, having relied so long on my catching his mistake. If he did it without me there to switch the similar green herbs with quite distinctive tastes, he would discover the mix-up with the key flavor in bánh mì sandwiches the hard way and would have to rush back to Howard's Supermarket while my mother tried to hold off impatient customers. These thoughts could trigger as much anxiety in me as my physics class.

So many afternoons, while waiting for customers behind the sliding glass window at our shop, I had observed similar breakthroughs of light on the ground beneath the awning. With my book open and my mind numb from studying, I looked past them toward the stream of shoppers in the parking lot. Behind me, I could sometimes hear my father's snores coming from the half-open cot, tucked out of view between the bathroom and refrigerator.

All around the supermarket, different customs and traditions of our adopted homeland unfolded from one season to another. During Christmas and New Year's, plants with deep green leaves and flaming red petals filled shoppers' carts. It occurred to me that in America, the poinsettias were analogous to *hoa mai*, a yellow flower ubiquitous around Tết in Việt Nam. On a certain Sunday in the dead of winter, I came to expect the parking lot to be devoid of shoppers. "The Super Bowl is on. People get together and watch it on TV. You should just close your shop and go home," a customer told me. "He went out, didn't he?" my father responded after I had happily relayed the message. "We still need to keep the shop open for customers like him." I also learned that the Fourth of July is not the only holiday bedecked with red, white, and blue. Memorial Day, Labor Day, and Veterans' Day all merited patriotic displays.

As my knowledge of America deepened, so did my understanding of my father. In the beginning at the shop, we scrambled and yelled amid burning bread and smoking oil. During the lulls, I retreated into my own world of homework and friends. Sometime in the afternoons of confinement in the tiny space, I turned to my father. I read to him stories I had written, weaving English and cultural lessons into plotline clarifications. I pointed out pop songs playing on the radio that I liked and dissected their lyrics for him. I talked about school and friends, dragging the reserved Vietnamese father across cultures and generations into the caldron of teenage drama. To gauge his attention, I would pause to offer quizzes on the web of adolescent ties and loyalties among my circle of friends. We both chuckled the rare times he passed the tests. In time, we learned to read each other. We could cobble together dozens of sandwiches, whip up multiple batches of fried rice in little time, our movements in lockstep, few words needed.

I started working at the shop at the onset of my teenage years and left as they ended. In that time, I had found my footing in our new home, but I sensed my father never quite secured his. Beneath the teenage swagger, I always wanted his stewardship. I remember waiting for my father to review my college essay before sending it off. By then my English skills had far surpassed his. "Good, good!" I knew was all he would say, but it was what I needed to hear.

"I think the students at Rice would really like to have a bánh mì shop on their campus," my father said one afternoon while we were cleaning up. It was a few days before I would leave for college. I was sure he was joking, but so jolting was the possibility that I had to turn around to look at him.

"Chanh, you know this stand can be pulled behind a truck if we just put some wheels on it. You can put all the stuff you want to move to school in there," he continued in a tone so matter-of-fact. But in his eyes, I caught the familiar twinkle of pride and mischief.

"So Ba, at college, I can just hop in and hang out with you between my classes?" I knew he wanted me to go along.

"Yeah, just like now," he said, smiling widely.

"Ông Ba Vườn, I don't think so," I said, referring to him by the nickname from what seemed like a different lifetime. But it was a lifetime I had often thought about. I wondered how our lives would have turned out had my parents not taken the gamble to cross the sea. In this alternate existence, my siblings and I might never have been able to leave our small village as my parents had hoped. Surrounded by fields and waters, we would likely have grown up knowing no other life except one of farming and fishing. But that didn't happen, and we reaped the benefit of my parents' decision. *Đời cha ăn mặn, đời con khát nước* (The father's generation eats salt, the child's generation thirsts for water). The proverb describing inherited consequences between generations took on a positive twist as we inherited not debt but fortune.

"Ba, I'm finished thinking about sandwiches when I leave here," I told my father that day. But our afternoons of preparing bánh mì would become intertwined with my memories of canoes, monkey bridges, and running from bees in the countryside of Việt Nam to form the mesh of my childhood experience, a blending of two homes from opposite ends of the world.

Of the different paths back to my dorm, my preferred route was through the main academic quad. I liked to linger on the bench next to Willy's statue, the memorial to the founder of Rice University. As I gazed up at William Marsh Rice, I thought of my father's comment: "We already won the lottery by being here in America." My father made the remark whenever I complained about trivial matters or got annoyed when a scratch-off lotto ticket failed to deliver on its promise of an easy win. For a long time, the refrain would only inflame my frustration. Beneath Willy's watch, I finally grasped what my father meant. In fact, our family had won the lottery, not once but twice. First, by defying the sea in escaping Việt Nam and, second, by arriving in America. The lady of liberty opened her arms to the battered refugees and nursed us back to productivity. Nowhere else could a family like ours have recovered as well in as short a time.

The acclimation process had not been easy. In a sense, we remained on the boat. Only the turbulence no longer came from the waters of the South China Sea but from the struggles of adjustment to our new life. After seven years, my parents and I had arrived at a juncture in our voyage. Ahead, the horizon shimmered with possibilities, but it beckoned only me. As I set out on my own for the first time, I expected to encounter many storms beyond the calm. At times I knew I would be tempted to retreat. "Turning around is not an option!" I hoped I would recall my father's admonition from another storm long ago when I was desperate to hear him surrender. This time, the reminder would roar in my ears as a rallying call and not as a betrayal. It would soothe and strengthen me, pushing me forward.

ACKNOWLEDGMENTS

A late comer to the world of writing, I've been lucky to have encountered many guides to whom I owe a great debt.

To my husband Adam—my biggest fan and fiercest critic, the editor behind every word that I've ever published: Despite our heated discussions, I loved editing the memoir with you. Without you, the book would not have been possible.

To my children (Lillian, Hannah, and Benjamin): Thank you so much for pulling up a chair to read and give me your feedback, even when you had just come home from school and were tired and grumpy. Over the four years that it took to write this book, you passed on to me your newfound knowledge at each stage of school.

To my brother-in-law Eric: I'm deeply grateful for your help clearing out the weeds of the first draft. Your insight and meticulousness never ceased to amaze me.

To my sisters and brothers (Chị Hai, Anh Trưởng, Chị Ba, Chị Tư, Chị Năm, Cu Anh, and Bảy): Thank you so much for entrusting me to tell our family's story. I cherish our time reminiscing about the past, all in the name of research. A special thank-you goes out to Bảy. You were as big a help to me as you had been while we were growing up.

To Violet: Your unwavering faith—our many late-night phone conversations when you told me not to give up—helped sustain me.

To Melanie Richards: Your kindness and grace inspire me every day. You often reminded me that writing gets easier with time. The advice gave me much comfort.

To my agent Glen Hartley at Writers' Representatives: Thank you so much for taking me on and helping me find my way to publication.

To Danielle Chin at Writers' Representatives: As your suggestions made the book so much better, your cheer did the same for my day.

To Laurel Ferejohn: Your copyedits and proofreading gave the manuscript the polish it needed and made it shine.

To Mark Lasswell: On the advice that a writer should start and end with the strongest arguments, I'd like to conclude by thanking you. As the op-ed editor of The Wall Street Journal, you published my first story and suggested that I should write a memoir, then helped edit the manuscript in its early stages and introduced me to the world of publishing. I treasure your mentorship, and above all, your friendship.

ABOUT THE AUTHOR

Oanh Ngo Usadi was born in Sài Gòn but grew up in an orchard in the Mekong Delta. When she was eleven, her family escaped Việt Nam as part of the mass exodus of boat refuges. In 1984, they settled in a small Texas town where her father, the eternal entrepreneur, opened a *bánh mì* sandwich shop.

Oanh's writings have appeared in the *Wall Street Journal, Washington Post, Forbes,* and elsewhere.

Contact Oanh

 facebook.com/oanhandonly

 twitter.com/OanhNgoUsadi

Made in the USA
Monee, IL
28 May 2021